GUNBOAT DIPLOMACY, 1919–1991

Gunboat Diplomacy 1919–1991

Political Applications of Limited Naval Force

James Cable

Foreword by Admiral of the Fleet Sir Julian Oswald, GCB
First Sea Lord, 1989–1993

Third Edition

St. Martin's Press   New York

First edition (Chatto & Windus) 1971
Second edition first published in the United States of America in 1981
Third edition 1994

Printed in Great Britain

ISBN 0–312–12141–5

Library of Congress Cataloging-in-Publication Data
Cable, James, 1920–
Gunboat diplomacy 1919–1991 : political applications of limited
naval force / James Cable ; foreword by Sir Julian Oswald. — 3rd
ed.
p.   cm.
Rev. ed. of : Gunboat diplomacy 1919–1979.
Includes bibliographical references and index.
ISBN 0–312–12141–5
1. Sea-power.   2. International relations.   3. Post-communism.
I. Title.
V25.C327   1994
327.1' 17—dc20   93–48526
                                                          CIP

For Viveca, as always

Also by James Cable

GUNBOAT DIPLOMACY
THE ROYAL NAVY AND THE SIEGE OF BILBAO
BRITAIN'S NAVAL FUTURE
DIPLOMACY AT SEA
THE GENEVA CONFERENCE OF 1954 ON INDOCHINA
POLITICAL INSTITUTIONS AND ISSUES IN BRITAIN
NAVIES IN VIOLENT PEACE
INTERVENTION AT ABADAN: Plan Buccaneer

As Grant Hugo

BRITAIN IN TOMORROW'S WORLD
APPEARANCE AND REALITY IN INTERNATIONAL
   RELATIONS

Contents

Foreword

Those who have known and admired James Cable's work in the past, and who have read both the first and second editions of *Gunboat Diplomacy*, might recall that while both volumes had a preface and an introduction, neither had a foreword. So the reader may justifiably wonder if a contribution in the form of a foreword is either necessary or justified. A foreword can have a variety of purposes: to outline the book, to explain its aims, or to introduce the writer. However, a different consideration occurs to me. By far the largest part of the book – the text, the references, the bibliography, the introduction and the preface – comes from the pen of the author, and all of these inevitably reflect his characteristic modesty. It is only in the publisher's blurb on the dustjacket and in the foreword that anybody other than the author can pay tribute to the quality of James Cable's work. It seems to me that in a book as important as a new edition of *Gunboat Diplomacy*, it is perfectly proper to have an external assessment of the significance of the task, and of how well the author has discharged it.

The third edition, like its predecessors, concentrates on the period since 1919, but in this edition the author takes us up to 1991; this new volume, therefore, comprehends the period of the recent and cataclysmic changes in international security relationships consequent upon the collapse of the former Soviet Union. In this edition, 'gunboat diplomacy' is described and explained not only in the twenty-year period from 1919 to 1939, but also in the post-Second World War period of the so-called Cold War and, most interestingly and importantly, in the post-Cold War state we now enjoy in which international security constraints are very different, and far less predictable, than those which pertained a few years ago. The early years of this period of new world order are a particularly appropriate time to revisit the concept of gunboat diplomacy and test it against the new strategic realities. In essence, these changes reflect the end of the confrontational stale-mate of the Cold War and the removal of the previous virtually automatic veto by one super-power or the other of almost any peacekeeping or other activity involving the deployment of armed forces. (Of course, there were exceptions, and the UN operations in Korea in the 1950s are perhaps the most celebrated, but the non-use of the veto on that occasion is a different, and fascinating, story). Of course, even the power of veto did not prevent action being taken in a considerable number of cases, as indeed this new edition of *Gunboat Diplomacy* well illustrates, but it did constrain the super-powers on many occasions, which might well have furnished additional examples of the use of gunboat diplomacy had conditions been different. The reader will appreciate that the veto is off both ways as it were, and we can now expect the Russians to consider the use of coercive force in ways that would not have been likely during the Cold War. Initially, this has already been evident in the deployment of Russian forces to counter insurrection within the borders of the former Soviet Union. Increasingly, we can expect to see these forces, not least the Russian Navy, playing their part in peacekeeping operations on the world scene. Additionally, because those Cold War constraints are lifted, we see many more situations developing in which the superpowers, or even medium powers, may feel that the use of force is both necessary and justified in the pursuit of peace. We have only to look at the former Yugoslavia. In the days of the Cold War it was a pleasant country ruled by Tito, a popular holiday destination. One could certainly not describe the former Yugoslavia in those terms now. In the words of the old saying, 'The cat's away, the mice do play.' Thus we see a world security scene in which the need for deterrence against, for example, general war between NATO and the Warsaw Pact with major hostilities – possibly even including the use of nuclear weapons – has all but disappeared, but where the number of lower-level, more limited (but still very damaging and potentially serious) disputes is increasing at a worrying rate.

It is worth giving a few moments' thought to the nature of peacekeeping operations, because to an important extent this affects the way in which gunboat diplomacy may be employed. We must begin from the unarguable premise that man is a land animal (and often, not a very sociable, caring or pleasant one at that!). He is capable of falling out with his neighbour and even his erstwhile friend on grounds of race, religion, language, politics, creed, economics and a host of other issues. Differences of ethnicity, tribe and culture are quite enough to have him at his neighbour's throat. He will squabble, and quite possibly fight, over land, food, water, economic rights and much more. The list of conflicts, even since the end of the Second World War, seems almost endless. The death toll has been estimated at between 20 and 30 million people, a figure that dwarfs that of many of the major declared hostilities in history. Because man lives on land (although he is often highly dependent upon the sea), the extent to which he can be influenced by gunboat diplomacy will frequently be limited – although watery countries like Vietnam and Cambodia provide interesting exceptions. However, it is not ships, sailors, submarines or even aircraft that will prevent rape and mayhem in Sarajevo or tribal massacres in Soweto, it is, if anything, soldiers – probably infantry soldiers and marines – on the ground. Even in an area remote from the sea, though, back-up operations and support from seaward may well be important, as we have seen with the operation of naval forces in the Adriatic in support of UN forces in former Yugoslavia.

As economies worldwide become more complex, more inter-related and more interdependent, the importance of maritime embargo operations is certainly going to increase. These may be UN-sponsored, as with those against Iraq, or unilaterally imposed, as was the US embargo against Cuba. Their organisation and implementation is tricky and may demand considerable resources, but they represent a powerful form of coercion that seems to be widely politically acceptable.

The other significant advance we have seen, if it is an advance, is a greater perceived reliance upon the United Nations. Demands abound that the United Nations should keep the peace, but countries and governments are often less than willing to provide the United Nations (which, after all, is only their agent) with the necessary force and authority. Nevertheless, we are increasingly seeing a world in which UN authority is important, and, although still flouted, is gaining in respect. Of itself, this makes little difference to the concept of the coercive use of naval force, but it will govern the conditions under which it may be employed.

It is worth briefly considering changes in the means whereby forces may be imposed or used at sea. Even since the previous editions of *Gunboat Diplomacy*, we have seen significant developments. One that immediately comes to mind is the development of the very large and powerful aircraft-carrier, typically that of the US Navy. The carrier, one might even say 'supercarrier', is interesting in terms of gunboat diplomacy because it has such enormous reach with its carrier air group – such that it can stay in international waters without infringing anybody's sovereignty and without the politically sensitive need for over-flight and foreign-basing facilities that so constrain land-based aircraft. The carrier and its support can poise offshore in-definitely and yet, when and if necessary, its aircraft can range hundreds, if not thousands, of miles. This is very different to the small warship reliant upon its guns or short-range missile system, which (with the possible exception of embargo operations) must approach close to the coast if it is going to exert much influence. Another important area in which the technical scene is changing fast is the availability and speed of dissemination of strategic and tactical intelligence. Enormous investment has been made in this area in recent years. The major navies now possess highly sophisticated systems for ensuring that the commander on the spot is fully acquainted with every aspect of intelligence relevant to his task. That much of this intelligence is collected from space-based sensors means that it can be acquired without infringing national territory and with little danger of interference. Operation Desert Storm saw the use of satellites to collect photographic, radar, electronic intelligence, communications intercept and other data that, when correlated, analysed and disseminated in near real time, played a major part in the coalition's success.

The next very significant improvement that should be men-tioned is in command control and, in particular, in com-munications, widely known as C^3. Virtually instantaneous high data rate space-based communications, which are both reliable and secure, again mean that the commander on the spot can understand exactly what his superiors are thinking and can communicate with them in a matter of micro-seconds. Thus the fine control – one might even say the fine *political* control – of the coercive use of naval force is very much improved; and governments should feel less inhibited about making forces available for such operations, because they can retain very close control under all circumstances. In embargo enforcement operations, for example, it may be necessary to make very rapid decisions about stopping, searching and detaining foreign merchant ships. While a well-handled operation will help to enforce the embargo and act as a useful deterrent to further sanction-breaking, a bungled job could have disastrous political consequences. Communications are the key.

Another area in which there has been significant recent activity is the use of the mine. History has shown us frightening examples of the efficacy of the mine and the ease with which it can be employed – and also the difficulty of mine counter-measures. I think we can expect the mine to play an enlarged role in naval operations, particularly as it so favours the underdog. The technology is freely available, manufacture is not difficult, and laying mines is extremely easy. The significance of the mine used against merchant shipping, as well as against naval vessels, must not be overlooked.

An area that has been the subject of a great detail of discussion, exercising and thought is that of Rules of Engagement. These Rules are now considered essential in any situation in which forces may be opposed to one another, even in situations well short of hostilities. Rules of Engagement can be framed to try to contain, to escalate or to de-escalate a situation. With the widespread fitting of missiles, particularly those fired from submarines, and the extreme difficulty of defining hostile intent, the framing of Rules of Engagement for a particular situation will always be difficult. While the politician will, understandably, wish to ensure that his country's forces cannot be accused of starting the war, the military commander will be concerned that the outbreak of shooting does not result in his losing mission essential forces or any appreciable measure of military capability. Fortunately, intelligence and communications will come to our assistance and Rules of Engagement can be altered or modified very speedily as the situation requires. The importance of Rules of Engagement is easily illustrated by considering the complex 'no peace – no war'-type situations that appear to abound nowadays. Even when open hostilities occur, very frequently war has not been declared. Thus the military, at sea as on land, are dealing with a spectrum of conflict – ranging from glaring watchfully at each other at one end of the continuum, to high-intensity fighting at the other.

Another area in which attitudes are changing, and quite rapidly, is that of civilian casualties and collateral damage. Whereas a while ago these might have been accepted relatively phlegmatically, they are now of the utmost concern and (rightly) place a further constraint upon the military commander.

The coercive use of naval force, or gunboat diplomacy as it is so much more elegantly called, must be considered in the future in this changed and changing framework: new weapons, new vehicles, new rules and, above all else, a totally different strategic background, perhaps best illustrated by observing the differences between the published US Navy concept for the 1980s known as 'The Maritime Strategy' and that for the 1990s entitled 'From the Sea'. The first was very largely devoted to deterring, and if necessary fighting and beating, a single adversary in the deep water of the North Atlantic, the Pacific and the rest of the world's oceans, while the second reflects the need, in totally different circumstances, to project power from the sea to land to exert influence for peacekeeping or other purposes in countries around the world. The one is a blue-water strategy, and the other a brown-water alternative – quite new, quite different, and absolutely appropriate in the circumstances.

The importance of naval history as of any other type of history must lie in the extent to which its study can point a clear and helpful way ahead. Can it do so, one might ask, in the case of gunboat diplomacy? Well, possibly it can, and certainly it appears that history is the only guide we have, and we neglect it at our peril. Coercive naval diplomacy is in some circumstances an alternative to war. It may limit war or even prevent it, and we should ensure that we not only have the means (the responsibility of the Ministry of Defence and the government), but that we understand its strengths and weaknesses, how and where it should be applied, when it should not, and what it may achieve. In addressing these latter requirements, we owe a great deal to the author of *Gunboat Diplomacy*.

JULIAN OSWALD

Introduction

> We have no more reason to believe that the days of gunboat diplomacy are over than to believe that the threat of force will not be used on land and in the air.
>
> Millar[1]

Gunboat diplomacy is most familiar, but will never be employed in these pages, as a term of abuse, a metaphorical epithet for almost any kind of attempt by one government to exert an unwelcome influence on the policy of another. It is often applied to situations involving no threat or use of naval force, sometimes even to disputes in which the only pressures employed are economic or diplomatic.

This degeneration of a phrase that was once exactly descriptive stems from the belief that gunboat diplomacy is a technique as obsolete as the vessels that used to sustain it. Both are vaguely supposed to have vanished with the passing of Victorian imperialism, the first under the pressure of altered political attitudes, the second in response to the advance of naval technology. Although Chinese, Soviet and US gunboats saw action even in the 1960s, not every use of gunboats can be regarded as gunboat diplomacy, nor is it essential that the warships employed should actually bear this name. Gunboats, which are almost as old as the naval gun, have assumed many different forms in their long history, and have been employed for many different tasks – most of which are outside the scope of the present work.[2] We shall not be concerned with their employment in the conduct of war or for coastal defence, or on such routine operations as police, anti-smuggling or fishery protection duties inside the territorial waters of their own state. The purpose of this book is to consider the recent and future applications of limited naval force as one of the instruments of foreign policy.

The concept of limited naval force is one that requires, and will receive, a more extended definition. This, in turn, will be supported by an analysis of some of the many instances of gunboat diplomacy during the last seventy years,[3] so as to bring out more clearly not only the nature and scope of gunboat

1

diplomacy, but also the theoretical principles that might be regarded as determining its efficacy. Both the theory and the practice of the past, however, will be examined primarily for the lessons these offer for the future. This is not a work of history, not even of the relatively under-recorded history of limited naval force since 1919, but of speculation. The question to be explored is how, in the years to come, the naval powers might wish, or be able, to exploit their naval resources in furtherance of their foreign policy. What does analysis of the past suggest as the future role of limited naval force? Against whom might this be exerted and what indications can be discerned of readiness for its employment?

If this is not a history, neither is it a manual of naval strategy or tactics, which will be considered only in their relation to the achievement of political and diplomatic objectives. Above all, this book is not concerned with naval warfare, for any kind of war, particularly in the second half of the twentieth century, constitutes the failure of foreign policy and the abandonment of diplomatic expedients. Limited naval force, as it will be considered in the present work, is a peacetime technique or, if employed during an actual war, one confined to the exertion of pressure on allies or neutrals.

Even this restriction still leaves an elastic field for inquiry. Neutrality has always tended to be disputed or disregarded when this suited the purpose of belligerents, but the difficulty of distinguishing between the state of war and the state of peace has increased still further since 1946. The foreign offices of the world, or their legal advisers, were so impressed by the Nürnberg Judgement that not one of the many wars[4] of the last forty-five years was ever declared: a dubious triumph for international law, but an unmitigated nuisance to diplomatic historians. To describe gunboat diplomacy as a peacetime expedient thus offers only an uncertain and provisional ceiling to the domain of limited naval force, not a substitute for the more elaborate definition to be attempted in Chapter 1. Nuclear exchanges are clearly beyond the scope of our inquiry, as are most aspects of the Second World War or the conflicts in Korea and the Persian Gulf, but subtler tests are needed to discriminate between coercive diplomacy and undeclared war in the doubtful zone that lies beneath such heights of violence.

Such tests are not, unfortunately, to be found in the nature and number of the warships concerned or even in the duration of their employment. The political applications of limited naval force range all the way from the single gunboat that merely drops her anchor in alien territorial waters (as did SMS PANTHER at Agadir in 1911) to the use of as many as eighty-eight assorted warships in active hostilities in the Baltic from December 1918 to May 1921. Nor is gunboat diplomacy normally exercised only by warships at sea: the landing of sailors, marines, soldiers and supplies is a common feature, as is the use of helicopters and the availability of air cover. The subject matter of this book will not, therefore, be confined to purely naval operations, but it will exclude all threats or uses of force in which the availability of warships does not play an essential and, in most cases, a predominant part. Gunboat diplomacy can comprise much more that the mere arrival of a gunboat to reinforce the representations of an ambassador or consul, but it must not be divorced from the seas that have always sustained it.

Using the sea not only distinguished gunboat diplomacy from other forms of coercion but, in the past, actually made the process easier. In more recent years challenges developed to the idea of the sea as a favourable medium or of coercive diplomacy as a viable option. The sea was long regarded as no more than a protective cover for the manoeuvres of missile-firing submarines: diplomacy as an anachronism offering no useful alternative to the modern techniques of terrorism and rocket-rattling. These are some of the objections that will have to be stated and tested throughout the present work, but a preliminary outline may help to clarify the nature and scope of the ensuing argument. Technically, it is contended, the obstacles to naval operations on an unfriendly coast have steadily increased from the virtual zero of 1850, when an invulnerable British fleet blockaded Greece and seized Greek shipping,[5] to such a level that, on 21 October 1967, an Israeli destroyer patrolling at least 10 miles off the coast of Egypt could be destroyed at long range by only four missiles.[6] Politically, the once respectable practice of coercing weak maritime countries not enjoying the protection of a great power has become an outrage against sovereignty and a threat to peace, though this moral stigma is perhaps less important than the increased powers of resistance

that even the weakest states derive from the growth of nationalism and political organisation.

It is to assist in the erosion of these objections that 1919 has
been selected as a starting point for the analysis of earlier
applications of limited naval force. By then, mines, torpedoes,
submarines, coastal artillery and even aircraft[7] were already
hampering the operation of warships in coastal waters, and the
concept of the nation-state had taken firm root well beyond its
nurseries in Europe and North America. The seventy-odd years
since 1919 thus possess a degree of contemporary – and future
– relevance not enjoyed by earlier periods. If instances of
gunboat diplomacy towards the end of this era prove compar-
able with those at the beginning, it becomes arguable that this
technique has already been successfully adapted to changes
in the international environment and is capable of further
evolution in the future.

This is a capacity less easily deduced from the actual composition of contemporary navies or official statements of their
purposes. The strength and shape of a navy at any given
moment are often as much the result of chance as of design,
and one can seldom find anything approaching Admiral Fisher's
reconstruction of the Royal Navy at the beginning of the
century – when gunboats were deliberately and avowedly
sacrificed to battleships and the navy's diplomatic capacities
were reduced to augment its readiness for major war. Warships,
moreover, are such flexible instruments of coercion that even
these drastic and controversial reforms left considerable scope
for the continued use of limited naval force by successive
British governments. Changes in the order of battle of the
world's navies thus offer only partial indications of their
prospective employment.

These indications are most inadequately supplemented by
official statements, which are constrained to a hypocritical
ambiguity by the desire simultaneously to satisfy the prevailing
political cant and the professional aspirations of naval officers.
Given the pejorative overtones attached to gunboat diplomacy
in the second half of the twentieth century, its absence from the
public speeches of Ministers of Defence is scarcely surprising.
Their omissions, however, are often remedied by third parties
and the functions of one navy may occasionally be best deduced
from the more outspoken comments of apprehensive rivals.

This indirect evidence is particularly useful in the case of navies whose slender past achievements in gunboat diplomacy create no initial presumption of their readiness to undertake such tasks in future.

It is this need for deduction that has given the study of gunboat diplomacy its controversial flavour, allowing unlucky prime ministers and opinionated professors an easy escape into the cliché of declaring the days of gunboat diplomacy to be over. That whiskery objection had again to be answered when the second edition of the present work appeared in 1981, by instancing the repeated use of this expedient in the 1970s. Today, however, there is a new argument to be considered. The world has changed. The Soviet Union, bipolarity, the familiar ideological conflict, the looming spectre of a Third World War, all seem to have dissolved. Admirals have had to alter their ideas. In April 1991 the avowedly anti-Soviet Maritime Strategy of the United States, which Admiral Watkins had unveiled in January 1986, was decently interred by one of his successors as Chief of Naval Operations, Admiral Frank B. Kelso:

> We must shift the objective of our national security strategy from containing the Soviet Union to maintaining global stability. Our evolving strategy must focus on regional contingencies in trouble spots wherever our national interests are involved.[8]

When admirals recast grand strategy, theorists concerned with the lesser conflicts of what passes for peace must also review their thinking. Can the concepts suggested in the 1970s and 1980s as the principles of gunboat diplomacy be expected to hold good in the new era of international relations that is now unfolding? Some attempt to answer that difficult question cannot be avoided in a third and fully revised edition of *Gunboat Diplomacy*. The approach adopted has been point by point: restating the original theories, but testing each against the experience of the 1970s and 1980s; trying to determine the existence of trends; and finally, looking for any pointers to the pattern of the future.

In its navigation of the relatively uncharted waters of the recent past, no less than its groping into the mists and shoals of the future, this book must steer an inevitably controversial course, but one objection ought to be anticipated – for it can

scarcely be avoided. This book attempts to assess the effectiveness of limited naval force in terms of its ability to achieve
the results originally intended by the initiating government. It
does not question the purposes of such governments. This
treatment of force merely as a tool – and its measurement only
as a lever – implies no moral judgement. Nor do the terms that
will often be employed: assailant and victim. The assailant is he
who first uses limited naval force, the victim is he who suffers it.
Nations are not typecast for either role. Any country with a
coastline – and occasionally some without – can be a victim. Any
country with a sea-going navy – even one not called by that
name – can be an assailant.

Gunboat diplomacy can be described either as an infringement of national sovereignty or as the maintenance of international law and order; as aggression or as self-defence. Such
distinctions are irrelevant in a book concerned with means
rather than ends and, if we are to believe the greatest of all
authorities on the application of force, probably possess little
intrinsic meaning:

> ... the exercise of this force may be considered both as resist-
> ance and impulse: It is resistance in so far as the body, for
> maintaining its present state, withstands the force impressed;
> it is impulse in so far as the body, by not easily giving way to
> the impressed force of another, endeavours to change the state
> of that other. Resistance is usually ascribed to bodies at rest
> and impulse to those in motion: But motion and rest, as
> commonly conceived, are only relatively distinguished; nor are
> those bodies always truly at rest, which are commonly taken to
> be so.[9]

1 Definitions

'When I use a word', Humpty Dumpty said in rather a scornful tone, 'it means just what I choose it to mean – neither more nor less.'

Carroll[1]

More bathers have heard of the jelly fish, even seen it, than could depict its shifting outlines, translucent as the sea in which they merge and blur, or grasp the slipperiness of its floating substance. Gunboat diplomacy is equally familiar and no less amorphous. Its scope and nature are not easily discerned: they resist the simplicity of a single, a *priori* definition. Instead, the subject must be enveloped and, step by step, isolated from its fluid and shadowy environment. This process of definition by elimination is necessarily arbitrary. In the absence of any consensus of received opinion, doubt and disagreement are not merely permissible, but justified. It is the need to fix a starting-point, not its self-evident validity, that demands precision, even pedantry, at the outset of an inevitably speculative venture across the horizons of the future. The more categorical the statements that follow, the more they will need (but, to avoid tedious repetition, will not receive) the perpetual qualification: 'for the purposes of this inquiry'.

If, therefore, we begin by asserting that gunboat diplomacy is an instrument of governments, this is not to ignore the role of limited naval force in the hands of those who seek to overthrow or to coerce their own regime. When the cruiser AURORA trained her guns on the Winter Palace,[2] the political consequences were momentous and, seventy-five years later, can still be felt; this, though, was a revolutionary act, not an exercise of gunboat diplomacy, which is the exclusive prerogative of those already in effective control of the state.

The threat or use of naval force by governments in the repression of their own subjects – as when the British government menaced the strikers of Liverpool with the guns of HMS BARHAM and HMS RAMILLIES in 1926[3] – is equally beyond the scope of the present work. Gunboat diplomacy is something that governments do to foreigners. This is a proposition that must be

7

interpreted with some care and with more regard to the realities
of a situation that its appearance. If a political organisation
commands the powers of a government and behaves as one in its
relations with other governments, its legitimacy is a secondary
consideration. If it acts in the furtherance of a dispute involving
other states, the international character of its action is not
necessarily diminished if this takes place within the national
territory and is ostensibly directed only against its own nationals. For instance, when Admiral Muselier seized the islands
of St Pierre and Miquelon on 24 December 1941, Gaullists could
regard this as a mere assertion of domestic authority, whereas
Pétainists could regard it as an act of rebellion. In either view, in
a simplified or purely legalistic interpretation, this was a dispute
among Frenchmen. In reality, of course, it was nothing of the
kind. The only significant opposition came from a foreign
government, that of the United States, who had rejected
Admiral Muselier's prior request for their concurrence and
suggested a Canadian intervention instead. This was not simply
because the US government then recognised Marshal Pétain as
the ruler of France: their disapproval would scarcely have been
diminished if the situation had been reversed – if Vichy warships
had seized power in a Gaullist island. Indeed, one of the motives
of US policy – deriving partly from the mystique of the Monroe
Doctrine – was to freeze the status of French territories in the
Western Hemisphere and to prevent any change of allegiance
for the duration of the war. What was at issue was not which
French government should control France – St Pierre and
Miquelon were the merest grains of dust in those scales – but
the right of any French government to disregard the suzerainty
temporarily claimed by the United States over French territory
in the Western Atlantic. General de Gaulle was the virtual
government of France in this instance, because he could and did
assert the independence and authority of his own nation-state in
a dispute involving a foreign government.

One of the advantages of this otherwise rather unusual instance of gunboat diplomacy is that its exceptional characteristics facilitate more precise definitions. The nature of the
initiating authority, the nationality of the ostensible victims and
even the territorial jurisdiction at the point of action, are all
shown to be secondary to the crucial question: was force applied
in the furtherance of a dispute between different nation-states?

Here it clearly was. The Free French had originally sought the concurrence of the British, Canadian and US governments for the assumption of authority over St Pierre and Miquelon and, when this was refused by the US government, proceeded clandestinely to assemble a naval force capable of seizing the islands before US opposition could take a more concrete or effective form. But for US opposition, indeed, naval force might have been unnecessary: the Vichy governor capitulated in twenty minutes and a plebiscite produced an overwhelming Gaullist majority.[4]

Therefore to establish an act of force as an instance of gunboat diplomacy, one minimum qualification is that this should have occurred in furtherance of a dispute between different nation-states. Such a dispute may be directly and explicitly between two governments, or one government may usurp the prerogatives of another in circumstances that imply a conflict between nation-states even in the absence of inter-governmental dispute. For instance, in 1927 British warships used or threatened force on the rivers or territorial waters of China on at least twenty occasions. Only a minority of these incidents involved any direct or open dispute with the Chinese government: the purpose generally being to rescue or protect British subjects whose safety was menaced by riotous mobs or rebels. It is arguable, therefore, that the Chinese government might themselves have wished to take similar measures if they had enjoyed sufficient authority in the areas concerned, and that British warships were acting in lieu of the Chinese government rather than against them. However, this is a dubious argument, not merely on the basis of the facts of these particular incidents, in which the prior approval of the Chinese government was seldom sought and never regarded as an essential condition for action, but also on the grounds of general principle. When force is used by one state within the territorial jurisdiction and against the nationals of another, this creates the presumption of a dispute between nation-states, and this presumption cannot be rebutted merely because the government of the second state consented to or even requested forcible foreign intervention. Governments do not acquiesce in, let alone invite, foreign coercion against their own nationals on their own territory unless they have already lost some of their domestic authority and, therefore, forfeited the exclusive claim to represent their own nation-state. Nor do foreign governments take such action without regard to their own national interests or without exciting a degree of sympathy with the victims of coercion among the nationals of the other state. British warships never went into action in Chinese waters without leaving the impression on at least some Britons and some Chinese that a dispute existed between Britain and China. It would thus be plausible to contend that any use or threat of force against foreign nationals within the territory of their own state implies the existence, at least in embryo, of a dispute between nation-states.

We may, however, free ourselves from dependence on such subtleties by expanding our preliminary definition of the political conditions for gunboat diplomacy. Any use or threat of limited naval force, otherwise than as an act of war, may constitute an instance of gunboat diplomacy if it is committed either in the furtherance of an international dispute or else against foreign nationals within the territory of their own state.

With these words, however, we can no longer postpone the most difficult and controversial stage in the process of definition by elimination: when and why is the use of force in an international dispute not an act of war? The intractability of this question can of course be reduced by discarding a whole category of meanings: we are not concerned with the distinctions lawyers try to draw between the kind of force that is permissible in peace and the kind that is only lawful in war. For our purpose, an act of war is either the use of force against an alien enemy during an existing war or, alternatively, one that, although committed in time of peace, has the result of producing a state of war. Peace and war, however, have become regrettably hard to distinguish. Almost everyone would agree that from the moment Israeli aircraft attacked Egyptian airfields in the early morning of 5 June 1967, until the ceasefire took effect on the evening of 10 June, there existed a state of war between Israel and Egypt. However, did President Sadat's visit to Israel in November 1977 inaugurate a state of peace and had this ever existed before? When, and on what criteria, can it be said that other Arab states have ever been at peace with Israel? What about China and the United States? For twenty years those two nations neither recognized one another, nor were in diplomatic relations, nor permitted any normal intercourse between their respective citizens. Their regular forces met and fought an undoubted war in Korea, and for two decades their mutual resentment was punctuated by hostile pinpricks. But was it a war or was there ever peace before Kissinger went to Peking?

The more one considers actual cases, the more one is driven to the reluctant conclusion that the peaks of undoubted war and demonstrable peace are separated by a valley of uncertainty, where the classical definitions offer no guidance that is either absolute or precise. 'An act of violence intended to compel our opponents to fulfil our will'[5] includes an Arab bomb in a London store; 'armed conflict between nations'[6] almost justifies those journalists who, in 1958, talked of Britain's 'Fish War' with Iceland.

On the other hand, there is one criterion that, though neither objective nor exact, might offer some assistance. This is sometimes described as the profit motive. At least in theory, there are two broad categories of motive that might prompt a government to employ violence against foreigners. One is positive: to gain something for the initiating state. The other is negative: to injure the foreigners or their state. In total war, these two motives become one and the same. Injury to the enemy is regarded as inherently advantageous, and cost-effectiveness as the touchstone for choosing to inflict one kind of injury rather than another. In extreme cases, hurting the foe may seem desirable even in the absence of any conceivable advantage:despatching the last missiles from a country already irretrievably destroyed in a nuclear holocaust. In limited war, the restraints are greater and more various: many possible methods of injuring the enemy will be rejected if these entail incidental disadvantages. Poison gas may not be used, privileged sanctuaries allowed, third powers permitted to assist the enemy. However, there will still be a presumption – even if this can now be more easily and more often rebutted – that the enemy's loss is automatically our gain. In peace, on the other hand, the likelihood of injuring foreigners does not provide a self-sufficient motive for employing violence against them. On the contrary, it may even be a disincentive. Those advocating the use of force are thus compelled to argue that the result will either bring positive advantage to the initiating state or else prevent it from suffering otherwise predictable loss. In peace, governments have to explain why they have injured foreigners; in war, why they have not.

Any attempt to identify wars by reference to the state of mind of the participants has obvious inconveniences in practice. It may even appear more than a little absurd. After all, if tanks grind across frontiers, shells fall on cities, and men of different nationalities kill one another in repeated and protracted conflict, what need is there of sophisticated and psychological analysis? Yet all these things happened in Hungary in 1956 and nobody called that a war; none of them occurred in 1939 on the Western Front, where everyone believed that Britain and France were at war with Germany.

The truth of the matter is that war and peace can be defined in many different ways, each appropriate to a different purpose, but that no single definition is likely to satisfy all purposes or to be immune from the challenge presented by particular situations difficult to accommodate within the framework of a general definition. To suggest, therefore, that war is a violent conflict between states in which policy is determined by the desire to inflict injury rather than the hope of positive advantage, is to set up a yardstick for only one dimension of a multi-faceted complex. Nevertheless, it may be more useful, when attempting to distinguish between the diplomatic and the warlike character of a particular act of force, to inquire its purpose (as seen both by the initiator and by the victim)- than to count the forces involved, the shots fired or the casualties sustained. From 1840 to 1949, for instance, few years passed without British warships employing armed force in Chinese waters, but it would be as misleading to regard this as a hundred years' war between Britain and China as it would be to ignore the occasions on which this pattern of coercive diplomacy was broken by outright acts of war.

For our purposes, therefore, an act of war is the use of armed force against or in a foreign state for the primary purpose of injuring that state, whether as part of an existing policy of injuring the other state as and when opportunity serves, or to initiate such a policy or, and this is a new and important point, without regard to the risk that the reaction of the victim state will go beyond mere self-defence to a reciprocal adoption of injury rather than profit as the prime motive for policy. In other words, an act of war may either continue an existing war, be deliberately intended to start a war, or liable to provoke the victim into starting one.

An act of coercive diplomacy, on the other hand, is intended to secure some specific advantage from another state and forfeits

its diplomatic character if it either contemplates the infliction of injury unrelated to obtaining that advantage or results in the victim attempting the infliction of injury after the original objective has been either achieved or abandoned. Coercive diplomacy is thus an alternative to war and, if it leads to war, we must not only hold that it has failed: we may even doubt whether it ever deserved that name.

Governments, no less than reasonable men, must be presumed to intend the predictable consequences of their acts and, if the seizure of St Pierre and Miquelon had led to war between the United States and the Free French, Admiral Muselier would have been hard put to it to maintain his honoured place among the successful practitioners of gunboat diplomacy.

His actual success was, of course, entirely dependent on the use of warships. US opposition made it impossible to use any base near enough to the islands for an airborne expedition, and the danger from German submarines was too great for unescorted merchant vessels to cross the Atlantic. There is no need, however, for so exacting a test in order to determine that a particular instance of coercive diplomacy was also one of gunboat diplomacy. It is enough that the actual choice fell on the use or threat of naval force and that, even if other means were available or employed in addition, the presence of warships played an essential part. This part must, however, include their availability to support at least a threat of force, if this is needed to resolve a particular dispute. When US warships appeared off Santo Domingo on 19 November 1961, they did not actually do anything, but US representatives ashore made it quite clear that they might intervene if the surviving relations of the dictator Trujillo failed to facilitate the establishment of a government acceptable to the United States by leaving the Dominican Republic.[7] The visible presence of warships was thus a threat of naval force and, therefore, an instance of gunboat diplomacy, which mere naval visits are not if, as so often happens, their only political purpose is a general reminder that the government concerned possesses a navy.

This incident usefully illustrates the lower boundary of our subject: a threat, however delicate and discreet, that naval force might actually be applied in support of specific diplomatic representations. The upper edge, as we have seen, falls short of the brutal, if sometimes uncertain, threshold of the act of war.

The earlier description of gunboat diplomacy as the application for political purposes of *limited* naval force will nevertheless require further elucidation of that often ambiguous epithet. Though of the greatest importance, this may nevertheless be reserved for the next chapter. Having explained who uses gunboat diplomacy and against whom, having distinguished this expedient from naval action in revolution, repression and war, having at least outlined the upper and lower limits of its operation, we can now repeat, with only minor modification, our earlier definition:

Gunboat diplomacy is the use or threat of limited naval force, otherwise than as an act of war, in order to secure advantage or to avert loss, either in the furtherance of an international dispute or else against foreign nationals within the territory or the jurisdiction of their own state.

2 Principles and Precedents

Limited is a victim of *slipshod extension* ... a lazy habit of treating *limited* as a convenient synonym for many more suitable and more exact words ... to limit is to confine within bounds.

Fowler[1]

I DEFINITIVE FORCE:[2] ALTMARK and PUEBLO

At twenty minutes to four in the cold darkness of the morning of 14 February 1940, a Norwegian coastguard rang up the curtain on one of the classic dramas of gunboat diplomacy – perhaps the purest instance in recent times of the definitive use of limited naval force in isolation from all other means of pressure.

As the morse stuttered to and fro, the accustomed routine was methodically applied. *'Et ukjent skip war kommet in på Frohavet fra sjøen'*[3] – an unknown ship had come in from the sea to enter the Frohavet, the stretch of water that divides the Froan islets from the mainland and constitutes the northerly approach to Trondheim. The news was confirmed by the coastguard station at Tustna, and the torpedo boat TRYGG sailed from Kristiansund on yet another of the routine investigations by which the Norwegian Navy were accustomed to uphold the neutrality of their country in those early months of an undoubted, but still dormant, European war. Her report that afternoon was reassuring. The unknown ship was a tanker bound for Germany from the United States; she had conformed with the requirements of Norwegian neutrality by dismounting her anti-aircraft guns; she had no passengers on board; her name was ALTMARK.

But Admiral Tank-Nielsen, the Norwegian area commander, was a stickler for detail. TRYGG had reported ALTMARK as an armed merchant ship, but had not provided satisfactory answers to all the seventeen questions specified for such vessels in article 21 of the relevant standing instructions.[4]

15

Two further visitations, this time by the torpedo boat SNØGG, in the evening of the 14th and the morning of the 15th, still failed to satisfy the Admiral, who put to sea himself in the destroyer GARM and, at 1 p.m. on the 15th, sent his Chief of Staff on board ALTMARK, which had meanwhile been continuing her southward journey through Norwegian territorial waters under the escort of SNØGG. By 4.15 that afternoon, both the Norwegian Commander-in-Chief in Oslo and Mr Bull, the Secretary General of the Norwegian Ministry of Foreign Affairs, had received Admiral Tank-Nielsen's initial report. It was brief, but it revealed the reason for his stubborn persistence. Three words of muted brass were enough to mark the first entry of this essentially Wagnerian drama's *leitmotiv: 'Antakelig fanger ombord'* – 'probably prisoners aboard'.

Admiral Tank-Nielsen was more than meticulous; he was alert and farseeing. Over a month earlier he had spotted a story in the Oslo newspaper *Aftenposten* that the German naval auxiliary ALTMARK was expected to cross the Atlantic with 400 British prisoners en route to Germany. He had immediately addressed a special circular to his command, calling attention to this report. By one of those mischances familiar in all navies – and other organisations as well – this circular never reached the commanders of TRYGG and SNØGG. However, it explains Admiral Tank–Nielsen's reluctance to accept the repeated denials, as relayed to him by his subordinates, of ALTMARK's captain: 'No passengers; there are no persons on board who belong to the armed forces of another belligerent country, nor are there civilians of a belligerent country.'

It explains his demand to inspect the ship and, when this was refused on the grounds that ALTMARK was a state ship flying the *Reichsdienstflagge*, his decision that, without inspection, ALTMARK might not traverse the waters of the Bergen defended area, a decision that would have required her to follow a course only just inside Norwegian territorial limits. The Admiral's attitude was not determined by *Aftenposten* alone: his Chief of Staff had heard and seen for himself, as Oslo was informed later that evening, SOS signals from ALTMARK's fo'c's'le and noted the efforts of the crew to hide them by working the winches and slamming the deadlights.

However, Admiral Tank-Nielsen was also a prudent and circumspect officer, careful not to let his personal sympathies override the obligations of discipline and responsibility. He neither disregarded the legal force of Captain Dau's refusal of a search nor sought to present his superiors with a *fait accompli*. His decision – to refuse passage through the defended area – was a compromise that neatly avoided any direct clash on the delicate central issue, which he nevertheless indicated to his superiors with concise clarity: '*Antakelig fanger ombord*'.

There is no suggestion in the Norwegian documents[5] that these ominous words were discussed between the Commander-in-Chief, Admiral Diesen, and Mr Bull before the latter went off to change for his dinner at the Brazilian Legation. Their conversations had turned on the right of naval auxiliaries (as opposed to actual warships) to passage through the defended area, on the signal of protest despatched by ALTMARK's captain, and on the desirability of speeding this ship on her way before detection by the British gave rise to an awkward situation. At 5.30 that afternoon Admiral Diesen telegraphed his order: 'Let the vessel pass in her capacity as a State ship. Escort.'

At 6 p.m. he told Admiral Tank-Nielsen by telephone that his order covered passage through the defended area. At 10.30 p.m. Admiral Diesen was able to reassure the German naval attaché, who had telephoned to complain of the delays imposed on ALTMARK, that the vessel was again on her way south. The closing note of Act One was quietly reassuring: '*Han takket*' – 'He thanked me'.

Across the North Sea, the stagehands were still setting the scene for Act Two. The British Admiralty had long been acutely aware that ALTMARK was on her way home with British prisoners transferred to her from the pocket battleship ADMIRAL GRAF SPEE, but there had been no news of ALTMARK's whereabouts since December 1939 and no one knew that bad weather had enabled her to elude British patrols in the Iceland–Faeroes passage during the night of 12/13 February. It was thus a most unpleasant surprise to learn, on the evening of 15 February,[6] that ALTMARK had not merely gained the shelter of Norwegian territorial waters, but had progressed as far as Bergen by noon that day. At a rate of 25 knots, of which speed the British believed her capable, not many hours of steaming – and most of those in Norwegian territorial waters – now divided her from the potential shelter of German air cover. Immediate decisions were clearly needed, and at 12.10 a.m. the curtain went up for

the Second Act. Captain Vian, then patrolling northwards from
the Skagerrak in HMS COSSACK with four other destroyers and
the cruiser ARETHUSA under his command, received the signal:
'ALTMARK your objective. Act accordingly.'[7]

Admiral Forbes, the Commander-in-Chief of the Home Fleet,
was as concise in his signals as Admiral Tank-Nielsen, but
perhaps a trifle less explicit. Captain Vian, after all, had not
been sent out to look for ALTMARK, but for German iron-ore
ships. His presence off the Scandinavian coast was coincidental.
He did not even know what ALTMARK looked like and, on finding
a picture of two ships in an old copy of the *Illustrated London
News*, unfortunately chose the wrong one as his intended
victim.[8] Curiously enough, it was Admiral Diesen's order of the
previous evening that helped him to correct this error. Even at
3 p.m.[9] on the afternoon of 16 February, visibility was poor
south of Stavanger, where the Norwegian coast sheds its islands
and begins an eastward curve towards the country's southern
tip and the entrance to the Skagerrak. Without the conspicuous
– and significant – presence to seaward of the escorting FIRERN,
even that sharp-sighted officer of HMS ARETHUSA might not have
identified ALTMARK as she slipped through the gathering dusk
while hugging the coast. But ARETHUSA closed to read the name
on ALTMARK's stern, and to be reported, with her accompanying
destroyers, by FIRERN as five British cruisers. The full cast was
now assembled on the stage, and we may skim over the largely
irrelevant moves before the next curtain: the torpedo boat
SKARV taking over escort duties, the exchange of signals (often
mutually incomprehensible) with the British warships, their
unsuccessful attempts to stop ALTMARK or detach her from her
Norwegian escort, ALTMARK's flight into Jøssingfjord closely
followed by SKARV, the newly arrived torpedo boat KJELL, and
then two British destroyers. Act Three began only at 5 p.m.,
when Captain Vian responded to protests against British violation of Norwegian neutrality by informing KJELL's commander
of his orders from the British Admiralty[10] to liberate 400
British prisoners on board ALTMARK. This time it was the full
orchestra that blared out the *leitmotiv* first introduced by
Admiral Tank-Nielsen twenty-four hours earlier.

When KJELL's commander had replied that he knew of no
prisoners, had rejected a proposal for a joint inspection of
ALTMARK, and had demanded British withdrawal from Norwegian

territorial waters, there followed a pause. The two British destroyers left Jøssingfjord to join their consorts on guard outside the 3-mile limit; two more Norwegian warships joined KJELL and SKARV inside; ALTMARK lay motionless against the ice, as close to the shore as she could get. COSSACK's telegraphists worked frantically at their keys, but the Norwegian commander's wireless was blanketed by the mountainous sides of the fjord. Amid all his other preoccupations, he could only obtain instructions by rushing ashore to find a telephone. He got through to the local defence HQ at Kristiansund, who confirmed the standing orders on the upholding of Norwegian neutrality: he was to go on protesting, but not to resort to force.

The orders elicited by Captain Vian's signaller, orders personally drafted by Mr Churchill after he had obtained the Foreign Secretary's concurrence by telephone, were rather more elaborate:

> Unless Norwegian torpedo-boat undertakes to convoy ALTMARK to Bergen with a joint Anglo-Norwegian guard on board and a joint escort, you should board ALTMARK, liberate the prisoners and take possession of the ship pending further instructions. If Norwegian torpedo-boat interferes, you should warn her to stand off. If she fires upon you, you should not reply unless attack is serious, in which case you should defend yourself using no more force than is necessary and cease fire when she desists. Suggest to Norwegian destroyer that honour is served by submitting to superior force.[11]

The finale is too well known to require recapitulation in detail. At 11 p.m. COSSACK re-entered the Jøssingfjord, her searchlights blazing. When KJELL's commander went on board to reiterate his protests, he was informed by Captain Vian that his orders required him to liberate ALTMARK's prisoners with or without Norwegian consent. British and German ships crunched together, the boarders went in, a few shots punctuated the brief scuffle, and at 12.35 a.m. COSSACK was steaming out of Jøssingfjord with 299 British subjects in excess of her proper complement. Churchill's careful conditional clauses had not, it seems, been needed,[12] though we shall have to return to them later. Instead, this opera closes on the chord first struck by Admiral Tank-Nielsen: 'COSSACK had meanwhile manoeuvred

herself on to ALTMARK's port bow and now there appeared a
crowd of people – presumably prisoners – *"antakelig fangene"* ...'[13]

This drama was introduced to these otherwise prosaic pages
as a classic example of the use of limited naval force. This is an
adjective demanding elucidation. To the victims of any kind of
force, the description *limited* often seems more questionable
than it does to the wielders of force. The argument of this
chapter is that force may nevertheless be objectively regarded
as limited, provided that certain conditions are met. The first of
these is that the act or threat of force should possess a definite
purpose, of which the extent is apparent to both sides. On the
night of 16 February 1940, both British and Norwegian naval
officers understood that no more was intended than the release
of British prisoners from a German ship. Admittedly, the
Norwegians were sceptical of the existence of these prisoners
(KJELL's commander was one of the many unfortunates who had
never received Admiral Tank-Nielsen's circular), but they did
not question the intentions of the British, only the evidence on
which these intentions were founded.[14]

So far as they were concerned, the challenge presented by
Captain Vian was radically different from that offered seven
weeks later by the entry into Oslofjord of the German cruiser
BLÜCHER. She was sunk outright because her undeclared intentions seemed – partly because of the tension with Germany after
the ALTMARK affair – to represent an unlimited threat: not to
the letter of Norwegian neutrality, but to the independence of
Norway. Both decisions, incidentally, were taken by naval
officers alone.[15] Norwegian Ministers in 1940 were seldom
available at moments of crisis and the Minister for Foreign
Affairs left the capital to address the Trondheim Students'
Union just two hours before COSSACK re-entered Jøssingfjord.
As a general rule, however, it will be convenient to assume, in
the absence of evidence to the contrary, that the decisions,
intentions and reactions of responsible officers and officials
were broadly representative of those of their governments. In
the heat of action, Captain Vian may not have used all Mr
Churchill's words, but he did make clear the limited intentions
of the British government.

Secondly, the purpose of those employing force must not only
be recognised as limited, but also as tolerable. This is a vaguer
and more difficult concept. The purpose is obviously unwelcome

or the use of force would scarcely be necessary. However, there is a difference between the kind of result that can, however reluctantly, be accepted under duress and the circumstances in which, to use an outmoded cliché, 'I would rather die'. The use of force is not limited if its purpose is likely to be regarded by the victim as demanding an unlimited resistance.

This is naturally not a criterion of general or absolute validity: different peoples at different periods and in differing circumstances have reacted in a variety of ways to otherwise similar challenges. What affronts are tolerable and which call for desperate resistance is a question requiring separate study and an individual answer in every particular case. That same year of 1940, for instance, elicited from the various peoples of Europe a remarkable range of responses to the single stimulus of German invasion. Broadly speaking, however, a tolerable result is one that, in the eyes of the victim, is less undesirable than resort to war. This was clearly the view taken of acquiescence in British action by all the responsible Norwegians involved.

The concept of purpose has a military as well as a political aspect. The force employed must be regarded by both sides as capable of achieving its objective. If COSSACK, for instance, had not been expected to reach ALTMARK and to return with the prisoners, then Churchill's order of 16 February, unless it had been a mere gamble, would have implied a readiness to follow an initial failure by the employment of more extensive force. Before the attempt was made, the choice was between abandoning the prisoners and offending Norway by their rescue. After an unsuccessful attempt, the option of avoiding Norwegian anger would no longer have existed and its adverse consequences could only have been aggravated by either of the choices that would then have remained: to accept defeat or to seek victory by using greater force. Whether or not the latter course led to actual war, it would have involved the use of force for objectives, and to an extent, that the British government could not have defined in advance. Both would have depended on Norwegian reactions, which would have been much harder to predict, because they might no longer have been determined by the original cause of dispute.

A government embarking on an act of genuinely limited force should thus have a reasonable expectation that the force initially employed will be sufficient to achieve the specific purpose originally envisaged without regard to the reactions of the victim, whose options are thus confined to acquiescence, ineffectual resistance or a retaliation that can only follow, and not prevent, the achievement of the desired result. In such cases, the use of force is not merely limited, but is also *definitive*: it creates a *fait accompli*.

It is, however, important that the probability of immediate military success should be equally apparent to the victim. If ALTMARK had been capable of effective defence, or under the protection of shore batteries, or if the escorting Norwegian warships had been strong enough to sink COSSACK out of hand (though this would presumably have meant coping with her consorts as well), the problems confronting the Norwegians would have been different. Neither Churchill's suggestion 'that honour is served by submitting to superior force', nor the Norwegian proviso that violations of neutrality were not to be resisted 'against a considerable superiority of force',[16] would have applied. Indeed, if it had seemed likely to be successful, Norwegian resistance could have been justified by other arguments than those of honour or compliance with the regulations. Suppose that, instead of a destroyer supported by four others and a cruiser, a single weak warship had entered Norwegian territorial waters and had there been sunk, thus allowing ALTMARK to reach Germany before the arrival of British reinforcements, the *fait accompli* would then have confronted not the Norwegian government, but the British government, with a situation that they might resent, or even seek to revenge, but that they could no longer undo. The sword of limited force would then have been turned against Britain, to present the choice between ineffective protest and unwanted war.

As events actually turned out, however, the Norwegians had no doubts regarding British ability to achieve their limited objective without regard to Norwegian reactions. Indeed, thanks to FIRERN's mistaken report of five cruisers, they may even have overestimated their opponents' strength. The choice presented to them was thus between a relatively painless acquiescence and the certain casualties of a futile attempt at resistance – casualties that, by arousing an emotional demand for retaliation, might then have exposed Norway to the prospect of greater suffering in a wider conflict. Moreover, even if Norway would be the political victim, the human targets of British force would be German and not Norwegian.

The desire to avoid casualties or suffering may, however, seem less compelling if these have already been inflicted. In such cases, a fourth test is often suggested to establish that force is actually limited. This is the more familiar condition, and, conventionally, the more important one, that the force employed should manifestly be the minimum needed to achieve the desired result.

In applying this test, it is naturally important to distinguish between force and violence. The fact that more force – in the shape of five additional warships waiting outside the Jøsingfjord – was available than was actually employed to liberate the ALTMARK's prisoners, did not detract from Churchill's insistence on the use of minimum force. From the standpoint of the victim, the greater the force available to the opponent, the stronger become the arguments for his own acquiescence. But, when this force is employed in actual violence against the victim, this may produce both an emotional and a rational reaction in favour of resistance. If COSSACK, for instance, before boarding ALTMARK, had taken the militarily defensible precaution of torpedoing KJELL, this would have further reduced the chances of successful intervention by the remaining Norwegian warships, yet made it more likely that even the coolest and least berserk of their commanders would have felt bound to attempt it. In doing so, he would have been responding to a different duty in a new situation: instead of adopting an attitude of prudent restraint towards a technical offence – the violation of neutrality – he would have been reacting to an act of war, an infliction of injury not demanded by what had previously seemed a limited and tolerable objective. On the other hand, if KJELL had suffered damage, or even casualties, from a collision with COSSACK while attempting to bar the way, there would have been much less reason for any fundamental change in the Norwegian attitude, either then or afterwards.

An act of force may thus forfeit its limited character if the damage inflicted during the actual operation seems to the victim to be disproportionate, because the excess of violence may suggest the existence of hostile intentions not confined to the achievement of an immediate and limited result. Even if the conclusions drawn by the victim do not increase the effectiveness of his resistance to the actual operation, they make it more likely that he will retaliate. Therefore, when limited force is employed as an alternative to war, it will often be desirable to make this clear to the victim by accepting military risks that would never be run in war: allowing the victim to fire first, and even suffering some fire without replying. If the immediate objective can be achieved whatever happens, it becomes more important for the assailant to avoid the infliction of casualties than the incurring of casualties.

Unfortunately, this ideal combination of sufficient force and minimum violence – a force that the victim cannot hope to withstand, but a violence he can expect to survive – is not always feasible. Even when limited force is used definitively – to remove the cause of dispute rather than to persuade someone else to do so – the infliction of damage and casualties may be a foreseeable, even an inevitable, feature of the operation. The victim's capacity for resistance may be so great, for instance, that only a surprise attack will secure the objective, or this may be a fort that must actually be destroyed. In such cases it is not resistance (which must be overwhelmed) that has to be avoided, but retaliation, and it does not necessarily follow that this will best be achieved by minimum violence. The infliction of any casualties or damage is bound to arouse anger, and it will largely depend on the circumstances and national characteristics of those concerned as to whether the resulting desire for revenge will be diminished by the argument that the assailant could have caused even more suffering than he actually did. It may sometimes even seem desirable to increase the level of violence, so that the inevitable resentment is accompanied and balanced by fear. The most that can be ventured as a general proposition is that, if violence is confined to the time and place of the actual operation, this will tend to reinforce the idea of its limited character, whereas preparatory or diversionary attacks will suggest a general hostility more akin to the start of a war. The level of violence in the actual operation, on the other hand, is difficult to measure by any standard acceptable to both sides, who can seldom be expected to agree on its necessity. If, as in the ALTMARK incident, the victim suffers no violence at all, this may usefully reinforce his readiness to believe that the objective was limited and tolerable. Otherwise, the concept of minimum violence is probably more useful after the event – to the lawyers and propagandists who must assert or deny its justice – than it is to those who, in the heat of conflict, endeavour to distinguish between limited force and acts of war.

This was a distinction established with exceptional care and clarity in February 1940, but the liberation of ALTMARK's prisoners is a classic case of gunboat diplomacy rather than an entirely typical one. The friendly relations between Britain and Norway, the similar traditions and political outlook of the two peoples, even the fact that most of the Norwegians concerned could speak English: these unusual features made it much easier for the British to explain the limited character of their operation and much easier for the Norwegians to believe British assurances. Although there was a war on, in spite of the mutual suspicions engendered by earlier disputes regarding Norwegian neutrality, notwithstanding the importance – for both sides – of the issues now at stake, there was throughout this operation an exceptional degree of mutual comprehension, confidence and forbearance. It is not very usual to find a victim (Captain Halvorsen of KJELL) testifying to his assailant's courtesy: 'the conversation (with Captain Vian) was throughout conducted by both sides in a polite, but firm manner'.[17]

Any such comment would have been inconceivable in a later instance of the definitive use of limited naval force: the seizure, on 23 January 1968, of the USS PUEBLO off the coast of North Korea. The incident, however, is less remarkable for its lack of amenity than for the success with which North Korea exploited a local and momentary advantage against a victim otherwise incomparably more powerful. Gunboat diplomacy is traditionally a weapon employed by the strong against the weak, and this somewhat exceptional instance thus demands careful analysis to establish whether it resulted from a chance combination of circumstances unlikely to be repeated or whether it can be fitted into a theoretical framework of more general application – even if this framework then entails some modification of the principles derived from the rather different ALTMARK episode. This is not an easy task. Our evidence of even US intentions and assumptions is incomplete, while those of the North Koreans can only approximately and tentatively be deduced from their actions and public statements. These last offer a particularly uncertain guide. To Western ears, the vocabulary of communist diplomacy – except on those occasions when peaceful coexistence used to be hymned in the glutinous vibrato of an early Wurlitzer – resembles the gamelan orchestra: it includes only the instruments of percussion. The sheer stridency of abuse is so deafening that courage often contributes more than expertise to the detection of those trifling reductions in pitch or volume that may signify restraint or a readiness to compromise. The interpretation that follows is thus necessarily conjectural.

The background, however, is clear enough. Relations between North Korea and the United States had long been devoid of sympathy or mutual understanding. Neither would feel inhibited in the conduct of a dispute by any recollection of past friendship or hope of future goodwill. Lack of contact made each inherently liable to misinterpret the other's intentions and, when they erred, to do so by exaggerating the extent of the opponent's hostility. Perhaps this was particularly true of the US government, for there was no equivalent in North Korea to the wealth of information published to the world by the US press and radio. US interpretations were thus necessarily based on only a fraction of the corresponding data available to the North Koreans and were, in addition, liable to distortion by a factor from which the Koreans, who only had to concentrate their efforts at analysis on the United States, were immune. In Washington the actions of Asian communists then tended to be explained as the response to directives from Moscow or Peking. Even if this assumption had been valid – and it is arguable that often it was not – there was obviously added scope for confusion and misinterpretation in trying to relate specific actions or statements to the patterns of behaviour characteristic of not one centre of decision, but three.

Thus, when the North Korean radio broadcast on 9 January 1968 [18] an attack on the activities of US electronic surveillance vessels off the coast of North Korea, there may have been at least two reasons for not taking this seriously. First, it was the practice of the North Koreans to denounce everything done by the Americans, so that any significant message was easily obscured by the volume of indiscriminate abuse. Secondly, Americans and Russians had established a pattern of mutual tolerance of espionage outside their respective territorial waters. Any expectation that the North Koreans would violate these conventions thus required either the admission that they were capable of pursuing independent policies or else the assumption that the Russians had wider and more sinister motives for permitting such a breach. It was the latter notion that, after the event, seemed to come more naturally to the Americans, who meanwhile failed to react to the admittedly imprecise warning they had received.

On 23 January 1968, therefore, PUEBLO was placidly carrying out her accustomed task of electronic surveillance at a point that, in the light of North Korean signals intercepted by the Americans, was almost certainly just outside the territorial waters of North Korea. For all practical purposes she was un-armed, her crew were not trained in self-defence, she was not escorted, and no arrangements had been made for her protec-tion or rescue. Her commander and his superiors relied entirely on the immunity conferred by international law, an essentially European concept that had been little applied, and less imita-ted, in Asian waters. This illusory confidence was scarcely ruffled when, about noon, she was located, challenged and identified by a North Korean patrol vessel. This visitor, however, was not content with shadowing PUEBLO. Reinforcements were summoned and the luckless US vessel soon found herself surrounded by four patrol craft escorted by two fighter aircraft. She was again summoned to heave-to and, when she ignored the signal, was fired on until she complied; and now, obedient to further directions, followed her assailants towards the coast before being boarded and taken into Wonsan as a prize. There she remained, while her crew had to endure a barbarous capti-vity for eleven months until the US government, having unsuccessfully attempted a variety of other expedients, finally purchased their release on the terms demanded from the outset by the North Koreans: 'all you have to do is to admit military provocations and aggressive acts committed by your side, apolo-gise for them and assure this table that you will not recommit such criminal acts'.[19]

Bearing in mind that no satisfactory evidence exists of North Korean motives, two interpretations of this remarkable story are possible. The first is that the North Koreans recklessly committed – perhaps even on the initiative of a relatively junior commander – a potential act of war, and that they only escaped its consequences because of a fortuitous combination of US weariness with hostilities in Asia, US uncertainty about the intentions of China and the Soviet Union, and US humanitarian concern for the lives and liberty of PUEBLO's captive crew. The US Secretary of State, Dean Rusk, early described the incident as being 'in the category of actions that are to be construed as acts of war';[20] US warships and military aircraft effected a threatening concentration against North Korea; reservists were called up; the Security Council convened. That all these gestures expired in empty air; that North Korea escaped all retaliation and achieved her full objectives; that events finally demonstrated this to have been an act of limited force: these, it may be argued, were the chance results of a desperate gamble in circumstances so favourable that they could scarcely be repeated, could not form the basis for more general deductions, and hardly qualify for inclusion in the annals of gunboat diplomacy.

Another interpretation is that the factors that made the United States willing to wound, but afraid to strike, were not beyond the wit of the North Koreans to foresee and that, in deciding to impose their will on a superpower, they were taking a risk they had calculated in advance. If this was indeed a deliberately planned operation, we must presume – even if we have no equivalent of Churchill's order of 16 January 1940 to rely on – that the objective, the method and the obstacles to be expected had been envisaged in advance. The objective seems obvious, though it has been disputed: to put a stop to PUEBLO's espionage, to capture her secrets and, by this example and by exploiting her crew as hostages, to deter the US government from replacing this vessel by any other with similar tasks. If this assumption is correct, then the North Koreans intended both an act of definitive force – the removal of PUEBLO – and one of purposeful force – inducing the US government to desist from this type of espionage in the future. These were defined and limited objectives.

They were not, however, initially clear to the US government. This was partly a result of the apparently constitutional inability of the North Koreans to explain themselves in a manner comprehensible and convincing to US ears. The signal they may have desired to convey, whether in the broadcast warning of 9 January or in General Pak's statements of the 20th and 24th,[21] was swamped by the background noise of seemingly irrelevant and ambiguous abuse. However, their failure probably owed something to the obsessive US belief that all communist actions were centrally directed from Moscow. On this view, it was inconceivable that the Soviet Union, which had long practised seaborne electronic espionage on the largest of scales, should jeopardise US tolerance of these activities by permitting an act of violence on the high seas unless this had some purpose far wider and more sinister than mere counter-espionage. As a result, the US press, no doubt reflecting official speculation, canvassed the wildest hypotheses: this was the opening move of a new Korean war, a Soviet probe of US resolution, a gambit to reduce US pressure on North Vietnam. The idea that the North Koreans objected to being spied upon and had acted independently to rid themselves of this nuisance was often mentioned, only to be dismissed. Even President Johnson spoke of the incident as the culmination of a 'stepped-up campaign of violence against South Korea and American troops' that might be intended 'to divert South Korean and US military resources from the Vietnam war'.[22]

These speculations may have been far-fetched – the doctrine of total control from Moscow had already taken some battering in Asia – but their prevalence demonstrates the extent of the North Korean failure to communicate to their victim the limited character of their objective. Perhaps they did not try very hard, because they believed that a further war in Asia would, in any case, prove less tolerable to the United States than making concessions, and that the United States would not retaliate on mere hypotheses unless these were confirmed by further acts of violence. Such a calculation could reasonably have been based on the assumption that no middle course was open to the United States between all-out war and concessions to obtain the release of the crew. Indeed, the crucial weakness of the US position was the predominance over most other considerations of their anxiety to preserve the lives and obtain the liberty of these hostages. It is this factor that, at first sight, seems to differentiate the PUEBLO affair from the ALTMARK incident, and to make of the former an isolated case difficult to fit into the general pattern of gunboat diplomacy.

This may be a misleadingly superficial analysis. The exploitation of hostages is an expedient regularly employed against governments sensitive to the welfare of their individual nationals, and there is no reason to expect its use to be less frequent in the future than in the recent past.[23] When employed in connection with an act of limited force, it serves the purpose of rendering acquiescence by the victim's government relatively less intolerable than other courses of action unlikely to preserve the lives or secure the liberty of the hostages. Moreover, on this issue the North Koreans took greater pains to make clear the limited character of their objectives. Although the first definite indication that PUEBLO's crew would be released if the United States admitted its fault, apologised, and promised there would be no repetition seems to have been given only on 31 January,[24] this was surely implicit in General Pak's statement of the 24th. It is at least arguable, therefore, that the North Korean conduct of this operation, when allowance is made for the hostile and mutually uncomprehending relationship between assailant and victim, can be interpreted as presenting a rough approximation to the principles derived from the ALTMARK incident. The North Koreans did have a defined and limited objective, which they did, however inadequately and unsuccessfully, endeavour to explain before and immediately after their act of force. They had reason to regard the results of their action as less intolerable to the Americans than war and they exploited their seizure of hostages to provide an additional incentive for US acquiescence. They could be confident that their military resources were adequate to create a *fait accompli* that the Americans could neither prevent nor undo and that would confront the US government with a choice between acquiescence and an escalatory retaliation. The opening of fire and the infliction of four casualties by a superior force that had surrounded a defenceless ship may reasonably be ascribed to mere nervousness and incompetence on the part of assailants who must surely have been ordered to secure vessel, crew and secrets intact. This view receives some support from General Pak's subsequent pretence[25] that the almost unarmed PUEBLO had carried 'large quantities of weapons' and had fired first. These lies may have been prompted by the consciousness that more violence had been employed than was in fact necessary. They were not essential to his main thesis that PUEBLO had been captured within territorial waters.

This is a conjectural interpretation, but it is not an impossible one. Naturally we cannot deduce from Korean actions any consciousness of the ALTMARK principles, let alone any formal proof of their validity. Indeed, we cannot expect every feature of the almost ideal case of the ALTMARK to be reflected in other uses of definitive force. In 1940 a major (albeit secondary) preoccupation of the British government was to minimise the harm to Anglo-Norwegian friendship, a purpose that found no echo twenty-eight years later in Pyongyang, but that necessarily demanded greater precautions. The North Koreans had only to consider how to avoid US retaliation, for which purpose their exploitation of the hostages may have seemed a sufficient means of rendering acquiescence less intolerable than any alternative course. It may thus be preferable to treat an act of force as possessing a limited character if it has a defined objective of which the achievement is expected to evoke only a limited response, and to regard the ALTMARK principles as aids to predicting that response rather than indispensable elements of a definition. Provided the North Koreans expected to achieve their objective without retaliation, their failure to communicate to their victim the limited character of this objective would not require the exclusion of the PUEBLO operation from the category of acts of limited force. It was a needlessly clumsy and brutal operation, as was the Israeli attack on the USS LIBERTY in 1967, but in each case the assailant achieved his objective without suffering retaliation. The glaring differences between the ALTMARK and PUEBLO incidents are partly attributable to the very different character and mutual relationship of assailant and victim, but also to the distinction between the purely definitive nature of the force employed in the ALTMARK affair and the transition from definitive force, which captured PUEBLO, to purposeful force, which wrung concessions from the US government. These differences, though, are less important than the underlying similarity: in each case, limited naval force was successfully employed to achieve, without retaliation or other consequences undesired by the assailant, a defined objective scarcely attainable by any other means.

What is more, in spite of the passage of twenty-eight years and the major changes that have transformed not only warships and their weapons, but also the structure of international relations, a comparison of the ALTMARK and PUEBLO affairs suggests that the potential efficacy of gunboat diplomacy has actually increased. The greater elegance and smoothness of the Royal Navy's operation should not blind us to the fact that their victim was far less formidable than that of their North Korean successors. The British merely liberated some prisoners in the face of ineffectual and even half-hearted protests by a far weaker state; the North Koreans seized a US naval vessel in international waters, stopped US seaborne espionage against their country,[26] and used the hostages they had taken to extract significant and humiliating concessions from a superpower.

Acceptance of this view, however, demands an answer to one obvious question. If the efficacy of gunboat diplomacy had not merely survived, but actually increased, why was the world's strongest naval power unable to use this expedient against North Korea? There are two explanations: one particular and technical, the other political and of more general application.

The first is paradoxical. Gunboat diplomacy is the weapon of the strong against the weak, but strength is to be measured not by potential, but by the ability to apply appropriate force about the point at issue. By this yardstick the North Koreans were stronger and had used their naval forces that, though relatively insignificant, were on the spot, to create a *fait accompli*. Long before any of the innumerable ships of the US Navy could reach North Korean waters, the hostages were aboard a train rattling into the interior of the country.[27] The tactical situation was thus entirely different from that obtaining in 1926, when the Royal Navy rescued British prisoners (at considerable cost in casualties) from two merchant vessels captured by the Chinese at Wanhsien high up the Yangtse, or in 1949, when HMS LONDON and BLACK SWAN failed in their attempt to rescue HMS AMETHYST, then aground under artillery fire in the same river.[28] In both these cases, the location of the captives was known and accessible to nearby British warships. To liberate PUEBLO's crew, however, the Americans would have had to emulate the exploits not of the Royal Navy, but of Otto Skorzeny, whose successful rescue of Mussolini in 1943 was facilitated by precise intelligence not available to the US government in 1968.

The second explanation is that, when an act of definitive force has created a *fait accompli*, any reaction by the victim can only take the form either of purposeful force – inhibited in this case by concern for the safety of the hostages – or of retaliation. The latter operates in a different moral and military climate. Tension has already been aroused by the initial act of limited force, the assailant is on the alert and prepared to resist any counter-attack, the entire corpus of international law and morality exerts a vague but (on Western governments) sometimes efficacious disapproval of the whole concept of retaliation. Above all, retaliation is liable to assume the character of an act of war and thus excites the apprehension and mobilises the dissuasive energies of allies, of international organisations and of large sections of public opinion, both within and beyond the borders of the victim state. All these factors combine to support the argument that, however infuriating, outrageous and immoral the original act of limited force, mere retaliation would be fruitless, dangerous and even wicked. This is not necessarily a valid argument, nor one that invariably prevails, but it probably exercised considerable influence on the US government in 1968. Their acquiescence, then, can thus not be attributed to any flaw in the concept of gunboat diplomacy as an instrument for the furtherance of foreign policy.[29]

In its definitive form, therefore, we may provisionally conclude that limited naval force, where this is employed (as in the case of PUEBLO) to seize the property or nationals of the victim, or, as happened at Mogadishu in 1991, to rescue the nationals of the assailant,[30] has lost none of its ancient effectiveness in recent years as long as the assailant is able to support an informed resolution with appropriate naval force at the decisive point and the critical moment. The capture of PUEBLO, however, though itself an act of definitive force, was subsequently exploited by the North Koreans to extract concessions from the US government, thus making it also a purposeful use of force. It is to the purposeful application of limited naval force that we must now turn our attention.

II PURPOSEFUL FORCE: CORFU

Limited naval force is employed purposefully in order to change the policy or character of a foreign government or of some organised group whose relationship to the assailant is, for practical purposes, that of a foreign government. In its purposeful application, force does not itself do anything: it induces someone else to take a decision that would not otherwise have been taken – to do something or to stop doing it, or to refrain from a contemplated course of action. This is a less direct, and hence a less reliable, expedient than definitive force, which itself removes the cause of dispute, because purposeful force depends for its success on a choice made by the victim. Once the North Koreans decided to attack PUEBLO, there was no option available to the US government that could have been exercised to prevent the capture of the vessel and her crew, but the subsequent exploitation of the hostages only succeeded because President Johnson decided that their lives and liberty were worth the concessions demanded, a choice he might not have made.

There are, however, many situations in which the desired result can only be achieved with the co-operation of the victim. If a safe is to be opened, for instance, definitive force can be used to seize a key or blow the lock, but a memorised combination can only be obtained if force – or some other inducement – convinces the holder that revealing it has become the least disadvantageous course open to him. On this analogy, the most direct application of purposeful force is to the leaders of the victim state or organisation. They may be induced by personal threats or violence to take the desired decisions or they may be removed and replaced by others able and willing to do so.

In October 1983, for instance, the United States mounted a large amphibious operation, Urgent Fury, under the command of Vice-Admiral Metcalf, to invade the island of Grenada and to replace its communist government by leaders more acceptable to President Reagan. The level of violence was rather high and a number of casualties resulted, but the objective was quickly achieved, the new regime was welcomed by most of the people of Grenada, and normal relations were soon restored. Although the resistance to be overcome was less than formidable and the operation attracted much international criticism, this successful use of limited naval force to change the character of a foreign government[31] deserves to be contrasted with the failure of many other attempts, some involving outright war – for instance, against North Vietnam in the 1960s and early 1970s.

Even the success achieved by the US Army (the Navy were not involved) in December 1989, when they removed one president of Panama (General Noriega) and replaced him by another, entailed the use of 23,000 troops with air support, much heavier casualties than in Grenada, and an estimated cost (including damage in Panama) of 2,000 million dollars.[32] When it comes to overthrowing a foreign government, the traditional methods remain the best whenever the circumstances allow the assailant to rely on a cunning and unobtrusive use of force, rather than a massive use of force. In 1944, for instance, a small group of parachutists commanded by the resourceful Otto Skorzeny kidnapped Admiral Horthy and replaced him by Hungarian leaders more amenable to German wishes.[33] In 1953 the British and US secret services collaborated in financing and inspiring the *coup d'état* that toppled Mohammed Mossadegh, that obstreperous Iranian Prime Minister.[34]

Whether overt or covert, all outside interventions to change the character or policy of a foreign government are necessarily purposeful rather than definitive, because their success is ultimately dependent on the acquiescence of the inhabitants of the victim state. If we take five years as the measure of lasting success (one British Prime Minister, Harold Wilson, said a week was a long time in politics), then the Soviet Union managed a durable change of leadership in Hungary in 1956 and in Czechoslovakia in 1968. However, they failed in Afghanistan in 1979, when the leadership changes effected by Soviet armed intervention only exacerbated the Afghan insurgency they had been intended to quell. History is rich in other examples of intervening foreigners who got their man into the palace, but could not keep him there.

On the whole, however, the political developments of recent decades have been unfavourable to the use of foreign limited force against governments as opposed to their states. The number of intrinsically vulnerable governments – those without a centralised administration or the ability to count on a degree of popular support against foreign intervention – is steadily declining. Most modern nation-states are hydra-headed: remove one set of leaders and another, equally obnoxious, set may replace them. Overt intervention – and limited naval force is necessarily overt – is liable to generate a reaction, not only among the people of the victim-state, but also from other governments. Even if the victim has no powerful foreign protector, the modern doctrine of absolute national sovereignty may generate a degree of embarrassing international sympathy for a government evicted by foreign violence. This may not be important – if the force available is sufficient – but it constitutes a disincentive that has probably reinforced the contemporary tendency towards increasing reliance on other methods: covert assistance to indigenous movements anxious to replace the obnoxious government or overt force that, without attempting the eviction or personal coercion of the leaders, induces them to change their policy by altering the balance of national advantage in the options open to them.[35] The potential naval contributions to subversion and its prevention will be considered later: what now concerns us is the role of limited naval force in convincing a foreign government that new circumstances require them to take altered decisions.

Such force can sometimes be applied directly to the cause of dispute. During the Spanish Civil War, for instance, the Italian government wished to dissuade other countries from sending aid to the Spanish Republicans, so, from August 1937 onwards, Italian submarines were intermittently employed, without their use being officially admitted, to sink ships bound for Republican ports. Because Italy had insufficient submarines and did not wish to risk an open rupture with other powers, this practice was not fully effective, though it did constitute both a deterrent and an impediment to the supply of arms and equipment to the Republican forces. So far as British ships were concerned, these sinkings were discontinued when the British government (together with the French) countered with their own threat of limited naval force: that submarines found submerged in the area patrolled by British and French destroyers would be sunk.[36] In principle, however, the more nearly that purposeful force can be related to the actual cause of dispute, the more likely it is to achieve the objective while retaining its limited character.

The patrol maintained off Beira after 1966 by the Royal Navy[37] was not a particularly effective way of stopping oil from reaching Rhodesia, but it does seem to have prevented its importation by this particular route and to have done so without any of the direct confrontations with dissenting governments that other methods might have entailed. When a particular course of action can demonstrably be prevented, a reasonable government will not wish to persevere in a fruitless endeavour. It is no coincidence that one of the traditional conditions in international law for the recognition by neutrals of a naval blockade is that it should be effective.

Limited naval force, however, can only be directly applied to disputes in which the sea or the use of navigable waters is an intrinsic element. British warships may protect British trawlers fishing in Icelandic waters or assert the right of innocent passage through territorial straits; the US Seventh Fleet may throw a defensive girdle around Formosa; the Soviet Mediterranean squadron may interpose its warships between Port Said and the Israeli Army on the opposite bank of the Suez Canal. However, there would have to be some special factor before any of these navies could directly influence the outcome of a purely terrestrial dispute. The elephant is not vulnerable to the crocodile until his trunk dangles near the water's edge.

In its indirect applications, however, the influence of limited naval force can be extended to disputes far beyond any high water mark. This is mainly achieved by damage infliction, which need not be directly related to the actual cause of dispute. Instead, injury is threatened or performed until the victim purchases immunity by the desired concessions. Methods employed in the past include blockade, harassment of shipping, the capture or sinking of vessels flying the victim's flag, coastal bombardment, the occupation of islands or coastal areas, the landing of punitive expeditions and, of course, the seizure and exploitation of hostages. In its more extreme form, damage infliction comes close to war and – when the reactions of victims have been wrongly estimated – sometimes develops into war, as happened when the United States tried to end the insurrection in South Vietnam by inflicting damage on the North. In the nineteenth century, when a fleet at sea was almost invulnerable to anything but a stronger fleet, the use of limited naval force for damage infliction often allowed an assailant to put pressure on his victim with impunity, but both political and technological developments have since impaired the effectiveness of this expedient. As its future usefulness is not necessarily exhausted, a brief examination of one of the classic cases of modern times – the Corfu incident – may serve to illustrate the principles involved and the extent to which these require adaptation to the different environment of the late twentieth century.

On 27 August 1923, General Enrico Tellini, the Italian President of the Commission of Delimination appointed by the Conference of Ambassadors (on which Britain, France, Italy, Japan and the United States were represented) to mark out the frontiers of Albania, was ambushed and murdered, together with those of his staff who had accompanied him, in a wood at Zepi. This was in Greek territory, though not very far from the

Albanian border, and the General was on his way to a meeting of
the Commission at the time of his death. For reasons that need
not concern us, the Italian government decided, with little evidence to support their view,[38] that the Greek government were
morally responsible for this murder and should be required to
make reparation to Italy. On the evening of 29 August the Italian
Minister at Athens accordingly presented a note demanding an
apology, the presence of all members of the Greek government at
a funeral for the victims in Athens, naval honours, an investigation, capital punishment for the culprits, 50 million Italian lire,
and military honours for the corpses on their final embarkation
for Italy. A reply was required within twenty-four hours.

A conciliatory answer was received from the Greek government within the time-limit specified, but this did not accept all
the Italian demands. On 31 August, therefore, Mussolini
despatched a personal message to all Italian diplomatic missions
abroad, which was communicated to the Greek government that
afternoon:

> To the just demands formulated by Italy following the barbar-
> ous massacre of the Italian Military Mission committed in
> Greek territory, the Hellenic Government has replied in terms
> that correspond in essence to the complete rejection of the
> same. Such an unjustified attitude places upon Italy the
> necessity of recalling the Hellenic Government to a sense of
> its responsibility. I have therefore communicated the order for
> the landing on the island of Corfu of a contingent of Italian
> troops. With this measure of a temporary character Italy does
> not intend an act of war but only to defend its own prestige
> and to manifest its inflexible will to obtain the reparations due
> to it in conformity with custom and international law. The
> Italian Government hopes that Greece does not commit any
> act that may modify the pacific nature of the measures.[39]

At three o'clock that afternoon Captain Foschini of the
Italian Navy landed on the Greek island of Corfu and informed
the local authorities that the Italian Fleet, commanded by
Admiral Solari, were on their way and would carry out the
occupation of Corfu in thirty minutes' time. Unless a white flag
was raised by 4 p.m. to signify the surrender of the island,
bombardment would begin. It did. Thirty-five shells were fired,
killing sixteen people and wounding about fifty, before the

white flag appeared. Militarily this shelling was unnecessary and contrary to Mussolini's orders, but the Greeks offered no resistance to the occupation of Corfu and the adjoining islands, an occupation successfully maintained until 27 September, by which date the Greek government had complied with every one of the original Italian demands, which had meanwhile been endorsed by the other four governments represented in the Conference of Ambassadors and presented to the Greek government by that organisation as their own. The Council of the League of Nations, to which Greece had appealed, took note of the intervention of the Conference of Ambassadors and welcomed their success in reaching a solution.

A number of interesting points emerge from this singular story. First of all, limited naval force had achieved complete success for Italy in a manner that no other expedient could have. The role played by the Conference of Ambassadors was essentially a moderating one – they induced the Italian government not to press some of their supplementary demands (the payment by Greece of the cost of the Italian operation, for instance) and they smoothed the way for Greek surrender by giving an international veneer to Italian pressure, but they would never have endorsed the demand for 50 million lire except as the only means of terminating the occupation of Corfu. The almost simultaneous repudiation of responsibility by the Swiss government for the murder in Lausanne of a Soviet diplomat, V.V. Vorovsky, suggests the likely fate of unsupported diplomatic representations.[40]

Secondly, the Italian conception of the operation (though not the clumsy brutality of the Italian admiral) conformed closely to the ALTMARK principles. The objective was defined, limited and tolerable; it was carefully communicated to the victim (the phrase 'Italy does not intend an act of war' is particularly noteworthy); the forces employed were manifestly capable of achieving their military objective without regard to Greek reactions; and acts of violence unrelated to the operation were avoided.

These are factors obviously still relevant today, but there are other aspects of this episode for which it might seem difficult to find a recent parallel, or imagine an imminent parallel. To begin with, no great power was seriously prepared (though the British government made tentative and ineffectual gestures) to support Greece. In the days of bipolarity, when most small states expected to appeal to one superpower against coercion by the other or by a lesser power, this seemed an unlikely contingency. Yet, was it so different from the ineffectual condemnation of intervention in Hungary in 1956, in Cuba in 1961, in the Dominican Republic in 1965, in Czechoslovakia in 1968? Or, if it be objected that, even in 1923, Italy scarcely ranked as a superpower, were Scandinavian objections then any more futile than those expressed by many members of the United Nations to US invasion of another island, Grenada, in 1983? In 1923 France had her reasons for extending diplomatic support to Italy, just as, in a more recent era, the United States had for backing Israel, or the Soviet Union for backing North Korea. The international kaleidoscope has shifted, but it is the patterns that are new, not their character. The combination of a relatively strong Italy, whom no one particularly wished to quarrel with, and a relatively weak Greece, whom no one felt especially bound to defend, is one that could still be reflected in future.

On the other hand, the inability of the Corfiotes to defend themselves against the Italian Navy and their ready, if reluctant, acceptance of the inevitability of Italian occupation (the Prefect of Corfu was authorised by a meeting of government officials 'to bow before superior force')[41] might find fewer parallels today, when otherwise weak states (Albania in 1946, the Lebanon in 1983) can be the source of disconcerting reactions to the manoeuvres of warships off their coasts or the landing of marines. Weak states can sometimes do so, but not always: the US Navy operated with impunity off the shores of the Dominican Republic; the 1980s saw the failure of repeated efforts to make the US Sixth Fleet feel the fierceness of Libyan resentment.[42] Exceptional circumstances are nowadays required for the successful exercise of limited force, but so they were in 1923. There were not many other countries against which Mussolini could then have executed a similar coup.

One factor of importance in the Corfu episode does however seem to have disappeared, at least temporarily, from the contemporary scene. This is the degree of responsibility that states were then expected to assume for the safety and immunity within their territory of diplomatic representatives or international emissaries, even of ordinary foreign nationals. The Italian view that the Greek government had a duty to guarantee the personal safety of 'all legally accredited missions in its territory' and the opinion of the Conference of Ambassadors that 'every State is responsible for the crimes and political outrages committed on its territory' did not pass unchallenged by the international lawyers (what opinion ever will?) but they commanded acceptance from many members of the League of Nations otherwise critical of Italian conduct. At the very outset of the dispute, and before Italian intentions were known, the French government proposed that the powers represented in the Conference of Ambassadors should 'reserve to themselves to present eventually any demands for sanctions and for reparations that will appear necessary to them' and the final exaction of the indemnity of 50 million lire was justified by the Conference of Ambassadors on the ground that *'les coupables n'étaient pas encore découverts'*. 'The right of the Conference to reparations for the murder of General Tellini was never questioned during the settlement of the crisis.'[43]

The nature of international society has greatly changed since 1923, and ambassadors, diplomats and representatives of international organisations may nowadays be maltreated with impunity. Since 1965 six US ambassadors have been murdered at their posts and over seventy other Americans attached to diplomatic missions of the United States – the world's strongest naval power – have been killed abroad. The representatives of lesser states have suffered proportionately. 'The world at large, which in the past took steps of a cooperative character to uphold the rights of diplomats, stood idly by.'[44]

This change – and the absence of any recent reaction of the Corfu variety to similar provocations – probably constitutes a source of more unalloyed satisfaction to coastal dwellers than to the smaller number of people likely to be charged by their governments or by international organisations with the conduct of such dangerously invidious missions. Borrowing the words of a more illustrious author, 'I leave it to be settled by whomsoever it may concern, whether the tendency of this work be altogether to recommend paternal tyranny or reward filial disobedience.'[45] The only moral that need be pointed out here is that, thanks to the use of limited naval force for damage-infliction, the Italian government successfully exacted, in spite of a climate of international opinion much less indulgent than the Conference of Ambassadors, all the considerable concessions they had originally demanded. In similarly exceptional circumstances, though doubtless from different motives, other governments might still emulate Mussolini's exploit against victims incapable of coastal defence, unwilling to contemplate popular resistance and devoid of resolute allies. So far, however, the Corfu incident remains a unique example of the extent to which damage-infliction by limited naval force can be carried without provoking war or any international complication capable of detracting from the complete success of the assailant in all his original demands.

III   PURPOSEFUL FORCE: THE UPPER LIMIT

Limited naval force is an alternative to war, and purposeful force in particular may sometimes be used or threatened in an effort to resolve a dispute that, if allowed to fester, could lead to war. It is a risky expedient – fighting fire with fire – and the risks are aggravated when the parties to the dispute are of more or less equivalent military strength. These dangers were strikingly apparent during the confrontation that occurred in October 1973 between US and Soviet naval forces in the Mediterranean. The circumstances were admittedly exceptional, so much so as to raise the question as to whether the final phase of this episode can properly be classified as gunboat diplomacy or whether some of its features should instead be regarded as a threat of war.

Even the opening moves took place at a time when both navies had more ships than usual in the Mediterranean and its approaches. Both also sent reinforcements as the crisis developed. The trigger was the attack launched on 6 October by Egypt and Syria against Israel. On the 10th another Soviet cruiser and two destroyers entered the Mediterranean. On the 13th a third US carrier (there were two in the Sixth Fleet already), the JOHN F. KENNEDY, left British waters for a holding position just west of Gibraltar. In the third week of October both navies became involved in resupplying their Middle Eastern clients. All the belligerents had sustained heavy losses of equipment, particularly tanks and aircraft, in the intense fighting. In this task the part played by the US Sixth Fleet had one element that was not merely unprecedented, but one that no other navy could have attempted.

Israel desperately needed combat aircraft, having lost many to the surface-to-air missiles acquired by Egypt from the Soviet

Union. The United States was now willing to fly these aircraft out to Israel, but the *Skyhawks* and *Phantoms* would have to refuel at least three times on the way. Under US pressure, Portugal agreed to let the Azores be the first stop, but this still left a 2,000-mile gap that other European allies refused to fill. So the carriers of the Sixth Fleet turned themselves into staging points and the aircraft hopped from the Azores to the KENNEDY (after her arrival outside the Straits on 18 October), to the ROOSEVELT in the central Mediterranean, and then on to the INDEPENDENCE south of Crete. More ships of the Sixth Fleet were stationed in the intervals to provide navigation aids, communication facilities and, if needed, other support for the US air-lift. This included many large transport aircraft bringing equipment and supplies. These aircraft did not need the carriers as staging points, but profited from the protection against hostile interference that the deployment of the Sixth Fleet afforded.[46]

No such interference was attempted by the Soviet Fifth Squadron, which was content in this opening phase to keep the two US carriers inside the Mediterranean under surveillance. Soviet warships were also involved in resupplying Syria and deterring interference from the Israeli Navy. The Americans did, however, have to be on their guard against the possibility of Arab attacks, for the course of their air-lift to Israel was flanked by Morocco, Algeria, Tunisia, Libya and Egypt. If the employment of aircraft-carriers as staging points was an unique instance of the definitive use of limited naval force to overcome the refusal of the European allies to facilitate US resupply of Israel, the deployment of the Sixth Fleet was a routine threat of purposeful force.

This opening movement, in which the navies of the super-powers had independently busied themselves in ensuring the resupply of their respective clients, was abruptly ended on the evening of 24 October, when a message from Brezhnev to Nixon announced that, failing US agreement to a joint despatch of troops to enforce the ceasefire in Egypt, the Soviet Union would intervene on their own. As three Soviet airborne divisions had earlier been placed on alert, it has been suggested that two might have arrived within three days. The US reaction was to bring all their forces (nuclear missiles included) to a state of alert (Defcon Three) – a clear, if only implied, threat of war. The Sixth Fleet, already 'in an advanced condition of readiness', was ordered to concentrate in the eastern Mediterranean.

highest level, the crisis was quickly eased by another ⸀rom Brezhnev. This blandly announced the despatch ᴏⱼ ꜱoviet representatives to *observe* the implementation of the ceasefire in Egypt. The idea of military intervention seemed to have sunk without trace. In the Mediterranean, however, the storm was slower to subside:

> On October 26 the Soviets began large-scale anti-carrier exercises against the INDEPENDENCE carrier group with cruise-missile submarine participation. These exercises – the Soviet Navy's equivalent of training its guns on the US fleet – continued until November 3.[47]

The Soviet Navy also deployed anti-carrier groups to shadow ROOSEVELT and KENNEDY (which had joined INDEPENDENCE south-east of Crete) as well as the amphibious group of the Sixth Fleet. Only the INDEPENDENCE, which entered port at Athens on 3 November after the Sixth Fleet had been ordered to disperse, was made the target of mock attacks, presumably because she had been the nearest to Egypt throughout.[48]

Roberts, on whose admirable analysis this account has drawn heavily, comments that:

> After October 25, the crisis took on an entirely new character, setting the stage for a possible confrontation between the two superpowers.

> When Soviet ships began carrier exercises using US units as targets, this was the most intense signal the Soviets had ever demonstrated with their naval forces in a crisis.[49]

Clearly this signal could be interpreted as a threat of war. It was conduct forbidden – simulated attacks on the other party – by the *Incidents at Sea Agreement*, which the Soviet Union and the United States had signed on 25 May 1972, and it had long been regarded as provocatively bellicose. In 1893, when a French cruiser off Siam had turned her guns on a British cruiser, Kaiser Wilhelm II told Queen Victoria there was no way out of the incident but war.[50] Such behaviour by Soviet warships, at a time when acute tension ought to have been subsiding, invited the worst suspicions and could have had disastrous consequences. Fortunately, the US carrier group showed great restraint, even though they ran considerable risks by holding their fire. As Admiral Moorer, chairman of the US Joint Chiefs of Staff, pointed out, 'Victory in a Mediterranean encounter in 1973 would have depended on which Navy struck first and a variety of other factors.'[51]

Now that fossicking has begun in the Russian archives, we may one day learn what the Fifth Squadron intended by their conduct and who ordered it. Meanwhile one possible explanation seems worth considering. Although Brezhnev had apparently abandoned the idea of armed intervention in Egypt, he was clearly still concerned by the predicament of the Egyptian Third Army. This had been cut off and surrounded by Israeli forces, who were trying, even after the ceasefire, to starve the Egyptian formation into surrender. On 26 October, the day the anti-carrier exercises began, Brezhnev sent Nixon a message calling for US action in 'the next few hours' to ease the Israeli stranglehold on the Third Army. Kissinger himself was worried. He put strong pressure on Israel and the first food convey was allowed through to the Third Army on 29 October, though this provided only temporary relief and the issue remained acute throughout the period in which INDEPENDENCE was subjected to Soviet harassment.[52]

It is conceivable, therefore, that the anti-carrier exercises were a threat of naval force – limited only to the extent that it was a bluff not meant to result in action – intended to keep up the pressure on the United States to do something about the Third Army. If there is any truth in this speculative interpretation, the evidence is lacking to suggest that such a dangerous plan had any success in influencing US policy. Kissinger, whose memoirs make only fleeting and perfunctory references to the Sixth Fleet, had earlier repudiated the idea of naval influence in a few ill-chosen words: 'I have seen statements that in 1973 the United States was affected in the conduct of the Middle East crisis by its fear of the Soviet Navy. This may have been true of our Navy: it wasn't true of our government'.[53]

Remarkable as they were in themselves, these Mediterranean naval activities were only part of the superpower confrontation of October 1973 – probably the most dangerous since the Cuban Missile Crisis of October 1962, in which the US Navy also played a significant role. Nothing on this scale has happened since, and the disintegration of the Soviet Union makes any early recurrence unlikely, but the purposeful use of limited naval force, as a glance at the Chronological Appendix to this book will demonstrate, has naturally continued. Indeed, it has often entailed greater violence, for neither assailants nor victims were inhibited by the fear of starting a major war that, in October 1973, persuaded the superpowers to keep their safety-catches on.

IV CATALYTIC FORCE: FROM THE BALTIC TO BEIRUT

So far, we have been concerned with the use of limited naval force to achieve objectives defined in advance: to liberate prisoners, seize a ship, extract precisely formulated concessions, deter a foreign government from an expected course of action. However, force is often deployed for vaguer purposes. A situation arises pregnant with a formless menace or offering obscure opportunities. Something, it is felt, is going to happen, something that somehow might be prevented if force were available at the critical point. Advantages, their nature and the manner of their achievement still undetermined, might be reaped by those able to put immediate and appropriate power behind their sickle. These are situations peculiarly favourable to the exercise of limited naval force. Warships can cruise for long periods awaiting the moment most auspicious for their intervention. As long as they remain on the high seas, they are not committed. Even after they have intervened, they can easily be disengaged and withdrawn. Air forces and armies, unless they enjoy the advantages of an adjacent frontier, are cumbrous instruments, dragging a long tail behind their teeth, ill-adapted to the tactics of tip and run, to the limited, tentative, non-committal probe. A ship, a squadron or a fleet can as well float off one coast as another.

Of course, even for navies, the circumstances must be suitable. In 1991 it would have been inadvisable for a US squadron to cruise off the coasts of the Soviet Union in readiness to exploit the turmoil ashore in the interests of US policy. Yet this is very much what the British, then the leading naval power, did in the Baltic – and elsewhere – from 1919 to 1921.

The situation, admittedly, was unusual, but, in international affairs no less than in anatomy, it is the exception that is the rule. The Baltic is normally the preserve of the limitrophe powers and, ever since the eclipse of Swedish imperialism, had been contested between Germany and Russia. After the conclusion of the armistice of 11 November 1918, both these states were temporarily incapacitated by defeat and civil strife. The sea and its shores were open to the influence of their lesser inhabitants – and of outside powers. In Russia, the Bolshevik *coup d'état* was hotly contested by a clutch of generals and admirals, each with their ragtag and bobtail of miscellaneous supporters. In East Prussia the locally undefeated German armies were trying, under ambitious leadership, to snatch compensating advantages from the disaster that had overtaken their comrades on the Western Front. The long repressed nationalism of Estonians, Finns, Latvians, Lithuanians and Poles was hissing and seething. The situation was abnormal and seemed unique. With the ice cracking and the bergs plunging in all directions, anything might happen and the British government concluded that the chances of an outcome favourable to British interests would be improved by the presence of a British naval squadron in the Baltic.

For many months that was about all they did decide. When Rear-Admiral Sinclair sailed for the Baltic in command of a light cruiser squadron and nine destroyers, his orders could scarcely have been vaguer: 'to show the British flag and support British policy as circumstances dictate'.[54] He was, admittedly, furnished with a supply of army weapons and authorised to give these to the Estonian National Council (who had earlier requested British assistance) and to the Latvian authorities to facilitate their defence against the Bolsheviks, but his instructions regarding Russia were as confused as the policy of the British government. It was the Admiralty and not the Foreign Office who told him that 'a Bolshevik man-of-war operating off the coast of the Baltic Provinces must be assumed to be doing so with hostile intent and should be treated accordingly'.[55]

The trouble was that, throughout the period of our story, three mutually incompatible policies were open to the British government, whose inclination towards first one then another was determined less by the intrinsic merits of each than by the rivalry within the British Cabinet of Churchill and Lloyd George and by the gradual unfolding, around the brackish waters of the Baltic, of events neither foreseen nor determined in Whitehall. There was a case for backing one or more of the White Russian leaders against the Bolsheviks, but this meant ignoring the claims to independence of their subject Baltic peoples; there were arguments for assisting the movements of national liberation of Estonians, Finns, Latvians, Lithuanians and Poles, but this outraged the imperialism of the anti-Bolshevik Russians; there was a view, insignificant at first, but increasingly influential as the months went by, that Lenin and his blood-stained henchmen were going to win and ought not therefore to be irretrievably alienated. Until this last opinion was finally established by the force of events long after the conclusion of the Baltic episode, the presence of British warships seemed to offer British policy a wider range of options.

To begin with, Admiral Sinclair interpreted his mission, as did his successor, Rear-Admiral Cowan, exclusively in terms of the first and second of these conflicting objectives. Having landed arms for the Latvians and Estonians, British warships shelled Bolshevik troops near Narva on 13 December 1918 and, when attacked at Reval by the Red Fleet on 26 December, captured two of their destroyers. Subsequently, action had to be taken both against German troops (whose leaders wanted to make the Baltic states a German protectorate) and against dissident Latvians. On 29 December HMS CERES opened fire on barracks containing mutinous troops 'with excellent effect'.

In January 1919, when Admiral Cowan took over command, the previous orders were amplified: 'British interests,' he was told, 'may be summed up as follows: to prevent the destruction of Estonia and Latvia by external aggression.' He interpreted these orders liberally. On 9 February naval gunfire drove the Bolsheviks out of Windau. In April he rescued Latvian Ministers and ships from the Germans. Admittedly, in May, British support was refused to Mannerheim's plan for a Finnish advance on Petrograd, but in the same month the Bolshevik fleet was chased back to harbour from the Estonian coast and German troops shelled by HMS EREBUS.[56] It is scarcely surprising that, in March, the Admiralty should have protested to the Cabinet: 'It is essential, if our naval force is required to undertake operations of war, that it should do so in pursuance of a definite and coherent policy.'[57] Admiral Cowan's spectacular interventions were, after all, subsidiary to the main political and military struggle ashore, where the raw and scanty troops raised by Estonia and Latvia had to rely on the sporadic and dangerously self-interested assistance of German and White Russian forces in order to resist a Bolshevik invasion that came by land and not by sea. As British troops were not to be employed, some of Admiral Cowan's help had to go to these doubtful allies, and it would have been convenient to know which he should prefer, against whom and to what extent. Above all, was he or was he not to lend himself to the attempted overthrow of the Bolshevik regime in Russia itself?

In London, precision was unfashionable. Not until 4 July 1919 did HM government decided that 'a state of war did exist between Great Britain and Bolshevist Government of Russia', a decision that they then nullified by not announcing it. These ambiguities seem to have worried Admiral Cowan less than they did the Admiralty. Admittedly, it was after the non-declaration of war that he bombed the Red Fleet in Kronstadt harbour and later sank two of their battleships in the same base, but he had sunk a cruiser at Kronstadt as early as 17 June and his consistent strategy of neutralising the Red Fleet seems to have been endorsed, sometimes reluctantly, rather than initiated by a divided Cabinet, whose belated decision may however be thought to provide some legal basis for the institution of a blockade of Petrograd on 10 October. Meanwhile, for all the vigour and effectiveness of British naval operations, the British government continued to hedge their political bets: the White Russians, the newly independent Baltic peoples, the German military adventurers, were all in turn encouraged, restrained or exploited. Even the Bolsheviks, though more often attacked, occasionally received emissaries as well as bombardments.

Gradually, however, there emerged the conviction that British interests would be best served by avoiding involvement in the struggle for power within Russia, concentrating instead on the maintenance of the newly created Baltic States. To writers in this field it can only be a source of gratification to find that the view that ultimately prevailed was first enunciated by the author of *The Twenty Years Crisis* and *Conditions of Peace*: E.H. Carr, then a Third Secretary in the Foreign Office. In April 1919 he had minuted:

It is most undesirable that General Yudenitch (Commander of the White Russian North-Western Army) should be in any way encouraged to interfere in Finland or Estonia or to make either of these countries a base for offensive operations

against Petrograd ... the result ... would probably be the
sweeping of Estonia, and possibly Finland, by Bolshevism.

Ullman,[58] from whom this quotation is taken, records that
reaction within the Foreign Office was uniformly approving,
and Carr's minute may perhaps be regarded as the first crystal-
lisation, by the customarily implicit and instinctive process, of
British policy. Even though this objective was never formulated,
the effect was to establish the existence as independent countries of Estonia, Finland, Latvia and Lithuania. This result was
beneficial to British interests and could scarcely have been
achieved without the application of limited naval force to neutralise the otherwise preponderant Red Fleet, to support
coastal operations, to deny, as necessary, the use of the sea to
Russians and Germans, and to hearten and assist Estonians,
Latvians and Lithuanians against their two more powerful
opponents. Page[59] repeatedly emphasises the crucial importance
of British naval assistance and only Finland could perhaps have
dispensed with it.[60]

On 2 February 1920, Estonia, on 30 June Lithuania, on 11
August Latvia, and on 14 October Finland, were all able to sign
treaties with the Soviet Union establishing peace and the
recognition of their independent sovereignty. In 1921 British
naval forces were finally withdrawn from the Baltic, their long
uncertain mission accomplished. Altogether, 238 warships had
been employed, the number in the Baltic at any one time
varying between twenty-nine and eighty-eight. Seventeen ships,
including one light cruiser, were lost (mainly to mines) and 128
naval officers and men were killed. Twenty-six French, fourteen
US and two Italian warships served under Admiral Cowan at
one time or another, but were less heavily engaged.

These were extensive operations and – if we accept as the
objective that which ultimately emerged rather than anything
that might have been envisaged, though never authoritatively
formulated, at the outset – considerably more successful than
simultaneous adventures against the Bolsheviks elsewhere on
the periphery of Russia. But was this the exercise of limited
naval force or was it an undeclared war?

Both views are arguable and the justification for preferring the
former may be sought in the arguments of Chapter 1: this was
not a conflict between states in which policy was determined by

the desire to inflict injury rather than the hope of positive advantage. The British government wanted, with varying degrees of conviction, to change the Russian regime: they had no desire to injure Russia. Indeed, their readiness to assist the Baltic peoples was constantly inhibited by their reluctance to commit themselves, until a very late stage, to the detachment of provinces from the Russian Empire. The Baltic episode, though treated here in isolation, was part of a pattern of behaviour – it can scarcely be called a policy – that had originated during the war against Germany and had stemmed from the desire to keep Russians fighting Germans. As time passed and circumstances changed, so motives proliferated and conflicted, but war with Russia was never one that the British government were prepared to admit to the British people. At most, they were intervening in a civil war. In the Baltic they were fishing in troubled waters and with rather more success than in the Barents, the Black, the Caspian or the Japanese Seas.

British ability to undertake this remarkable adventure (in which, incidentally, no fleeting reflection of the ALTMARK principles can be discerned) depended on two particular features of the unusual state of affairs that followed the armistice with Germany: a disposable surplus of British naval capacity, and the absence of rivals capable of effective opposition. The new nations of the Baltic welcomed the activities of British ships; the German adventurers could not count on the backing of even their own defeated state; Russia, already exhausted by a disastrous war, was torn and distracted by civil strife; the Western Allies favoured and even abetted British intervention. The one real opponent – the new Bolshevik regime in Russia – was neither capable of responding to British acts of force by escalation to a wider war nor, in all probability, ready to risk a course likely to maximise British support for their Russian rivals. British success in confining so violent and protracted an intervention within the bounds of limited naval force was thus due to the exceptional advantages offered by an unusual situation and cannot be ascribed to any special skill in the handling of the affair. In most other circumstances, operations that (as the British government themselves recognised) involved what would normally be considered acts of war, would have led to actual war.

This brings us to the distinctive feature of the Baltic episode and to the main justification for choosing such an exceptional and even marginal instance of gunboat diplomacy for extended analysis. This is the first example we have considered of a major operation in which the assailant could afford to ignore reactions by his victim, the risks of retaliation, and the possible repercussions elsewhere. Mussolini in 1923 was not particularly concerned about the Greeks, but the possibility of British objections might have been a worry. In 1983 Grenada presented no military problem for the United States, but the criticism that Operation Urgent Fury attracted, even from their allies, was a little disconcerting. In the Baltic, however, Admiral Cowan enjoyed a free hand, with his only restriction being the persistent refusal of the British government to contemplate the landing of British troops. This effectively limited both the extent of British involvement and the ability of the victims to inflict injury on British forces, but the ban was imposed for entirely British reasons and not with any idea of persuading the victims that British objectives were limited and tolerable. It follows, therefore, that the circumstances of the victim are no less important than the intentions of the assailant in determining whether a particular intervention can be confined within the bounds of limited force or whether this must assume the character of an act of war.

In 1956, for instance, Britain and France jointly employed force against Egypt in a way that can only be described as catalytic – 'to bring Nasser to his senses'[61] – the objective initially stated by Eden, scarcely qualified as purposeful. But the reason why this operation failed – and the reason for placing it beyond the shadowy line that divides gunboat diplomacy from an act of war – did not reside merely in the weaknesses of its planning and execution. The original conception of the British government certainly neglected some of the principles earlier suggested as important to the establishment of an act of force as limited, but greater efforts were made than in 1919, even if they did not succeed, to impress on the victim the limited and tolerable character of British objectives. Force was more tardily applied than in 1919, but its effect might have been expected to appear sooner. Even the resources available were greater, both absolutely and in relation to the area of their deployment. However, the circumstances of the victim were utterly different. Instead of an internationally friendless regime struggling for its very life against half-a-dozen domestic rivals, Britain had attacked an established leader enjoying national support and the favour of important foreign governments. The Soviet Union rattled nuclear rockets, the US Sixth Fleet made an expressive threat of force, and a variety of international pressures were orchestrated to raise the stakes for Britain and France. If the sword failed, it was because it fell on thicker armour, not because it was wrongly wielded or because weapons were out of favour.

In every era and in all the oceans, we shall encounter instances of assailants who miscalculate the odds. What matters is whether or not the passage of time and the evolution of international relationships have consistently reduced the frequency of opportunities – which have always been relatively rare – for the successful employment of limited naval force.

That is an issue for the next chapter, but, at this stage, it is worth emphasising that political change, though unending, is not a very predictable process. The pattern that in 1971 seemed established was scarcely recognisable in 1991. Yesterday may offer better precedents than today for tomorrow's problems. In 1950, when China's situation reflected Russia's in 1919, and Japan's that of Germany, the Baltic episode became more relevant than it had been in the 1920s and 1930s. It was not so much sheer power as the combination of political circumstances that made the US Seventh Fleet as effective as Admiral Cowan's ramshackle collection in rescuing a new state from the wreck of a shattered empire. Formosa, now Taiwan, which owed her independence to naval midwifery, as did Estonia, Latvia and Lithuania, has already preserved it longer, not through any repetition of Soviet quiescence in the Baltic between 1920 and 1939, but because the US Navy interposed their shield of limited force between Formosa and the irredentist fury of a resurgent China.

For all its intriguing parallels with the Baltic episode, the defence of Formosa was nevertheless a straightforward example of purposeful force and, for our next instance of the catalytic mode, we must return to the Mediterranean, where, before two years had dried the ink on the lessons of Suez, Nasserist Arab nationalism was again the victim, but this time in circumstances sufficiently altered to permit a genuinely limited use of naval force.

This was an operation in which the relationship between objective and outcome is as complex and controversial as it was in 1919: the US intervention of 1958 in the Lebanon. Not the least of its difficulties is its intricate involvement with Lebanese politics, a mystery that only a Lebanese historian could expound. (When a few decades have drained the passions this year still inspires, perhaps this will occur.) Meanwhile, the uninitiated can best envisage the situation confronting the US government in terms of three concentric circles. The innermost was the Lebanon itself, where President Chamoun strove to maintain Christian ascendancy and the traditionally pro-Western orientation of his country (perhaps also to prolong his personal rule) against the increasingly violent opposition of discontented Muslims, Arab nationalists, leftists and those more moderate Lebanese who, for a variety of reasons, preferred a more flexible policy of adaptation to the altered circumstances of a new era. The middle circle was the Middle East, in which Nasser, far from displaying any gratitude for US help at the time of Suez, seemed to Washington to be whipping Arab nationalism into adventures ever more adverse to US interests. And, in the outermost circle, the spectre of advancing Soviet imperialism, to which Eden had vainly pointed in 1956, soon seemed so real to President Eisenhower that, on 7 March 1957, the celebrated 'Eisenhower Doctrine' was endorsed by the US Congress.[62]

When the Lebanese government, on 16 March 1957, accepted US material aid and declared their readiness to defend Lebanese political independence, their opposition to outside interference in Lebanese internal affairs and their determination to co-operate with the United States in resisting the menace of international communism, they gave to all three circles a common centre. President Chamoun had publicly committed his country in the Cold War, he had defied President Nasser's leadership and, by making any stand at all, he had alarmed as many Lebanese as his choice either delighted or outraged. Egyptian indignation and the apprehension excited among even Christian Lebanese were increased by two further developments during 1957. At the end of April the US Sixth Fleet arrived off Beirut in avowed readiness to assist King Hussein of Jordan, who had just overcome an attempted *coup d'état* of allegedly Egyptian, Syrian and even Soviet inspiration. Also, in July, the Lebanese parliamentary elections produced a majority capable, when they came to elect a President in 1958, of giving Chamoun a further six-year term.

The Lebanon was agitated and divided and her dissensions were actively inflamed from Egypt and from neighbouring Syria. Then, on 1 February 1958, the Lebanon's two Arab enemies proclaimed their fusion in the United Arab Republic of Egypt and Syria. Although this achievement was to prove ephemeral, its announcement and Nasser's visit to Damascus on 24 February were as exciting to Muslims and Arab nationalists in the Lebanon as they were alarming to those who already despaired of maintaining Lebanese independence against the advancing tide of Nasserism. Over 300,000 Lebanese made the pilgrimage to Damascus and the taxi-fare from Beirut reached five times its normal level.[63] On 28 March rioting broke out in Tyre and other Muslim districts, on 9 May it was repeated in Tripoli, where the US Information Office was burned down, and on 12 May in Beirut. When the Syrians attacked the Lebanese frontier post at Masnaa, disembowelling and castrating the five Lebanese customs officers they found there,[64] fighting was widespread, the chief leaders of the revolt being Muslim politicians and the Druze feudal chieftain and fellow-traveller Kamal Jumblatt. President Chamoun was supported by the police and by many of the Christians, with the Lebanese Army preferring to stand aloof from a conflict calculated to divide its own ranks as much as it did the nation.[65]

The origins and nature of the civil conflict thus summarily described will be long disputed, but President Chamoun was in no doubt that he was facing a *'coalition des forces communistes et de celles de la République Arabe Unie'*,[66] the very contingency for which the Eisenhower Doctrine had been designed. On 11 May the US Ambassador was asked whether his government were prepared to assist the Lebanon. On 13 May the US Sixth Fleet and HQ Second Provisional Marine Force (Task Force 62) were alerted. On 14 May President Chamoun was told that the Sixth Fleet would stand by, and on 18 May the Commanders of the Sixth Fleet and of Task Force 62 (whose HQ had by then reached the Mediterranean) began the planning of Operation Bluebat.[67] This assumed that the enemy most likely to be encountered – if, indeed, there was any opposition at all – was the Syrian First Army, which was credited with 40,000 men and 200 tanks.

There followed a pause, in which both Americans and Lebanese seemed to have second thoughts about their first impulsive reaction.[68] On 21 May the Lebanese government

appealed to the Arab League, and on 22 May to the Security
Council. The first of these bodies was unable to reach agreement; the second decided on 11 June (the representative of the
Soviet Union abstaining) to send a group of observers to the
Lebanon to prevent the illegal infiltration of men, arms or
materials of war. On 3 July the Secretary-General, who had
himself visited Beirut, announced that no mass infiltration
could be detected – a report received with considerable scepti-
cism by both the US and Lebanese governments.[69]

Meanwhile the civil war continued, as did requests from the
Lebanese government for various forms of US assistance.
These caused considerable perplexity in Washington, where
the US government, though anxious to uphold the validity of
the Eisenhower Doctrine, wished neither to override the
United Nations, for which they had professed such respect in
1956, nor to involve themselves needlessly in what, as their
Embassy in Beirut warned them, might turn out to be
primarily an internal conflict susceptible to eventual resolution
by one of the mysterious compromises in which Lebanese
violence so often ended. Even President Chamoun, though
formally authorised by the Council of Ministers on 16 June to
seek military assistance from friendly powers, continued to
shrink from an irrevocable step that, as he was well aware,
would no longer be welcome in Washington and, as occasional
successes against the rebels encouraged him to hope, might
still not be essential.

On 1 July the US Sixth Fleet relaxed its state of alert, most of
its ships were dispersed to Italian ports, and only the 6th
Amphibious Squadron with the 1st Marine Battalion Landing
Team aboard remained at sea. There was no such relaxation in
the Lebanon, where pitched battles were fought in the hills and
the rebels turned an entire quarter of the capital into an armed
camp, whence they sallied forth to kidnap or assassinate rivals,
to blow up their houses, and to attack official buildings. Arms –
and probably men as well – were freely imported across a
frontier largely controlled by the rebels, who were continuously
encouraged by broadcasts from Cairo and Damascus. These
activities were countered to the best of their ability by the
supporters of Chamoun and, though the good sense of the
Lebanese people (and the occasional intervention of the
Lebanese Army) kept the level of violence well below that of

civil wars in other countries, as many as 3,000 Lebanese were to be killed during the six months the conflict lasted.

Whether the fighting would have ultimately burnt itself out in compromise, or whether, in the absence of any counterpoise, it would have grown under Egyptian and Syrian pressure to proportions incompatible with the survival of an independent, precariously united, but genuinely prosperous Lebanon, we shall never know. On 14 July chance (though in Beirut and Washington it appeared to be the most sinister of designs) intervened. A revolution broke out in Iraq, and the King, his family and his pro-Western Ministers were massacred. The British Embassy was destroyed, Moscow and Cairo radios rejoiced at the fall of the reactionaries, the Lebanese rebels were excited to frenzy and, in Chamoun's words:[70]

> une grande peur s'était en revanche emparée des milieux attachés à un Liban paisible et indépendant. Leur moral, longtemps mis à dure épreuve, atteignait subitement les limites de la débâcle.

President Chamoun took only two hours to make up his mind: at 9 a.m. he asked for US military assistance within twenty-four hours.[71] The response of the US government was equally prompt: at 2 p.m. Chamoun was told that help was on its way and by 12.30 a.m. (Beirut time) Admiral Holloway, commanding the operation,[72] had been ordered to start landing his marines by 3 p.m. on the 15th.

To the dismay of the US Ambassador – whose wireless link with the Sixth Fleet had broken down and who had been given insufficient time to reconcile the startled and indignant Commander-in-Chief of the Lebanese Army, General Chehab, to the prospect of US intervention – the Admiral was only four minutes late. The landing craft grounded on the dingy sands of the remote and unfashionable bathing beach at Khaldé, the marines charged inland past the Coca-Cola stalls and cooked-meat sellers, and across the road and up the sand dunes to secure the international airport of Beirut, some miles south of the city proper. The advance into the city was delayed for negotiations with the Lebanese Army, but the following evening a further contingent of Marines, preceded by the US Ambassador in his car with his dog and a somewhat reluctant General Chehab as a passenger and mediator, secured the harbour, the bridges on the Tripoli road at the opposite extremity of Beirut, and the US Embassy. On 20 July the first airborne reinforcements arrived, and by the end of the month 10,000 Americans were holding a 20-mile perimeter around Beirut. The force reached its peak of 15,000, including a regiment of tanks, on 8 August; one marine battalion was re-embarked as a floating reserve on 14 August; withdrawal began on 14 September and was completed by 25 October. In spite of occasional confrontations with indignant Lebanese officers (who had initially wished to resist the landing), and one or two exchanges of shots with the rebels, the Americans were never called on to fight, encountered no significant opposition, and had only one man killed at Lebanese hands. Although shortage of tanks and essential items of equipment during the first few days worried US commanders ashore, there was ample air cover from the carriers of the Sixth Fleet (altogether fifty warships were involved) and no real reason for military concern, though US naval commentators have rightly emphasised that, as at Kuwait in 1961, only a naval landing could have met Chamoun's deadline:

> It was five days after the landing, in full force, of seaborne Marines from 18-knot transports, before the first lightly-armed airborne troops reached Lebanon and that only after delicate and uncertain negotiations, in a tug-of-war against Communist political pressure, for overflight permissions from each country in the paths of the transport planes.[73]

What were the objectives of this imposing operation (which cost the United States 200 million dollars),[74] and what did it in fact achieve?

There is no certain answer to either question and any conjecture is necessarily controversial, because the situation that provoked US intervention was never as clear-cut as, in the lurid glare from Baghdad, it briefly appeared at the moment of decision. In the message to Congress that preceded the arrival of the first marines on Khaldé beach, President Eisenhower appeared to accept in its entirety the thesis, that had hitherto been questioned in Washington, of President Chamoun: 'It is clear that the events which have been occurring in Lebanon constitute indirect aggression from without, and that such aggression endangers the independence and integrity of Lebanon.' In the same message he explained that:'US forces are being sent to the Lebanon to protect American lives and by their presence to assist the government of Lebanon in the preservation of Lebanon's territorial integrity and independence.'

In another statement issued on the same day, the President added a phrase with which the reader will by now have become familiar: 'These forces have not been sent as any act of war.'

All these statements – and there are many other explanations and qualifications that have been omitted – provided an objective for US intervention that was limited and tolerable and envisaged a minimum use of force, but was not, perhaps, very precisely defined. Indeed, the words 'by their presence to assist' might almost be the motto for the catalytic, as opposed to the purposeful, use of force: a threat existed, all the more disturbing because it was formless, and the outcome seemed likely to be more favourable with the Marines than without them.

There was a further consideration, which President Eisenhower put to his Special Representative in the Lebanon, Mr Robert Murphy, on the following day:

> sentiment had developed in the Middle East, especially in Egypt, that Americans were capable only of words, that we were afraid of Soviet reaction if we attempted military action. Eisenhower believed that if the United States did nothing now, there would be heavy and irreparable losses in Lebanon and in the area generally. He wanted to demonstrate in a timely and practical way that the United States was capable of supporting its friends.... My oral instructions from the President were conveniently vague, the substance being that I was to promote the best interests of the United States incident to the arrival of our forces in the Lebanon.[75]

Once again, a clear case of catalytic force and a remarkable echo of British instructions to their Baltic admirals forty years previously. Although no one said so, US Marines had not landed in pursuance of a defined objective: their job was to hold the situation and to gain time for the US government to decide what their objective should be.

The tentative and exploratory character of US intervention was not generally appreciated, and it is the misunderstanding of this point that still bedevils so much analysis of the actual US achievement. Most Lebanese, for instance, whichever side they were on, imagined that the Americans had come to crush the rebellion and restore the authority of President Chamoun. When US forces placidly continued to man their perimeter, while Mr Murphy helped to negotiate a compromise favourable to the rebels, many Christian Lebanese denounced US betrayal and loss of nerve;[76] many Muslims and Nationalists rejoiced at US failure. Mr Murphy's instructions, however, had mentioned only 'the best interests of the United States' and these were well served by the actual settlement – once this had been adjusted by a last-minute counter-revolt of the Christians. It was this final factor that caused many Lebanese – a nation more solicitous of, than grateful for, foreign assistance – to argue, once the dust had settled, that this had always been an internal dispute needlessly complicated by an US intervention in panic response to irrelevant events in Baghdad.

That remains a conceivable hypothesis, though the intemperate reactions to US intervention of Egypt, Iraq, Syria and, above all, the Soviet Union, scarcely support it. If this was no more than a domestic squabble, why did Mr Khrushchev, not content with the customary fulminations and with breaking the windows of the US Embassy in Moscow, find it necessary to tell President Eisenhower on 19 July that US intervention had brought the world 'to the brink of catastrophe'?

When everything was over, Khrushchev's demand for an immediate Summit Conference had expired in the sterility of diplomatic exchanges. Hurriedly arranged Soviet manoeuvres (including those of the Black Sea Fleet) had failed to shake US resolution, US forces, which had never found it necessary to resort to violence, had withdrawn in their own good time. A new Lebanese President had settled down with a coalition government to rule a more tranquil, but still independent, country of substantially unaltered social structure. It then seemed that neither of the two extreme conclusions suggested at the outset was entirely valid. Not everyone in the Lebanon agreed that 'the United States was capable of supporting its friends', but were the Kremlin still convinced that 'the time has passed when the fire of colonialist gunboats and the landing of armed detachments can crush the uprisings of oppressed peoples'?[77] In the innermost circle, the eventual resolution of the Lebanese crisis might seem curiously unrelated to the activities of the US

Sixth Fleet, but elsewhere governments had been forcibly reminded that, as long as the Soviet Navy were confined to the impotence of manoeuvres in the Black Sea, it was not the Americans who 'were capable only of words'.

That, however, was in 1958. Nothing better illustrates the overbearing nature of political change than the total failure, during the 1980s, of intervention by the Sixth Fleet (which included repeated bombardment of shore targets and the landing of US Marines) to promote the interests of the United States in the Lebanon or to mitigate the sufferings of a people plunged into anarchy and chaos by the collapse of the artificial compromise that alone sustained the existence of a state that never became a nation. What had changed, however, was not the general climate of international opinion, but the political situation in and around the Lebanon. Optimists might argue that, in 1958, the United States held the ring, thus giving the Lebanese time to reach their usual compromise. In 1983 compromise was a long forgotten word, and there was nobody left in the Lebanon to play the part of General Chehab. No limited intervention would now suffice, and the memory of Vietnam, even more than the presence of a Soviet squadron in the Mediterranean, discouraged any deeper commitment.

The incidence of secular change in the conditions governing the exercise of limited naval force is a subject to be considered in the next chapter, but a word of caution is needed meanwhile against the snares of geographical and historical coincidence. When the Soviet Union disintegrated in 1991 and the Baltic States again sought their independence, the situation was very different from that of 1919. The Soviet state was in ruins, but the armed forces, though a little demoralised and undisciplined, still had their weapons and some of their combat potential. Even a fragmented Yugoslavia was a tougher proposition in 1991 than the ruins of the Austrian Empire in 1919. In 1919, moreover, armed intervention in Russia was undertaken by a Britain whom four years of savage war had hardened to the point of running risks and incurring losses (17 ships lost and 128 killed) that would have seemed intolerable to the politician contemplating *limited* naval force in 1991. Circumstances alter cases.

V EXPRESSIVE FORCE: DEUTSCHLAND to DEDALO

The last and least of the uses of limited naval force in furtherance of the objectives of foreign policy is the expressive, in
which warships are employed to emphasise attitudes, to lend
verisimilitude to otherwise unconvincing statements, or to
provide an outlet for emotion. Its distinction from the threat of
purposeful force on the one hand, and from mere flag-showing
on the other, is as vague and uncertain as the usual result of its
employment. Yet the task must be attempted, because the
expedient is more common than it is valuable.

On 3 August 1936, for instance, just twenty-five years after
PANTHER'S disturbing visit to Agadir, the German pocket-
battleship *(Panzerschiff)* DEUTSCHLAND and the torpedo-boat
LUCHS arrived at Ceuta in Spanish Morocco. The German
Admiral went ashore and lunched with General Franco and the
German Consul from nearby Tetuan, who duly reported: 'the
visit is considered direct support of the Nationalist uprising of
General Franco'.[78] The point had been made, though the
reasons for making it so flamboyantly remain somewhat
obscure. The German transport aircraft that were already
ferrying Franco's troops to Spain had actually given him the
backing that DEUTSCHLAND's visit only symbolised and that
Hitler was otherwise still at pains to conceal. Perhaps the
dramatic gesture of DEUTSCHLAND's appearance seemed an
irresistibly appropriate sequel to a decision Hitler had taken at
Bayreuth after a performance of *Die Walküre*.[79]

Ambiguity is a recurrent feature of acts of expressive force,
but the significance of this one was that it did not constitute a
threat of purposeful force – there was no suggestion of
German naval intervention at that stage[80] – yet, because it was
related to the specific objective of emphasising German
support for Franco, it was more than a mere reminder of
German naval might. If it was useful, it was presumably
because it conveyed a message with emphasis, but without
precision or commitment.

Not all naval messages are so clearly distinguishable from the
threat or use of purposeful force. When the Netherlands
government announced, on 5 April 1960, the despatch of the
aircraft-carrier KAREL DOORMAN and two destroyers to New
Guinea, the intention was presumably to deter Indonesia from

attacking that colony. As a threat of purposeful force, however, the announcement might have been more effective if made after the ships had arrived. As it was, the message was ill-received – not only in Indonesia itself, but in other countries due to be visited en route – and probably did more harm than good. But the incident could be assigned either to the purposeful or to the expressive category.

On the other hand, when HMS BERWICK initiated the Beira patrol on 9 April 1966,[81] by stopping the Greek tanker MANUELA, this was a purposeful use of limited naval force: to prevent oil from reaching Rhodesia. Yet, as the months went by and the evidence accumulated that Rhodesia was now importing oil by other routes, the purposeful character of the Beira patrol began to wear a little thin and its expressive function became more significant.

Similarly, when President Johnson sent the Seventh Fleet to the sea of Japan after the capture of PUEBLO in 1968, this was a clear threat of purposeful force against North Korea. When President Nixon repeated the manoeuvre after the destruction of a US aircraft in 1969, the events of the previous year had stripped his bluff of credibility: he was merely assuaging US indignation by a gesture of expressive force.

The same year, however, witnessed a rather more elegant and classical employment of this gambit, in that very Western outlet of the Mediterranean that seems almost consecrated to the expressive use of naval force. Changes in the Spanish government having prompted newspaper speculation that the claim to Gibraltar might no longer be so vigorously pressed, the Spanish carrier DEDALO and twelve other Spanish warships arrived in the Bay of Algeciras and dropped anchor in sight of the Rock. The British retort was as taciturn and equally traditional, almost blatantly so: when the Spaniards arrived, a match was being played ashore – between the football teams of HMS EAGLE and HMS HERMES.[82]

The Rock of Gibraltar has continued to lend its own dignity to recurrent displays of expressive force, but for the elegiac mode we must turn to tropical seas. At the very end of 1975 a Portuguese warship was sent to cruise in the waters adjacent to East Timor, the island colony Indonesia had seized. The purpose, a spokesman explained, was 'to maintain a presence – even though we no longer appear to have any land'.[83]

The reader must excuse these frivolities. In its expressive mode, limited naval force resembles the ceremonial and representational aspects of ordinary diplomacy: equally rich in anecdotes, equally unproductive of identifiable advantages, equally dear to the romantic schoolboys who become politicians, diplomats and naval officers. Such practices may legitimately be recorded, and their principles analysed, without too nice a regard for their utility: they are inherently likely to continue.

3 The Altered Environment

Historical facts and events are studied not for imitation and not in a quest for 'prescriptions', but to trace regularities and to use them as a basis for formulating the principles of armed struggle best suited to contemporary conditions.

Penzin[1]

I HISTORICAL

It would be surprising if the historical record of any activity so essentially irregular and *ad hoc* as gunboat diplomacy were to assume any clearly defined pattern. The conclusions to be drawn from the analysis of the preceding chapter, or from the more extensive summary of the Chronological Appendix, must accordingly be confined to a few cautious generalities. First of all, throughout the last seventy years, albeit with the fluctuations that inevitably result from changes in the international balance of power, a number of different governments have continued to find various political applications for limited naval force. Secondly, although the collapse of the Russian and Turkish Empires, the chaos of China and US policy in the Caribbean combined to raise gunboat diplomacy during the 1920s to sustained heights of activity not since achieved, the fluctuations of subsequent decades have not been uniformly downward. The lull of the 1930s prefaced a new peak in the last years of peace; the nadir of 1944 (the only year without an example) was followed by a fresh outburst as soon as peace returned and, if the exceptional circumstances of the Spanish Civil War are discounted, the 1980s have seen more use of limited naval force than the 1930s. Thirdly, the varieties of gunboat diplomacy practised at the beginning of our period may also be distinguished during its later years. Finally, and much more tentatively, it could be argued that for seventy years there has been no clear or obviously directional trend of change in the principles governing the use of limited naval force or in the relative incidence of success or failure in its employment.

It is tempting, but it would be unwise, to seek further lessons in the record of the past: to argue that more governments use gunboat diplomacy today than occurred a century ago; that the roles of victim and assailant are now more equally shared between great powers and lesser states; that warships must increasingly be used and not merely moved; that prestige in the 1980s had lost the potency it still possessed in the 1920s. These, however, are essentially impressions. They could be challenged on a different interpretation of history: they could be destroyed by the events of the coming decade. It is better to content ourselves with the one outstanding regularity that emerges from this survey of seventy lawless years: the continued and frequent use, in one form or another, of limited naval force as a supplement to diplomacy and as an alternative to war.

Nevertheless, this is not the conclusion, but only the indispensable foundation, of our inquiry into the future usefulness of this expedient. The evidence for the repeated and recent use of this type of force had to be deployed to refute the widespread illusion that gunboat diplomacy is already obsolete. It will not suffice to disprove its obsolescence. Similar arguments were used, with a success that was unfortunate, to convince the British government that the progress of mechanical innovation had not, even in the 1930s, diminished the traditional importance and effectiveness of horsed cavalry. Historical analogies can only constitute the first step towards the crucial question: have technological and political developments so altered – or are they likely, in the near future, so to transform – the environment in which limited naval force must operate, that this ancient instrument of diplomacy must now be regarded as nearing the end of its useful life?

The most practical approach to an answer may be to adopt the standpoint of the victim and to consider how far technological or political changes can be expected to increase his ability to resist or avoid the coercion of gunboat diplomacy. These will constitute the obstacles that future assailants must find new ways to overcome. The existence of potential assailants need not be argued. With their traditional preference for doing what was done last time, governments are certain to seek means of pressure more vigorous than diplomacy but less violent than war, and for this purpose, at least, to consider the use of their navies.[2]

The potential threat is thus taken for granted and we shall initially only be concerned with the means to meet it. These means fall into three categories: deterrence – measures to discourage the assailant from even attempting the use of limited naval force; defence – measures to prevent the assailant who actually uses force from achieving his objective; and counter-attack – measures to induce the assailant to disgorge what his use of limited naval force has already swallowed. If a rational assailant is convinced in advance that his victim's defence or counter-attack can be expected to succeed, he will naturally be deterred from attempting the use of limited force, unless he is prepared to proceed to war, so deterrence as such will be examined primarily as the threat of war – with other varieties being considered as aspects of defence and counter-attack. All three means of resistance will also be taken to include the help that the victim can expect from third parties, and will be discussed in the light of, first, technological developments, and second, political developments.

II TECHNOLOGICAL

The first category of developments to be considered might almost equally well be termed military, for they are mainly concerned with the threat or use of armed force. Yet it is neither the existence of exceptions nor mere modishness that prompts a preference for this fashionable adjective. We are, after all, dealing with change, and the purely military – or the purely political – principles of resistance to limited naval force were not unknown to the Counts of the Saxon Shore. Deterrence is a case in point. Where this means the threat of war, it has always been impaired by two factors of uncertainty. First of all, the victim – or his allies – might only be bluffing. Secondly, even if the threat were implemented, it might not prove very damaging to the assailant, who could hope to win the war, even if it involved others, or at least to terminate it in circumstances no more disadvantageous than those that might have resulted from an initial abstention from the use of limited naval force. Many governments have been more prone to exaggerate than to underestimate their chances of sinking the enemy's fleet, defeating his army, shooting down his bombers or exhausting his resolution. That was the mistake made by Iraq, for instance, in 1991.[3]

Naturally, it can be argued that the development of nuclear weapons has invested deterrence with a new verisimilitude: that the United States and probably Russia each possess an assured capacity for inflicting intolerable damage on anyone else; that Britain, France and China have a good chance of doing more damage than any user of limited force would care to risk; and that the likely further diffusion of these weapons may soon enable other countries, even if defeated in war, to inflict greater injury than most conquerors have previously been prepared to contemplate. For universal deterrence – *tous azimuts*, as they used to say in Paris – an inter-continental delivery system is needed, but nuclear weapons can pose a threat at less expense. If Iraqi efforts to develop them had been more successful, the ability of Iraq to reach Israel and Saudi Arabia with their Scud missiles would have had to be taken much more seriously in Washington. In principle at least, these are real changes from the days when a British admiral could guarantee the invulnerability of his country by saying, 'they cannot come by sea', or Bismarck could laughingly proclaim his intention of sending for the police if the British fleet appeared off the coast of Pomerania.

In practice, of course, even the most formidable of nuclear deterrents has its inescapable drawback. Nuclear weapons, unless controlled by a lunatic, are not a credible response to limited naval force. The victim who seeks to make his threat of war more terrible by brandishing his nuclear weapons risks a neutralising response. Even if his assailant is not a nuclear power, the idea that nuclear weapons might be used – as has never happened since 1945[4] – would trigger superpower intervention. In 1982 war proved a successful and internationally tolerable British reaction to Argentine use of definitive force against the Falklands, but the United States would never have allowed Britain to avoid war by sending a strategic submarine to threaten Buenos Aires with a Polaris missile. There has also been a general assumption that nuclear weapons would only be employed under extreme provocation. Just how extreme no one is sure and, to some extent, the principle of uncertainty cuts both ways. There was enough risk that the invasion of West

Germany, or even North Vietnam, would lead to nuclear war to constitute an effective deterrent in most circumstances. In the 1962 Cuban crisis the Soviet Union had already advanced a nuclear pawn, thus lending credibility to the larger menace of the US response. The implied US threat of 1973 was made against the background of actual war in the Middle East. But the further one descends the scale of provocation and crisis, the less credible becomes the threat of nuclear war, so that it has long been widely accepted that a deliberate process of escalation or an equally elaborate demonstration of prior commitment would be required, in circumstances short of mortal danger, to convince an opponent that the threat was seriously intended.

Escalation and commitment, however, are manoeuvres ill-adapted to most of the situations in which limited naval force might be employed. If the credibility of deterrence is to be reinforced by a prior commitment, for instance, it is not enough to issue a verbal warning in general terms. 'Wolf' was cried too often in the early years of the nuclear era. The adversary must be told precisely which of his actions will incur what retaliation and words must be emphasised by visible military preparations, often even by the physical interposition of troops or warships.[5] And the lower the level of the objectionable act that is to be deterred, the more elaborate must be the apparatus of commitment to convince the opponent that even this seemingly trivial move will bring down on him the murderous – and also potentially suicidal – weight of nuclear attack.

When the object of deterrence is the use of limited naval force, these considerations have two awkward consequences. First of all, it is hard to devise a credible commitment against the unforeseen. On the other hand, if the risk is identifiable, a nuclear power ought to be able to find a simpler and more effective deterrent. It is hard to imagine any process of prior commitment that could have made nuclear deterrence a more effective safeguard for PUEBLO than some escorting destroyers.

Prior commitment, moreover, is necessarily a publicised and provocative process that is more liable to be answered in kind, and thus to usher in a potentially neutralising escalation, than is the discreet deployment of a conventionally effective defence. The Russians, for instance, resented the US practice of sending warships to sniff around the coasts of the Soviet Union. When diplomatic protest proved unavailing, they rattled no rockets.

Instead, in February 1988, the frigate BEZZAVETNY and her consort took a leaf out of the Anglo-Icelandic book and bumped the USS YORKTOWN and CARON as they were indulging their recurrent urge to assert the right of innocent passage through Soviet territorial waters in the Black Sea.[6] Curiously enough, this seems not to have infringed Article III 4 of the 1972 Agreement, which only required the parties to avoid the risk of collisions on the High Seas.

This does not mean that the threat of nuclear war can never have any impact on the use of limited naval force, even in situations where the nuclear armoury of one party is balanced by that of the other. Without this menace of last resort, gunboat diplomacy might be used still more frequently and in less limited form. However, as long as a convincing threat of nuclear war is harder to contrive than other forms of response, it seems reasonable to conclude that, in most situations, it will be less useful as a deterrent. Indeed, it is arguable that their nuclear armoury actually made both superpowers more cautious and more tolerant of affronts, either to themselves or to their clients, than were the great powers of the nineteenth century.

This effect of nuclear technology is not necessarily lasting. The nuclear powers have so far been circumspect, because none of them (except the United States during the first decade of the nuclear era) has yet encountered a situation in which they could expect – still less induce others to expect – their use of these weapons to remain unilateral. Even in 1956, when the United States had temporarily turned on their own allies, they were prompt to counter a Soviet nuclear threat to Britain, which thus exercised less influence than US financial sanctions. However, this state of affairs could change. A nuclear power might temporarily acquire a relative invulnerability or nuclear weapons might pass into the control of leaders impervious to any rational fear of retaliation. Circumstances could drive a government to such desperation that a nuclear strike might seem a conceivable response even to an act of limited naval force. Civil war or revolution, for instance, might deprive a great power, even a superpower, of every other means of organised defence, yet leave potential assailants wondering whether their intervention might provoke a maddened ruler to the discharge of those missiles whose controllers might still be prepared to obey him.

These are conceivable contingencies, but so far they are only hypothetical exceptions to the tentative rule that nuclear war is not a credible deterrent to actions that, almost by definition, do not affect the central balance of power. Yet, suppose nuclear weapons, and the means of their delivery, were acquired by so many states that the central balance ceased to have any significance, that these weapons were regularly employed in the minor wars of lesser states – what use would then remain for gunboat diplomacy? There is no answer to a question involving so many unknown factors, except perhaps to recall that the widespread diffusion of firearms in the United States has not yet deterred US citizens from the use of their fists in petty quarrels. We are only concerned with the foreseeable future in which nuclear weapons are more likely to reduce, rather than increase, the effectiveness of the threat of war as a deterrent to the use of limited naval force.

Defence is a different matter. Here we are not concerned with nuclear weapons, which are instruments of war, but with new developments that might assist a victim to prevent the achievement of the assailant's objective or else might raise the cost of achieving this to the level of war. This kind of defence demands a local and limited response, although, for reasons to be discussed when we turn to political developments, the victim can often afford a higher level of violence than the assailant. A reaction that extends to war, though, is not for our immediate purpose one of defence, while any form of retaliation against the assailant, rather than against the forces actually employed in his intervention, will be considered separately as a counter-attack.

The first requisite of successful defence is, as always, detection. Without it, even a victim stronger than his assailant may be unable to prevent the latter from establishing a local superiority sufficient to achieve his purpose. Here radar, aerial reconnaissance, even observation from satellites, have impaired the traditional ability of warships to make a surprise appearance over the horizon. Only a submarine – and this is a vessel ill-adapted to most forms of gunboat diplomacy – could nowadays count with much confidence on an unobserved approach, and major warships of interest to the United States – and occasionally to other powers as well – have to assume the possibility of unseen surveillance and the communication of the results to their intended victim. As accurate intelligence of the opponent's movements is usually more important to the victim (who may be relying on fixed defences) than to the assailant, this is one way in which technological progress may operate to the detriment of gunboat diplomacy. The operative word, though, is *may*. In 1982 the approach of the Argentine task force was detected. The risk had been obvious for decades. The Falklands were not surprised, just undefended.

Nevertheless, even allowing for human error, political surprise and the use of electronic counter-measures by a sophisticated assailant, the average victim's chances of early warning have improved – as have his means of local defence. Cruise missiles, bomber aircraft, radar-controlled guns, coastal submarines, modern mines: all these are formidable (and nowadays not uncommon) impediments to the kind of offshore manoeuvre that gunboat diplomacy so often entails. Even as long ago as 1958 or 1961, the US and British navies found it prudent to intervene in formidable strength and at corresponding expense against potential opponents – Syria and Iraq[7] – that were not then powerful, and might once have been overawed by a single warship (though the Shanghai intervention of 1927 was on an even larger scale than the landings in Kuwait and the Lebanon). Yet, if the cost-effectiveness of these operations is compared with that of others where gunboat diplomacy could not be employed – for example, Confrontation against Indonesia, war in Vietnam – the expense of limited naval force is seen to have risen less than the international cost of living. Technological progress has certainly made it more difficult to employ limited naval force successfully (though even the nineteenth century occasionally witnessed the impotence or repulse of the Royal Navy), but it has not rendered it impossible in the favourable circumstances it has always required. In 1967 the destruction of the Israeli destroyer EILAT while patrolling off Port Said made a profound impression on naval opinion, but she was, after all, acting with an imprudence to be compared with that of the ill-fated patrol of the Broad Fourteens by HM Ships ABOUKIR, CRESSY and HOGUE.[8] Also, both these incidents occurred in war.

Nor have the effects of innovation been entirely one-sided. The helicopter carrier provides the assailant with a new, and most effective, means of bringing limited naval force to bear on objectives well inland. Landing craft enable him to avoid defended harbours and concentrate tanks on deserted beaches. The hovercraft, so far rather neglected, might be improved to become an equally flexible instrument for surprise landings from a fleet well out to sea. Even the submarine might come into its own for specialised operations – landing a small party unperceived in order to kidnap or rescue a leader, just as General Giraud was rescued in 1942.[9]

The difficulty of assessing the impact of technological advance on the prospects of gunboat diplomacy is naturally increased by the very different objectives of the technologists, whose innovations have often been prompted by the supposed needs of nuclear war, trade protection or the hazily envisaged contingency of a conventional war fought at sea by the main fleets of important naval powers. The US Sixth Fleet, for instance, was originally sent to the Mediterranean for political purposes,[10] and it has discharged a variety of diplomatic functions, but its composition and equipment were long modified by the different role of supporting US capacity to launch a nuclear strike against the Soviet Union. Even when the main deterrent burden had been taken over by Trident submarines, the possibility of instant war overshadowed the aircraft-carriers and their long-range aircraft. The ever-watchful radar on the screening destroyers and frigates, the anti-submarine patrols, the daily preoccupations of the commanding admiral: all these were influenced by the need for instant response to the fatal signal from Washington.

In 1991 it was still too soon to say that such a signal could never again be expected. The Soviet Union might no longer exist, but the survival of its nuclear weapons had to be assumed – even if the integrity of the system that once kept them under tight central control had become open to question. Nuclear-propelled strategic submarines, it was said, were still patrolling, and someone in Moscow presumably thought they would obey his orders. Some of the surface warships, confined to port by fuel shortages and indiscipline among the crews, to say nothing of rival claims to the Black Sea Fleet, might one day be available for a sortie. There was a huge potential, even if idleness and the paralysis of the Russian economy were fast eroding it, in both ships and sailors, but it was uncertain whether or when or how that potential could be regenerated as a navy capable of sending battle-worthy squadrons to sea.

Thus the carriers of the US Navy were no longer regularly shadowed, let alone confronted by anti-carrier groups. As one US admiral argued: 'Today there is no adversary anywhere in the world whose military power approaches that of the United States'. Sensibly enough, he added: 'we cannot rule out the possibility that such an adversary might emerge some day'.[11]

In this hypothesis must be included the risk that such an adversary might grow out of the ruins of the Soviet Union itself. It is not only the future of the armed forces and their weapons that is uncertain. We cannot be sure what kind of political leadership will survive in the new republics or what their intentions will be. The old Soviet Union was perceived as an adversary and, in terms of military hardware, a technological rival, but years of experience had made it seem almost a predictable adversary, probably even a rational one. Today, though, we are in uncharted waters.

Although we cannot guess how long it will last, we may safely say that a new era began in 1991. For nearly forty years readiness for total war had been the constant, the dominant, preoccupation of the world's two largest navies. That had constrained their movements, narrowed the focus of their strategic thought, dictated their structure, and limited their availability for other tasks. The Soviet Navy, as the weaker force, had felt the handicap most acutely, but even the US Navy had lost some of the freedom of manoeuvre of the 1950s and early 1960s. Now one of those navies was rotting in harbour and the other, no longer poised for Armageddon, had the time, the resources and the inclination to tackle the lesser but frequent problems of violent peace. For that task, the US Navy should in future be able to spare more ships, even if the Navy's total strength is sharply reduced.

The new era may also give the US Navy a fresh incentive to address one paradoxical weakness. Concentration on the ultimate technology – not merely for major war, but for a special kind of war against the Soviet Union – left the US Navy inadequately equipped for the economical use of limited force on more humdrum assignments. Admiral Zumwalt, once Chief of Naval Operations, identified the problem as early as 1962, and suggested a High–Low concept, in which 'moderate cost, moderate performance' ships 'could be turned out in relatively large numbers' to do the peacetime jobs, allowing strike carriers and nuclear submarines and the specialised escorts they needed to concentrate on readiness for *Der Tag*. This idea encountered much opposition – 'the US Navy has traditionally insisted on traveling first class'[12] – and the primacy accorded to the 'battle of the first salvo' continued to demand further sacrifices.

For example, Vice-Admiral Joy, reflecting in 1957 on the lessons of the Korean War, had argued that: 'no so-called subsidiary branch of the naval service, such as mine warfare, should ever be neglected or relegated to a minor role in the future'.

In the 1980s, after a warning from the General Accounting Office that 'the Navy would find it hard to conduct even the most limited type of mining or mine counter-measure operation' had been echoed in articles in *United States Naval Institute Proceedings*,[13] the US Navy remained unprepared. In 1987, when tankers they were protecting against other kinds of attack during the Iran–Iraq war struck mines in the Gulf, US warships were reduced to seeking their own safety by following in the wake of the tankers they were escorting.[14]

The exposure of that particular flaw (it was weeks before mine-hunting helicopters arrived) in the armour of the world's strongest navy was given a touch of ironic emphasis by the inability of carrier battle groups in the Indian Ocean to do anything that would spare the US Navy the indignity of calling on the services (rather sluggishly conceded) of British, Dutch, French and Italian minesweepers. Even after the Gulf War of 1991, another article in *United States Naval Institute Proceedings* deplored the deficiencies of the US Navy in mine warfare, instancing 'the USS TRIPOLI and the USS PRINCETON – the only US or allied ship casualties from any cause during *Desert Storm*, both of which were damaged by mines in the northern Gulf on the same day'.[15]

The history of gunboat diplomacy is rich in similar illustrations of the maxim that power has no absolute existence. What matters is not the aggregation of resources, but the ability to apply appropriate force about a given point; not the ultimate availability of great fleets, but 'the opportune presence of a ship of war' when and where needed. In 1967, for instance, the USS LIBERTY was casually crippled by Israeli forces quite unconcerned by the thought that the Sixth Fleet must be somewhere over the horizon. The following year North Korea captured the USS PUEBLO and exploited her crew as hostages without regard to the belated deployment of three carrier battle groups. In 1980 the distant menace of the US Navy did not deter the Iranians from seizing the US Embassy in Tehran, nor did the nuclear powered super carrier NIMITZ approach closely enough for the rescue helicopters she launched to reach the US hostages. Perhaps the outcome might have been different if NIMITZ had shortened the flight by ascending the Gulf, but a ship so important in the bipolar duel could not be risked on a side-show.

The shortage of ships that admirals could afford to risk sometimes allowed potential victims to thumb their noses at great powers. However, freezing naval deployments in cold war patterns also created occasional opportunities for lesser assailants. Argentina might not have found the Falklands so unprotected in April 1982 if the Royal Navy had been less preoccupied by a hypothetical Soviet threat in the Norwegian Sea. Even the most advanced technology offered few aids to definitive force as effective as the classical expedient of surprise. It was not for want of technical sophistication that Israel was caught napping in October 1973: over-confidence had dulled the edge of Israeli vigilance. If good political judgement is the first requisite of the assailant wishing to make a definitive use of limited naval force, it is no less indispensable to the victim hoping to offer a successful resistance. War often affords time to retrieve the mistakes made at the outset. In its definitive application, limited naval force tends to be inexorable – one way or the other.

The definitive use of limited naval force is so dependent on political judgement and the ability to seize a rare opportunity that its incidence may not be much influenced either by the proliferation of advanced technology (perhaps accelerated by the sale of warships from the former Soviet Navy) or by the new era of international relations inaugurated by the disintegration of the Soviet Union. Graham Greene once told the readers of *The Times* that adultery would continue whatever the rate of taxation and sudden descents from the sea will survive the ingenuity of scientists and the vagaries of grand strategy.

Purposeful and catalytic force (we may safely neglect the expressive mode) are a different matter. These require time to take effect, or for confusion to resolve itself, and time is now more likely to allow the victim to muster his defences than to sap his resolution. The reasons for this are mainly political, and as such will be considered in their proper place, but there is also a technical aspect. Modern warships are designed for swift and sudden combat on or beneath the open seas, not for lingering offshore. The deliberate approach, the manoeuvres for position, the leisurely broadsides of the traditional naval battle: these and the opportunities they offered for evasion or disengagement have receded into history. The ideal now is to destroy the enemy before he is in range; it is essential to do so before he opens a fire that warships are no longer constructed to withstand.[16] These are tactics ill-adapted to the use of limited naval force. If the defences are smothered at the outset – as at Suez – this may be construed as an act of war. If they are allowed the initiative, the cost may be heavier than anything risked by the gunboats of the 1920s. It is not technically difficult, or even particularly expensive, to threaten a fleet crippled by the dual handicap of confined waters and an initial commitment to minimum violence. At relatively little cost a determined victim can easily equip himself to deny to a far stronger assailant one of the classical gambits of gunboat diplomacy – allowing the looming menace of visible warships time to fray the nerves of those ashore. Admittedly jets can still scream across the roof-tops from a safely distant carrier, while helicopters or landing craft disembark marines to seize key points, capture warships at their moorings and neutralise fixed defences; but these manoeuvres demand a more elaborate and warlike operation and, above all, a deeper and more uncertain commitment. Today's assailant must often choose between running greater risks and using less limited force. In the 1980s, for instance, the US Sixth Fleet demonstrated their ability to repel any attack by Libyan shore-based aircraft – at a price. The Americans had to fire first. When the USS STARK failed to take this drastic precaution in the Gulf in May 1987, she was crippled by an Iraqi aircraft that may, as the Iraqi government subsequently claimed, have attacked the STARK by mistake. The lesson was learnt aboard the USS VINCENNES, which in July 1988 shot down an Iranian airliner mistakenly assumed to be a hostile military aircraft.[17] No doubt there is an ideal middle way between these extremes, but they illustrate the dilemmas that technology has created for the gunboat captains of the late twentieth century.

Inshore operations are not of course an inevitable feature of the purposeful and catalytic use of limited naval force. The various forms of distant blockade or of interception on the high seas should still leave the advantage with the stronger navy. There are also many nations without effective coastal defence, and some whose preparations might be nullified by political disunity. Even today, the advantages of the victim are not insuperable.

Nevertheless, recent decades have produced no wholly convincing example of the purposeful use of limited naval force against a defended coast. Perhaps the nearest approach was the punitive raid against inland targets in Libya carried out in April 1986 by aircraft from the US Sixth Fleet (assisted by US aircraft from British bases). The Libyan coast was defended, and the purpose – to deter the Libyan government from supporting terrorist attacks – seems to some extent to have been achieved, though this was never admitted by the Libyans. Against the Lebanon, also in the 1980s, neither bombing nor shelling had any politically useful effect, and when US Marines were landed they had to be withdrawn after suffering heavy casualties from a terrorist bomb. So far, technology has favoured those victims able and willing to exploit it. Because victims can nowadays make assailants operating against a defended coast run the risk of suffering casualties, those assailants have a new inducement to protect themselves by raising the level of their own violence. There seems no obvious reason to expect this trend to be reversed.

The effects of technology in counter-attack are less direct and more intimately intertwined with political factors requiring separate consideration. If we disregard retaliation by acts of war, the new possibilities of counter-attack are all centred on sabotage. The existence of broadcasting stations, the diffusion of domestic receiving sets, improved levels of technical knowledge, the ready availability of firearms and explosives: all these factors have made it easier for many victims to respond by acts of economic destruction or retorsion that will hurt the assailant more than the victim. Gunboat diplomacy has traditionally been employed to protect economic interests, but if an otherwise successful operation is likely to lead to the cutting of pipelines, the disruption of communications, to strikes and boycotts and the sabotage or hijacking of airliners, then this expedient becomes much less attractive. Terrorism is a fallible weapon and one that may turn in the hand of the user, but it is more easily exploited by some victims than by most assailants. Whether or not an otherwise defenceless victim can be expected to react to the exercise of limited naval force by damaging reprisals of this kind is primarily a political question, but technology will probably continue to provide fresh tools for willing hands.

III POLITICAL

Political considerations are predominant in all kinds of response to limited naval force, but the military distinctions between deterrence, defence and counter-attack are less relevant than the difference between internal and external political factors. It will thus be more convenient, while not losing sight of the military categories, to concentrate on two different kinds of political consideration: those that affect the victim's own capacity for resistance and those that influence the attitudes and actions of third parties.

Every act or threat – even the possibility of a threat – of limited force confronts the victim government with a range of options. The choice – between spending money on coastal defence or on something else; between resistance and surrender; between retaliation and acquiescence – depends on the general political outlook of the government, on the effectiveness of their administrative authority and on the nature of the political support they can command. There is also a fourth factor (though this is sometimes difficult to distinguish from external considerations): what experience has conditioned the government to expect. During the 1920s and 1930s, for instance, suffering the exercise of foreign naval force was such an everyday and long-established experience for any Chinese government that mere familiarity must have coloured the choices ostensibly taken in the light of other considerations. To the bureaucrats of any nation, whatever their ideology and however diverse their real resources, precedent will always be a compelling influence.

For our purposes, the general political outlook of the government has little to do with their preference for private enterprise or socialism, with their authoritarian tendencies, or democratic traditions. What matters is the choice they habitually make between maintaining the authority and independence of the nation-state on the one hand, and such potentially conflicting objectives as peace, prosperity, progress and external ideologies on the other. A government according a high priority to the preservation of national sovereignty is more likely to divert resources from economic development to coastal defence, to react to infringements (which are a necessary consequence for the victim of gunboat diplomacy) by threatening or initiating a war regardless of the likely outcome, by sacrificing the lives of its citizens in even a futile defence, by persisting in reprisals even at great cost to the national economy.

A small, weak state with a government of this kind may seem a less attractive victim than a stronger nation whose leaders are preoccupied by the material welfare of their people, shrink from violence, take decisions in the light of their immediate advantage, and enjoy a reputation for appeasement and compromise. However, there is also a third type of government: one divided between loyalty to the interests, however these may be interpreted, of the nation-state and the claims of some wider allegiance: ideological, racial, religious, linguistic, even federalist. Such a government may react differently to identical infringements of sovereignty by different assailants. Soviet intervention in Czechoslovakia was not the same as German intervention; interference by an Arab country in the affairs of another is one thing, a US landing in the Lebanon something else.

A prudent assailant will naturally give prior and careful consideration to all these factors in each intervention he contemplates: they vary from one country, one period and one set of circumstances to another. It would be a rash undertaking, though, and one subject to an intolerable complexity of qualifications, to postulate a general historical trend towards or away from resistance to external coercion. Too much has been made, for instance, of the defiance that is nowadays so frequent a reaction among Asian and African governments to anything savouring of interference by anyone associated with their former rulers or oppressors. We may admit the fact without making it the basis of a general rule. Certainly warships manned by white sailors can nowadays expect a rougher reception on many of these coasts, but the five West African nations who sent forces in 1990 to restore peace in much troubled Liberia were still fighting two years later in November 1992, when a Nigerian gunboat seized a Greek supply ship off the rebel-held port of Buchanan and other warships spent three days bombarding shore targets.[18] Any theory that relies on heightened Egyptian resistance to naval intervention must also explain why Japan was a victim in the latter half of the nineteenth century, a conspicuous assailant in the first half of the twentieth and now, as the second richest country in the world, again a victim. It is not enough to point to the defiant chauvinism of Mao Tse-Tung without recalling the even more reckless nationalism of the Dowager Empress. Even the increased diffusion of nationalist sentiment is only partly an obstacle to gunboat diplomacy; it inspires assailants as well as victims, and not all contemporary equivalents of nationalism find their expression in the defence of a particular nation-state. We may yet see gunboats achieving easy triumphs in the extension of Islam, of Arabism, of *Négritude*. So far, however, the aggregation of resources by the European Community has not endowed that organisation with a collective resolve equal to that once possessed by most of the individual member states.

In looking to the future we may thus find the incidence of change in the capacities and expectations of governments a better pointer than any alteration in their inclinations. Few governments, anywhere, anytime, have ever wanted anything more than the maintenance of their own authority or failed to feel resentment and bitter regrets on those occasions when acquiescence in external coercion seemed to offer better prospects of survival than resistance. Important though political attitudes are in determining the choices of particular governments, it may be easier to discern general trends in the means at their disposal than in their objectives. Administrative control, for instance, shows a general upward tendency that is more obviously widespread than the growth of popularly supported nationalism.

This is only partly attributable to technological progress, though telecommunications have naturally been important. The altered structure of most societies, which nowadays demand more centralised control to keep them going at all; the spread of literacy, which provides administrative cadres; the legacies and examples of colonialism: all these have greatly increased the number of states whose governments, as long as they command obedience at all (many do not), can nowadays expect it from more of their citizens, and more effectively, than ever before. This is a development almost wholly unfavourable to gunboat diplomacy, traditionally most successful when exerted by a disciplined and co-ordinated navy against a state whose resistance was enfeebled because its inhabitants either received no orders or else disregarded them. During the 1920s and 1930s, for instance, China was a helpless victim in spite of huge armies, vast quantities of weapons, a substantial number of reasonably modern warships, and a widespread and burning resentment of foreign interference. Neither nuclear weapons nor the *Thoughts of Chairman Mao* were needed to deny the Yangtse to British warships: a battery of field guns sufficed in 1949, as soon as there emerged an administrative machine capable of harnessing the will and employing the means that had long existed.

Naturally there are now, and will continue to be in the future, instances of states disrupted by civil war, even of states declining into anarchy. There are also states whose administrative structure rests on only the scantiest foundation of national consciousness or political commitment. Notoriously, these are targets for *coups d'état*, a process much simplified when control of the administration is a sufficient source of authority, but also potential victims of limited naval force whenever this is employed to assist or suppress a *coup*. On the whole, however, the growth of centralised administrative structures can be regarded as a trend that is likely to continue and calculated to strengthen the power of governments to resist the application of limited naval force.

An even more potent factor, though one that is less general and that has more ambiguous implications, is the growing diffusion of political consciousness. When this takes the form of nationalism it constitutes perhaps the most important single source of strength to a government anxious to resist the purposeful application of limited naval force. Not only does it provide the means of counter-attack – boycotts, strikes, sabotage, passive resistance, terrorism – and hence of deterrence, but it also supplies the incentive. A government expecting popular support for resistance to the foreigner will also see more prospect of continued authority if they defy than if they acquiesce.

However, not all political consciousness finds expression in support for the nation-state or for its government. In a state divided by internecine conflict, foreigners may be less repugnant to some factions than their indigenous foes. In some tranquil and stable societies, the will to resist may be inadequate. Pacifism, hedonism, sectarian interests, larger loyalties do not only sap the resolution of potential assailants: they can also make victims of countries not otherwise earmarked for that role. There could be no greater mistake than to suppose that, because some traditional assailants would now encounter greater difficulty in employing limited naval force against some of their accustomed victims, the general utility of this expedient has therefore declined. The division of the world's nations between assailants and victims is no less subject to change than the relative strength of the world's navies. What one government can no longer do may present fewer problems to another. Gunboat diplomacy is only a tool that anyone can occasionally use, not a privilege reserved to a particular class of governments or peoples.

In so far, therefore, as generalisations are possible at all in so complex a field, we may conclude that the predominant trends in the political development of nation-states have provided, and will continue to provide, governments with new means of deterring, resisting and counter-attacking the application of limited naval force. This is nevertheless a conclusion most applicable to those governments that formerly lacked the confidence to attempt defiance, because they were conscious that orders to this effect would neither be efficiently transmitted nor kindle a popular response. There are limits even to the predictable diffusion of administrative centralisation, whereas popular readiness to incur sacrifice to uphold the integrity of the nation-state is not a reliably directional trend. It is thus safer to suggest that the political obstacles to gunboat diplomacy have increased and, in certain countries, are likely to continue increasing, albeit with exceptions and qualifications, than to postulate any kind of mathematical progression leading ultimately to the extinction of this expedient.

In gunboat diplomacy, as in anatomy, the exceptions are often more conspicuous than the rules. After the humiliating US failure to rescue hostages from Tehran in 1980, who would have expected armed helicopters from the USS GUAM and TRENTON to achieve such a smooth opposed evacuation from the

US Embassy at Mogadishu in 1991? Who would ever have imagined that 1974 and 1975 would see five islands or parts of islands seized by China, Indonesia, Iran, Turkey and Vietnam respectively? 'To every action there is an equal and opposite reaction',[19] and the heightened toughness of many potential victims will surely be reflected in fresh audacities on the part of assailants, who will not necessarily be the same as in the past, nor need their victims be familiar.

There exists, it is often argued, a more formidable obstacle to gunboat diplomacy than the puny efforts of any single state: the force of international opinion, particularly as this is expressed in the United Nations. Historically, it is true, there has been a considerable shift in attitudes towards outside intervention. The hierarchy of nations and the privileged position of great powers are less easily conceded; recent decades produced fewer examples than the 1920s and 1930s of otherwise unfriendly governments combining to assert a common interest against such a victim as China. The idea of an international order, a common concern for the rights of property and of the individual, now seem less important than the prerogatives of national sovereignty. When the regular forces – and navies are almost always that – of one state enter the territory or the territorial waters of another, this is widely regarded as more reprehensible than any actions that, however significant their international repercussions, do not involve such an open and official crossing of frontiers. This is a widespread sentiment rather than a consistent doctrine. Not all interventions are condemned, nor is every victim encouraged to resist.[20] The 1991 Gulf War was a case in point. The sympathy of third parties usually depends on their ability to identify with either assailant or victim and the degree of practical expression given to that sympathy is prompted by interest rather than ethics. Nevertheless, whereas the use of limited force 'to restore order' once enjoyed the benefit of some doubt and had to be proved wrong, there is now an opposite prejudice.

One effect of this change has been in the use of violence. Assailants and victims have always condemned this in one another, but in the past third parties tended to weigh both sides in scales that, if not always equal, were seldom biased in the victim's favour. A naval bombardment – that of Nanking by British and US warships in 1927, for instance – would be explained, even excused, by the attacks previously made on foreign residents. Nowadays there is a widespread feeling that the use of violence by regular forces is less permissible than even worse violence by a mob or popular resistance movement. Terrorism and assassination are accepted as legitimate means of defence or retaliation, a further advantage to the victim. Other results have often been curious. Assailants have not desisted from the use of limited force when opportunities arose and circumstances seemed to require it, but they have justified their action in different terms and have been at pains to associate others in their intervention.

The right of one government to protect by force the lives or property of their nationals in the territory of another is nowadays less often advanced as a pretext for intervention (though President Johnson used this argument at the outset of the Dominican affair in 1965, as did President Reagan over Grenada in 1983). Instead, avowedly political motives are proclaimed: to help the victim to overcome externally inspired revolution (sometimes called Counter-Revolution); to overthrow a tyrannous regime; to deter aggression. Whenever possible, intervention ostensibly takes place at the invitation of the victim government or of some group composed of nationals of the victim state. If this cannot be arranged, or as an additional precaution even when it is, efforts are made to give the operation a multilateral cover. The United States make extensive use of the Organization of American States, Britain has tried to enlist the Commonwealth, and the Soviet Union went one better by inventing a 'Socialist Commonwealth' for the benefit of Czechoslovakia. Nor are these militarily redundant allies desired only because something done by several seems better than the same thing done by one. Their presence also encourages the notion that the intervention was prompted by 'principles' (preferably embodied in some treaty of convenient ambiguity) rather than by 'selfish vested interests'. None of these devices is entirely new (many British interventions in China extorted treaties by which later interventions could be justified), but they are employed with a frequency and sophistry that would have startled such candid practitioners as Lord Palmerston or Signor Mussolini.

Prejudice against intervention has another aspect, one that is slightly perverse, but more practical. Most members of the United Nations have a healthy horror of nuclear war and were

– it will be interesting to see whether the sentiment survives the Cold War – particularly anxious to manifest their disapproval of any *action* that seemed liable to provoke one. This tended to arouse feeling against the use of purposeful or catalytic force, to which nuclear threats or escalation sometimes seemed a conceivable response, while simultaneously discouraging retaliation against the definitive use of limited force. In 1958, when US forces landed in the Lebanon, Soviet threats caused more alarm outside the United States than in Washington. When PUEBLO was seized, third parties were less concerned with the morality of this North Korean action than with the risk that US retaliation might lead to war. In the first case, therefore, the United States were urged to withdraw, and to acquiesce in the second case. The reactions in some European capitals to the fusillade of miscellaneous threats with which Iraq tried to deter interference with their conquest of Kuwait in 1990, suggested that there is life in this gambit still. It can be expected to operate as unevenly in the future as it did in the past, because democratic governments are more amenable to exhortation than others less exposed to pressure from public opinion. The resentment aroused by this 'double standard' often impairs the effectiveness of a sentiment that nevertheless has some practical roots. Purposeful or catalytic force can pose a greater threat of war simply because it lasts longer and allows more time for tension to build up on both sides. Definitive force is all over when the fuss begins and the only threat of war thus comes from the victim. Although examples of the definitive use of limited naval force are insufficiently frequent to warrant firm conclusions, it may be significant that in only two instances has the assailant been subjected to significant pressure from international opinion during the last two decades: Argentina over the Falklands in 1982, and the United States over Grenada in 1983. In both cases, the issue was decided by force of arms and not by the United Nations.

The risk that some use of gunboat diplomacy might attract censure from the general sentiment of mankind is perhaps an occasional deterrent to sensitive assailants, but it offers little encouragement to victims, actual or prospective. However, there have been other, and more important, developments in international relations, some of which are still operative.

The first of these was bipolarity: the emergence of two mutually antagonistic superpowers, each with its own magnetic field of attraction for lesser states. This shifting of iron filings about two fixed and opposite poles was very different from the kaleidoscope of the 1920s and 1930s, when the relationships of the seven great powers were as variable as the estimates of their respective strength. After the comparative stability of the era that ended in 1991, it requires an effort of the imagination to realise that – as seen from London – France, Germany,[21] Italy, Japan, the Soviet Union and the United States all fluctuated between the roles of potential ally and principal antagonist. What is even more surprising is that, outside Europe, these shifting patterns actually offered the remaining countries of the world less scope for manoeuvre than the more stable divisions after 1945. The combinations that dissolved and reformed were mostly regional. Japan was only active in eastern Asia; after the early 1920s, the United States played no part in Europe, Africa or western Asia; Britain[22] and France left the Americas alone; Germany's influence was almost exclusively European; Italy made only one significant excursion farther afield and, from 1922 to 1938, the Soviet Union's occasional sallies were across her Asian borders alone. A handful of lesser states in Europe had a genuine choice of protectors and occasionally exercised it, China had more assailants than one to fear, but the general rule, to which Abyssinia provided a brief and ultimately abortive exception, required the weaker nations outside the European continent to adapt themselves unaided to the exigencies of whichever great power happened to dominate that region. Britain alone had pretensions to being a world power, and she had no thought of extending an authority she could already scarcely maintain.

From 1945 onwards, however, the United States and the Soviet Union progressively expanded their respective spheres of influence into a world from which their former rivals had progressively withdrawn. After the early years, when Germany, eastern Europe and Japan were occupied, they seldom did so by actual conquest, but by bidding against one another for the allegiance of third states, to whom they offered protection, arms, economic aid, the blessings of their respective ideologies, and occasional assistance in political change. The superpowers, though, never achieved a partition of the world between them.

Instead, their competition encouraged and stimulated the emergence of more independent states than ever before and offered to many, both old and new, additional means of asserting and safeguarding a national sovereignty that sometimes exceeded the expectations, and the desires, of both. China has not been so independent for a century, Cuba for five, Egypt for twenty.

In that era most victims of limited force ought to have had a potential claim to assistance, either because they were already among the clients of one of the superpowers or because, as neutrals, they might turn to one superpower if not aided by the other. In 1956 Egypt was sufficiently adroit to obtain, as had Israel in 1948, the support of both. Unfortunately for the smaller states, there were substantial exceptions to this rule. One superpower normally permitted the other to discipline its own clients (the Dominican Republic in 1965, Czechoslovakia in 1968) and both were far more reluctant than, for instance, the great powers of 1914 to allow the grievances of their clients to involve them in the extremities of mutual war. Egypt, Syria and North Vietnam were left to suffer more than limited force; Laos and South Vietnam found protection as double-edged as 'liberation'. Nor was it only victims who enjoyed, or expected, the qualified support of a superpower. An assailant could sometimes exploit his special relationship to employ limited force with a heightened sense of immunity from retaliation.

The importance to the future development of gunboat diplomacy of the altered international situation produced by the collapse of the Soviet Union is obvious from a backward glance at the 1970s and 1980s. So much then depended on the primacy accorded to superpower rivalry. The continuing dispute between China and Vietnam, with its frequent resort to limited naval force over the Paracel and Spratly islands, surfaced in 1974,[23] when the United States had abandoned their Vietnamese clients and China saw no further need to sacrifice her own claims to the wider cause. That was also the year when Turkey, always rather a footloose member of NATO, got away with a particularly blatant invasion of Cyprus, the client of Greece, also a member of NATO, but one who showed less understanding of US requirements than did Turkey. In Washington the territorial integrity of Cyprus seemed less important than keeping Turkey in the front line against the Soviet Union.

In 1982, with regard to the Falklands, the influence of the
Cold War again shaped US reactions to Argentina's use of
gunboat diplomacy, but only after weeks of uncertainty. On the
one hand, the military junta in Buenos Aires was a potentially
useful ally against communist regimes in Latin America. On
the other hand, Britain was an important ally against the Soviet
Union. In the end, the balance tipped in Britain's favour and
Operation Corporate went ahead. During the long war between
Iran and Iraq, however, both the Soviet Union and the United
States seemed to be paralysed by their own rivalry, making no
serious attempt to end a conflict that was, as it turned out,
doing neither of them any good. The belligerents were allowed
to wreak wanton havoc on neutral shipping, even on the
petroleum exports so important to the economies of allies of
the United States, and the US use of limited naval force was
belated, rather half-hearted and not very effective. In the
Indian Ocean, however, a huge naval deployment – of little
relevance to the protection of shipping in the Persian Gulf –
strained the resources of the US Navy and occasionally entailed
the maintenance of as many as three carrier battle groups in
the sea area most remote from both coasts of the United States.
Their presence presumably reflected President Carter's
declaration of 28 January 1980: 'an attempt by any outside force
to gain control of the Persian Gulf will be regarded as an
assault on the vital interests of the USA'.[24]

The disappearance of these tensions and constraints has not
been an unmixed blessing. The years that saw the end of the
Cold War also seemed to presage a time of troubles. New
sources of turbulence developed in the Baltic (Estonia, Latvia
and Lithuania); in the Black Sea (Georgia and the Ukraine);
and in the Sea of Okhotsk (the Kurile Islands). Inland, the
troubles were worse, often extending to actual fighting. The
Mediterranean remained liable to sudden storms and the
waters of the Gulf to further conflict. If potential occasions for
the use of limited naval force were often apparent, so were the
risks of war: not total war or world war, but war of a kind that
was better avoided. Of all the continents, Australia was alone in
practising gunboat diplomacy as an assailant without also
suffering it as a victim.

So far, the political alternatives on offer to the international
discipline once imposed by the Cold War have commanded

insufficient acceptance. Brian Urquhart, formerly an under secretary-general of the United Nations, remarked that there had been much talk in 1990 'of a renaissance of the United Nations', but concluded a sceptical analysis of the organisation's role in the run-up to the Gulf War by wondering whether this had been more than a fig-leaf for US policy.[25] The Arab League and other regional organisations have seldom been more than talking shops, and the Organisation of Petroleum Exporting Countries has not so far repeated the successful use made of the oil weapon after the 1973 Arab–Israeli War. All these groups are capable of agitation and propaganda. They can embarrass politically sensitive users of limited naval force, but they have not yet revealed much potential for effective deterrence or for offering viable alternatives by way of conflict resolution.

It may be significant that India, once so fervent an advocate of conciliation and non-violent diplomacy, made increasing use of coercion in the later 1980s. In March 1991 Lieutenant Sanjay Singh, writing in *United States Naval Institute Proceedings*, doubtless reflected his government's official stance when he declared: 'The Indian Navy is charged with [Inter alia] ... safeguarding the nation from gunboat diplomacy.'

However, he forgot to mention India's prowess as an assailant (see the Chronological Appendix), which offered some contrast to the record of the European Community, whose ten navies never attempted, when women and children were trapped in Adriatic ports bombarded from air, land and sea, to emulate in 1990–1 the kind of rescue operations the Royal Navy managed from Spanish ports in 1936–7.

IV CONVERSELY

By now, the prospects for gunboat diplomacy may seem gloomy. Warships are more vulnerable, less able to employ their visible presence as a sufficient menace, compelled to assemble in greater numbers, and to undertake more extensive operations. Only definitive force, the rarest form, may be immune from this bias of change, which is often, though less uniformly, reinforced by the effects of political developments. These give victims added incentives and facilities to acquire and use the weapons

now available for their defence. They encourage resistance and
(in some circumstances) retaliation, and permit a wider licence
in violence to the victim than to the assailant. Above all, they
hold out the hope of assistance. Although new techniques,
military and political alike, are also open to assailants, these
are not always so uniformly available: the principal naval
powers are often politically handicapped, while states with an
international licence for assault sometimes lack the warships to
carry it out.

So far, however, we have deliberately considered this problem
from the standpoint of the victim. As a result, the political
factors examined have often elicited arguments, not so much
against the use of limited naval force, as against the use of any
force at all. It would be agreeable, but optimistic, to suppose
that these arguments – or the more plausible reasoning of
writers of greater eminence – would prevail and that diplomacy
would no longer be disfigured by a resort to arms. By 1991,
when the diplomatic pressure exerted by the Soviet Union as
well as the United States, the mandatory resolutions of the
Security Council, the adoption and application of economic
sanctions, and the menacing deployment of an army of allies
with full air and naval support had all failed to influence
Saddam Hussein, so that Iraqi troops had to be forcibly
expelled with extreme violence from Kuwait, this was unfortunately an illusion requiring no refutation. The question is
rather whether *limited* force is still possible, or whether we must
resign ourselves to a choice between the obliterating brutality
of modern war or the protracted cruelty of guerrilla conflict.

This is not a question that can be argued here. Two comments
will suffice to illustrate (not to support) an optimism essential to
the composition of the present work. First of all, the increasing
caution of the superpowers confounded the Cassandras of earlier
decades. The bombs did *not* go off, and after 1973 even the
rattling of rockets was in abeyance. Secondly, the proliferation
and – except in Vietnam – the achievements of guerillas have
fallen short of earlier expectations, whereas limited force, in the
1970s and 1980s had some notable results. The status of the
Paracels and Spratlys, of eastern Cyprus, of East Timor and of
Grenada was swiftly and decisively altered by limited naval force.
However, outright war failed the United States in Vietnam, the
Soviet Union in Afghanistan, Israel in the Lebanon, both Iran

and Iraq during eight years of fighting, and Iraq against Kuwait; and Israel has survived guerrilla attacks since 1948.

If we assume, therefore, that governments will continue to attempt the coercion of foreigners, what expedients are available for this purpose? Economic measures need not detain us. Saddam Hussein was not the first to shrug them off. Sanctions against Italy in 1935, the prolonged Arab boycott of traffickers with Israel, the Berlin blockade, the Rhodesian fiasco, are only a few of the instances that have brought home the lesson learnt by China over a century ago, when even the withholding of the indispensably laxative rhubarb was found inadequate to bring Britain constipated to her knees.[26] There are too many alternative sources of supply and too many unscrupulous governments and traders to make this expedient effective in any but the most unusual circumstances. And then it invites, and has sometimes received (at Pearl Harbor, for instance), a forcible response. The economic weapon can be a useful supplement: it is not a reliable substitute.

Guerrillas and terrorists, though occasionally effective (even in the territory of an alien victim), require specially favourable political conditions to achieve success. They also constitute a weapon of considerable potential danger to the assailant himself. More governments than one have found these irregulars easier to recruit than to disband. In any case, their employment demands the sanctuary of a secure base, either in the victim's territory or in a contiguous state. Not every government, however, enjoys the luxury of an adjacent frontier and guerrillas or an army, its own or a client's, to march across it. Although Guatemala in 1954, Hungary in 1956 and Czechoslovakia in 1968 are conspicuous exceptions, the crossing of land frontiers, particularly by regular troops, is hard to confine within the bounds of limited force. This becomes even more difficult if the attempt is made to fly them into some more distant country. Unless airfields have been secured in advance by local sympathisers, this is a hazardous operation. Even if there are no problems about overflying other countries, the landing often confronts the assailant with a choice between initial and politically undesirable violence and the risk of an embarrassing repulse – and parachutists are easier to drop than to withdraw.

The decisive argument against the use of ground and air forces is often geographical. A distant victim may only be accessible by sea. Moreover, air forces cannot be employed on their own without at least the threat of extreme violence. Bombing, as the experience of Vietnam demonstrated, incurs widespread odium, may not cow a resolute victim, and is hard to depict as the use of limited force – indeed, as anything but an act of war. It is one of the peculiarities of contemporary political sentiment that, other things being equal, bombing raids launched from land bases attract greater indignation than those emanating from aircraft-carriers at sea. In April 1986 the US bombers that attacked Libya from British bases were denied overflying rights by the European allies of the United States, blamed for the civilian casualties, and bathed in a glare of adverse publicity that quite obscured the part played by aircraft from the Sixth Fleet.

Even in those cases where access by land or sea is possible, naval intervention may offer political advantages. The sea is still a neutral *place d'armes*, open to all, where forces may be assembled, ready for intervention, but not yet committed. With greater precautions, perhaps in greater numbers than before, warships can still test the temperature of the water before they venture too far. A ship that has approached the victim's coast, even a fleet that has entered territorial waters, is a lesser involvement than a platoon that has crossed the frontier or an aircraft that has dropped a bomb. Also, if intervention takes place, but things go wrong, warships are still easier to withdraw.

Naturally it is at the moment of commitment that the assailant must confront and, if he is to achieve success, bypass or overcome the new obstacles previously noted to the application of limited naval force: the political sanctity of national sovereignty and the military effectiveness of motivated and organised resistance. These obstacles can, however, be rather less formidable than was suggested in the earlier analysis, which concentrated on the worst case, which is in practice also rather a rare case: the purposeful application of limited naval force inshore without any expectation of assistance or acquiescence from the victim until the moment when he finally yields to coercion. Without anticipating the scenarios to be offered in a later chapter, it may be worth while describing some of the easier types of naval intervention that assailants might consider. Being types of operation, this is a military classification according to method, which does not coincide with the political classification employed elsewhere: definitive, purposeful, catalytic, expressive.

The first and most obvious comprises operations on the high seas: escort, convoy, interception, capture, blockade, surveillance and harassment. Neither the political nor the naval considerations governing such operations have greatly changed since the days of the Spanish Civil War, though some victims may have the missiles or the aircraft to keep warships farther out to sea. Provided that the assailant enjoys local naval superiority, that he has a colourable pretext for his actions, and that he avoids direct confrontation with a stronger naval power, he can still expect to get away with much more at sea than on land. During the struggle in Algeria, for instance, the French Army were subjected to constant international criticism for their ultimately unsuccessful attempt to restore French authority in what was legally French metropolitan territory, whereas the French Navy were not seriously challenged in their probably illegal activities on the high seas. Stopping a merchant ship at sea is just as much an infringement of national sovereignty in international law as crossing a frontier to kidnap a fugitive, but it is seldom resented so acutely, either by the victim or by third parties. At sea, there are also more opportunities of employing definitive force, which has fewer political and, if the conditions are right, military snags than the purposeful and catalytic applications.

Even inshore, it is also possible to evade or mitigate the obstacles to limited naval force. At the lowest level there is considerable scope for quasi-clandestine or crypto-diplomatic operations: naval assisted espionage, landing and rescuing agents, perhaps an occasional kidnapping. In September 1987, for instance, one Fawaz Younis was lured aboard a boat operated by the Federal Bureau of Investigation and, once far enough into the Mediterranean, was arrested and transferred to the carrier USS SARATOGA in order to be flown to Washington and charged with hostage-taking in Beirut two years earlier. In 1989 he was sentenced to thirty years' imprisonment.[27]

Another possibility is unobtrusive support for, or opposition to, a *coup d'état* or political uprising. One of the crucial factors in many struggles for power, for instance, is the natural concern of leaders for their personal safety or for that of their families. If a friendly warship happens to be in port on a routine visit and is known to be available for a last-minute rescue, leaders may be encouraged to hold out the few extra hours needed for success. Even the rescue of a defeated leader may be useful. The Royal Navy, as will be seen from the earlier pages of the Chronological Appendix, once made quite a practice of this, thus providing many foreign politicians with an added incentive to pursue pro-British policies. In the Soviet Union, the KGB used to derive considerable advantage from their own cultivation of a similar tradition.

These crypto-diplomatic activities need seldom involve actual violence, as they are conducted clandestinely or with the connivance or acquiescence of those ashore. The point of using a warship is not to overcome opposition by the armed forces of the victim, but to deter and, if things go wrong, to repel interference by the ordinary police, coastguards or mobs. Such methods are naturally only applicable in situations where the involvement of the assailant government can, if necessary, be admitted. If a political upheaval is in progress, for instance, the outcome may, in any event, decide the possibility of friendly relations with the assailant. If involvement assists the success of the right party in the victim state, future relations may be even more cordial: if not, they may not be much worse than they would otherwise have been. In such circumstances, particularly if the operation is intrinsically too dangerous for civilians, there could be a strong case for naval participation.

The next level would be overt (but still small-scale) operations for the protection of the assailant's embassy, nationals or property in circumstances when organised opposition is unlikely. These have been less common in recent years because of a combination of two political tendencies: a declining interest among some of the naval powers in the safety and prestige of their representatives and nationals abroad; and an increased touchiness in small states about any infringement of their sovereignty. That is why warships will sometimes remain over the horizon, their unseen presence providing reassurance to their embassy ashore, whose diplomats will stay while those of other nations are hurriedly flown out, but causing no provocation to the over-excited citizenry of the victim state. In other cases, a visible presence is preferred, as in 1987, when two Indian frigates lay off Colombo ready to evacuate the staff of the High Commission if the civil strife ashore got out of hand. There are many

situations in which a victim government temporarily loses
control, and only armed intervention from outside can rescue
foreigners from the mob. In maritime states, particularly those
with capitals on or near the coast, this is a classic case for the use
of limited naval force. This type of operation, no less than the
crypto-diplomatic, is also well within the capacity of small navies
– if they are near enough – as it calls for resolution, judgement
and good intelligence rather than powerful or numerous
warships.

It is at the next level, where significant opposition is likely, that
the problem becomes more complex. In August 1991 US Marines
had to be landed in Monrovia, even though the evacuation of
foreign nationals ought to have been an uncontroversial task,
because the violence ashore was so uncontrolled. Even greater
precautions are needed where the application of limited naval
force entails a partisan involvement in local politics. The obvious
method, and one often adopted in recent years, is to arrange for
naval intervention to take place at the invitation, or with the
acquiescence, of a significant group in the victim state. The
government may want assistance against a third state or against
an indigenous uprising; a dissident movement may need help to
supplant the government. At worst, therefore, opposition to naval
intervention will be partially disorganised and hampered by
internal conflicts already in progress. At best, the mere show of
naval force will be enough to tip the scale and deter the other
side from offering effective opposition. In this type of operation
political factors are often predominant and success depends more
on the ability to back a winner at the right moment and on the
right pretext than on specifically naval skills. Nevertheless, in
modern conditions, a full task force will often be needed, both
to ensure the protection of the ships and their ability to
disengage and also to provide the marines, helicopters, landing
craft and the like needed for small-scale operations ashore. The
special problems of the US and Soviet navies in the Mediterranean have already been mentioned, but the interruption of
that rivalry does not mean that no admiral commanding a small
landing force will ever again have to worry about the presence
of an equal or stronger fleet out at sea.

There is thus a wide range of inshore operations that should
still remain feasible in favourable circumstances (which are
always required for the exercise of limited force – only war is an

ever-open option) for many years to come. Their actual conduct, however, will demand more careful political preparation and more elaborate naval planning than in the past. Governments will seldom be able simply to 'send a gunboat' – or even an amphibious task force – and confide the outcome to the initiative and improvisation of her commander. Gunboat diplomacy, in common with other contemporary uses of force (even ordinary domestic police work), is going to demand skills more expressly professional than dash and seamanship. Just as amphibious warfare now requires a common training and a single co-ordinated command for soldiers, sailors and airmen, so gunboat diplomacy will need a fusion of political, diplomatic and naval skills. In 1958 the US landing in the Lebanon almost ran into serious trouble at the very outset because of insufficient co-ordination between the government in Washington, the Ambassador in Beirut, and the marines on the beach. A quarter of a century later, when US – and French – forces again attempted intervention in the Lebanon, the fiasco that resulted seems to have been the result not so much of a lack of coordination as of a radically flawed appreciation of the political and military situation in the Lebanon at that time.

Even the utmost skill and care might not, however, overcome the more formidable obstacles to the final category of operations: the inshore coercion of a recalcitrant and undivided victim. There has been no entirely satisfactory example of success in so difficult an undertaking since the Italian seizure of Corfu in 1923. The US punitive bombardment of North Vietnam after the incidents in the Gulf of Tongking in 1964 was a political failure: it extracted no concessions and was the prelude to US involvement in a disastrous war. In the 1970s operations against eastern Cyprus and East Timor were militarily successful and both territories are still held by their assailants, but only the land was conquered: the victims were not coerced into acquiescence. It may none the less be possible to imagine circumstances in which so difficult a feat might reasonably be attempted. A small state without powerful protectors or unduly formidable coastal defences might have a determined government whose policies attracted strong support from their ruling class and little effective opposition while earning widespread international detestation. In such circumstances an amphibious task force (including an aircraft-carrier) might land marines, both on the beaches and by helicopter or hovercraft, to seize key points inland, neutralise airfields or other defences by shelling or bombing and, having secured the capital, set up a puppet government to whom generous terms would be offered on condition that the objectionable policies of their predecessors were abandoned or revised. That sentence has not been altered since it was first written in 1970, but it offers a passable description of the US Operation Urgent Fury against Grenada in 1983.

Change, rather than decay, may thus be foreseen for gunboat diplomacy in the altered environment. A reshuffling of identities among assailants and victims, greater sophistication and elaboration in the mounting of operations, a degree of preference for the open sea and new heights of hypocrisy in public justification are all predictable trends. The political applications of limited naval force will be less simple, less straightforward, probably less romantic than hitherto, but they may even be more effective. Instead of providing a welcome break in the tedious peacetime routine for dashing young naval officers, they may become regular preoccupations – and offer the subject of serious study – for the political specialists of future navies. *Qui vivra verra*.

4 Operations and Capacities

An American child crying on the banks of the Yangtse a thousand miles from the coast can summon the ships of the American Navy up that river to protect it from unjust assault.

Wilbur[1]

The purpose of this chapter is to examine the resources available to various governments for the political application of limited naval force and to consider how far their previous words or actions indicate their readiness to employ this expedient. Obviously this cannot be a comprehensive survey. *The Military Balance*[2] lists over a hundred navies and, even if all those with good reasons for not venturing beyond their own territorial waters are excluded, too many remain for even cursory treatment in a single chapter. It may thus be better merely to attempt the definition and the illustration by example of zones of probability for the exercise of limited naval force. The object would be to establish the minimum naval resources required before a government could reasonably contemplate resort to this expedient at different levels. These are naturally purely naval calculations and necessarily subject to wide margins of error. A government may have enough ships, but lack the will to employ them; another may attempt operations beyond the true capacity of the naval resources available; a third may rightly believe that the personal qualities and professional skills of their sailors will outweigh the deficiencies of their ships. In principle, however, it should be possible to deduce from the state of a navy the kind of operational ceiling that was expressly proclaimed for Britain in 1966:

It is only realistic to recognize that we, unaided by our allies, could not expect to undertake operations of this character (the landing or withdrawal of troops against sophisticated opposition outside the range of land-based air cover).[3]

99

Gunboat Diplomacy

Admittedly, this was as much a political decision as a military one and few other governments have set such explicit bounds to their ambitions. However, it was supported by the argument that operations of the excluded type required the use of aircraft-carriers, which Britain did not propose to retain. If, therefore, we find that certain levels of operation demand particular types of warship, or the possession of a minimum number of warships, we may legitimately regard such operations as being above the normal ceiling of navies that do not meet these requirements.

This example, chosen in 1970, turned out to be an even better illustration than originally supposed of the political character and thus the ephemeral nature of this kind of ceiling. No change in doctrine had been announced when Britain, unaided, landed troops in the Falklands in the teeth of sustained air attack and with only the sparse air cover available from two ships the Navy had contrived to obtain or to preserve (just) under the pseudonyms of 'through-deck cruiser' (HMS INVINCIBLE) and 'Commando ship' (HMS HERMES).[4] In the Falklands, of course, that was a war, but in gunboat diplomacy it is more the rule than the exception for ships to discharge functions never mentioned when their acquisition was justified to the taxpayer and probably not even contemplated by their designers. When a need arises, admirals must use what comes to hand and often get more out of it than was originally intended.

I OPERATIONS

This is a reservation to be borne in mind when the reader contemplates yet another set of categories, this time intended to circumscribe zones of probability. When we were concerned with the political objectives of limited naval force and asked *why* this was employed, we spoke of definitive, purposeful, catalytic and expressive force.[5] In answering the question *how* this force was employed, distinctions were drawn between one type of operation and another: on the high seas and inshore, for instance.[6] The problem now is *what* resources are needed for different levels of operation, and the following seems the most useful classification, in ascending order of resources required:

Simple Ship   (use of individual warships where significant resistance is not expected)

Superior Ship   (use of individual warships able to overcome expected resistance)

Simple Fleet   (unopposed tasks beyond the capacity of single ships, e.g. blockade)

Superior Fleet   (tasks demanding numerous ships able to overcome expected opposition)

Simple Amphibious   (unopposed landings from ships unlikely themselves to be attacked)

Opposed Amphibious (landings where significant opposition is to be expected)

Simple ship operations are within the capacity of at least fifty navies, all of which have warships with enough speed, endurance, armament and seaworthiness to intercept merchant vessels on the high seas or to reach and enter the territorial waters of another state. Thirty-three of these navies have made at least a threat of limited naval force outside territorial waters since 1939, and twenty-one have actually used limited naval force during this period. These statistics of experience exclude some efficient navies (that of Sweden, for instance) that undoubtedly possess the capacity for gunboat diplomacy, but that have been prevented by circumstances or the policy of their government from exercising this art. At this very elementary level, therefore, further argument or illustration would be superfluous. Proved capacity for simple ship operations is widespread, and probable capacity even greater. And, as so many of these operations are regarded by the initiating government as self-evidently legitimate (arresting a ship in an area of the high seas over which the assailant claims special rights not recognised by the victim, for instance), domestic political inhibitions are often minimal. This is a game that almost anyone can play – and, in favourable circumstances, quite probably will.

Simple ship operations are not, of course, necessarily so innocuous. The 'unknown' submarines of the Spanish Civil War or the anonymous ships that mined the Corfu Straits in 1946 expected no resistance and, in the latter case, encountered none. In 1986 the French fishery protection vessel ALBATROS sank the trawler SOUTHERN RAIDER (suspected of gun-running) off Réunion, and in 1988 the Indian frigate GODAVERI, while foiling an attempted *coup d'état* in the Republic of the Maldives, sank a ship carrying mercenaries.

The field for *superior ship* operations is slightly more restricted, even though the principle of superiority relates only to the particular operation, or class of operation, envisaged. A superior ship does not have to be a supreme ship. Indeed, there is no warship afloat that cannot be sunk by something. On the other hand, a warship that might expect to emerge victorious from a desperate battle with a given rival is not a sufficiently superior ship for gunboat diplomacy, which aims at achieving results without extremes of violence liable to lead to war. Ideally, a superior ship is one to which no more than token resistance will be offered, because even the victim recognises that any attempt would entail certain defeat. This is not an outcome that can be safely predicted without considering a specific operation against a known victim, because national attitudes differ so widely in these matters. Some governments issue standing instructions that superior force is not to be resisted; others expect heroic sacrifices; many would probably attach as much importance to the identity of the assailant as to his strength. A Peruvian naval officer, for instance, might be excused for yielding to the demands of a US warship, but would risk the firing-squad if his assailant, however superior, had been Ecuadorean.

Nevertheless, however much circumstances can alter cases, serious resistance is inherently less likely if the assailant is manifestly superior, whereas, whatever the political conditions, officers of any nationality will always at least be tempted to open fire when challenged by a warship of inferior or even equal strength. For this purpose, the appearance of superiority may be more important than its reality. The hierarchy of warships is today more misleading than ever. Many modern warships are intended to operate in groups, in which some have specialised functions and few are self-sufficient. A US nuclear-powered attack carrier, for instance, may be the most powerful ship afloat, but she needs escorts to cope with certain kinds of threat and would be vulnerable at close quarters. Ships designed for an over-the-horizon battle of the first salvo are not always easy to compare if they meet in a narrow strait or a confined anchorage, and such confrontations ought ideally to be decided by bluff rather than blasting away. Traditional assumptions that the larger ship is also superior no longer meet the facts.

In gunboat diplomacy a superior ship must obviously and generally be recognisable as such, which usually means that there must be more than one. It is highly improbably that, in 1963, either the French or the Brazilians ever contemplated anything so extreme as a naval battle resulting from their dispute over lobster-catching,[7] but contemporary press reports suggest a remarkable Brazilian naval concentration (involving the cruiser BARROSO, five destroyers and two corvettes) in response to the despatch of the single French destroyer TARTU. Admittedly, the Brazilian press reported (and the French denied) that TARTU would be reinforced by a naval squadron (including the small aircraft-carrier ARROMANCHES) then off the West African coast. Nevertheless, just as the despatch of TARTU was prompted by the desire to *marquer le coup*,[8] so the Brazilian concentration may reasonably be regarded as the gathering of a force sufficiently superior to invest the withdrawal of TARTU (she was temporarily replaced by a warship so small as to be entirely symbolic) with the character of prudence rather than pusillanimity. The encounters of gunboat diplomacy often resemble those of the Condottieri of Renaissance Italy, which were not decided by fighting but by manoeuvre, with one side withdrawing or yielding once the other had assembled superior forces in an advantageous position.

A particularly good example of the definitive use of this superior ship technique occurred on 6 May 1937, when the British battleship ROYAL OAK and her two escorting destroyers interposed themselves between the Spanish Nationalist cruiser ALMIRANTE CERVERA and some Spanish merchant vessels carrying 2,500 Republican refugees (mainly children) away from Bilbao. The intentions of both sides were made explicit in an exchange of signals, with ALMIRANTE CERVERA protesting: 'I got orders from my government to stop any Spanish ship leaving Bilbao. I protest if you stop me in the exercise of my rights', and ROYAL OAK replying: 'I have orders from my government to protect them on the high seas'.[9]

ALMIRANTE CERVERA gave way gracefully and it is interesting to note how relatively amicable most of these encounters were, though a signal from one of ROYAL OAK's escorting destroyers (*not* to the Spaniards) during this incident records that ALMIRANTE

CERVERA's torpedo tubes were not loaded, thus showing that the British at least were alert to the possibility that this could be more than a show of strength.

The value of employing a superior ship was, of course, realised at the time. After an earlier encounter between British destroyers and ALMIRANTE CERVERA, British destroyers off the northern coast of Spain were reinforced first by a cruiser and then by the battle cruiser HOOD, the latter flying the flag of the Vice-Admiral Battle Cruiser Squadron. Soon afterwards, on 27 April 1937, Vice-Admiral Geoffrey Blake made this significant recommendation, which the Commander-in-Chief Home Fleet endorsed when he forwarded it to the Admiralty: 'to avoid "incidents", i.e. the Spanish warship opening fire on a British merchant ship, or warship, the British warship present must be unquestionably more powerful than the largest Insurgent ship'.[10]

In modern conditions, of course, it might be more difficult to establish superiority so clearly. During the Falklands War of 1982 the British nuclear-powered submarine CONQUEROR established not merely superiority, but a wide-ranging ascendancy by torpedoing the Argentine cruiser BELGRANO. This ability to sink ships by surprise is the great strength of the submarine in war time, but the assailant who does so, or even threatens to do so, in time of peace can scarcely claim to be using limited force. Even in 1937, when casualty lists from the Italian troops fighting in Spain were openly published in Rome, Italy did not admit that her submarines were sinking neutral ships.[11] Victims, of course, can get away with greater violence, and might thus make use of submarines for defence or deterrence, but they are unsuitable weapons for any assailant intent on avoiding war. This is particularly true of superior ship operations, which are most likely to end happily when the victim can plausibly plead *force majeure* to his own government and public opinion. Yet, as the Swedish Navy discovered in the 1980s, it is just such 'outsiders' that are difficult to persuade of the reality of submarines that remain submerged. And submarines that surface to manifest their threat will forfeit much of their superiority.

Although success can only be predicted, if at all, after considering the particular circumstances of a specific operation, failure is likely to await any assailant unable to employ a force that is at least plausibly superior. This immediately allows us to exclude some otherwise efficient navies whose resources or whose geographical situation make it unlikely that they could ever employ convincingly superior force in any operation to which resistance was expected. The Belgian Navy, for instance, makes an important contribution to the minesweeping resources of NATO, but has few vessels capable of outfacing another warship or overawing a foreign port. To qualify for the superior ship category, a navy must be capable of deploying a demonstrably stronger force against an armed victim within its operational radius. This does not mean an ability to defeat the entire armed forces, even the whole navy, of the victim, but only to cope with the opposition likely in some plausible contingency. In August 1987, for instance, a remarkable confrontation resulted from an attempt by the Colombian frigate CALDAS to assert disputed Colombian claims to territorial waters in the Gulf of Venezuela. The Venezuelan Navy deployed a superior force of warships supported by aircraft which, after a week of confrontation and the diplomatic mediation of the Argentine government, induced the Colombian President to withdraw the CALDAS before anyone opened fire.[12]

Superior ship operations, however, demand more than the ability to produce two ships in circumstances where the victim has only one. The best of navies does not have all its ships available all the time; the most reckless would usually be reluctant to commit all it had to a single operation in which, however limited the intentions of the assailant and the expected response of the victim, there would always be some risk of loss or damage. If two ships are sent, for instance, one would normally expect that more would be available to reinforce or rescue them and that the combined total would still be substantially less than national resources. Unfortunately, these ideas are desperately hard to quantify. A reckless assailant undertaking a brief operation against a weak victim within a couple of hours of steaming needs so much less than a prudent admiral would demand in different circumstances. The 1960s alone produced half-a-dozen instances of relatively small navies using, or threatening, limited force in conditions where resistance was possible. The most one can say is that, whereas inadequate resources only constitute a major obstacle to superior ship operations for a relatively small number of seaworthy navies, many more are likely to regard these as too difficult in most circumstances. However, any kind of list would be futile because it would be riddled with qualifications and exceptions. In purely naval terms and bearing in mind that favourable circumstances are always required for the exercise of gunboat diplomacy, the minimum resources demanded by superior ship operations are too low to constitute a useful ceiling.

Politically the case is different. Although no country that goes to the expense of maintaining a dozen seaworthy warships is likely to exclude the possibility of their employment against an inferior force outside territorial waters, the possibility of encountering resistance does introduce a psychological barrier that did not exist at the level of the simple ship. Mere declarations that navies are maintained for defensive purposes alone are worthless – governments seldom regard their own use of armed force in any other light – but there are many countries whose policies, traditions or national characteristics would inhibit them from naval initiatives involving an element of risk. Unfortunately, these inhibitions are neither reliable (governmental attitudes can change and risks be underestimated) nor directly related to the size and naval resources of states. Japan's Navy is large and modern, her past prowess at sea outstanding, but since 1945 she has made no significant use of limited naval force. Israel's Navy is small and has no roll of battle honours, but is in constant employment. Some countries (and not only, or even always, those important countries who have traditionally enjoyed this advantage) find it enough to hoist their flag to invest a warship with the appearance of a superior ship.

The prestige of the flag is a factor equally applicable to a class of superior ship operations not so far considered: the landing of a small party of marines or sailors capable of overcoming local opposition ashore. This is something much smaller than the opposed amphibious operations to be discussed later. The local resistance might not amount to more than a single battery or a small detachment of troops. Surprise and speed might be more important to the assailant than fire-power, and such operations would not involve the use of landing craft or any resources not normally available to an ordinary warship, which would be discharging the classical gunboat role of the 1920s. Recent examples are few and flawed, perhaps the least unsatisfactory being the capture of South Georgia on 3 April 1982 by marines landed from the Argentine frigate GUERRICO, which also shelled the defenders.[13] This could have been reckoned a successful operation if it had not been followed by war, an augury that will not necessarily deter imitators. There are many lightly guarded coasts open to raids by a single warship and, if the incentive happened to coincide with a plausible prospect of impunity, at least some nations with more ships than scruples. Indeed, if there is a standard for assailants to reach before contemplating this type of operation, it is qualitative rather than quantitative, political not naval.

The real naval boundary is that dividing ship operations from fleet operations. A *simple fleet* operation is more than an operation involving several warships. It is usually some kind of blockade or patrol system intended to bar access to a particular coast, port or sea area. The blockade may be total, or intended only to identify and intercept vessels flying certain flags or carrying certain cargoes. The operation may be prompted by a war or civil conflict, and constitute an exercise of limited force only in so far as it is conducted by neutrals (in the Adriatic in 1992, to prevent war material reaching Serbian forces) or applied to neutral shipping. Sometimes the operation may have a more limited purpose: preventing incursions into the danger zone around a nuclear test or satellite splash-down. During the late 1960s, for instance, as much as 40 per cent (by tonnage) of the French Navy was thus employed in the Pacific, and the warships despatched to the area *'pour des besoins de surveillance'*[14] included one aircraft-carrier, one cruiser, three destroyers and five frigates.[15] The distinguishing features of this type of operation are that it takes place on the high seas (or in foreign territorial waters), that either the area covered or the number of potential targets demands the co-ordinated use of many warships, and that armed resistance is not expected.

Such operations are liable to make heavy demands on naval resources. The newspaper *Figaro* pointed out on 30 November 1966 that the naval concentration required by French nuclear tests in the Pacific had seriously impaired the French Navy's capacity for amphibious intervention during the same period. The Beira Patrol,[16] which the British Navy began in March 1966, was another distant operation of similar character, but one that lasted until June 1975.[17] The operation, the British Secretary of State for Defence told the House of Commons, was 'not a blockade, it has the limited object of preventing the arrival at Beira of vessels believed to be carrying oil for Rhodesia'.[18]

This was in implementation of a Security Council resolution intended to promote the transfer of political power in Rhodesia to the African inhabitants. Initially, therefore, this was a purposeful use of limited naval force. Before long, however, it became obvious that Rhodesian imports of oil had been re-routed via South Africa. The Beira Patrol was then continued simply because it would have been politically embarrassing to the British government to lose such a conspicuous token of their identification with international indignation. As limited naval force, the operation thus became as expressive as the policies of most members of the United Nations.

For an expressive use of limited force it was remarkably expensive. Even though the aircraft-carrier initially employed was withdrawn as soon as land-based air reconnaissance could be arranged, two frigates or destroyers were regularly deployed in the Indian Ocean, together with their supporting Royal Fleet Auxiliaries, until March 1971, when a single frigate was deemed a sufficient sacrifice on the altar of international hypocrisy. Allowing for reliefs and repairs, two warships on station meant a continuing commitment of six warships to the Beira Patrol. Even though armed opposition was exceptionally unlikely and the skimmed milk of international approval as nearly assured as it ever can be, no navy with less than eighteen ocean-going warships could have contemplated such a task. If an aircraft-carrier had been needed for more than a few weeks, Britain would have been out of the running. Admittedly, *The Times* was unduly pessimistic in arguing on 11 March 1966 that: 'for continuous surveillance to be maintained over a period of more than three weeks, two carriers are required'.

During the Falklands War HMS INVINCIBLE was at sea for 166 days at a stretch, and even longer periods might be possible with a full fleet train. More frequent reliefs, however, are clearly desirable in time of peace. Moreover, as British readers will be well aware, carriers are particularly susceptible to the demands of modernisation and tend to spend long periods out of service. A total strength of three carriers is thus needed by an assailant wishing to be sure that he can, at short notice, keep one carrier on surveillance of uncertain duration. On paper, Britain and Russia might pass this test, but in 1991 the third British carrier was laid up and the availability of the four Russian ships was politically uncertain. Only the United States could be sure of sustaining a prolonged simple fleet operation beyond the reach of shore-based aircraft.

In other ways, the Beira Patrol was an exceptionally easy operation. Before it even began, the General Assembly of the United Nations had voted by 107 to 2 against Rhodesia, and Rhodesia's two supporters (Portugal and South Africa) were never considered in the least likely to attempt forcible resistance to the operations of British warships. Although by definition a condition of simple fleet operations, this is an assumption that is often eroded by time. A blockade, for instance, may be correctly assessed at its outset as sure to be unopposed, but, if it goes on too long, third parties may change their views, or the victim, though initially defenceless, may acquire or devise means of retaliation. In 1992 ten navies contributed ships to the Adriatic patrol intended to enforce the United Nations embargo on the export of arms to Yugoslavia. Perhaps Operation Sharp Fence will achieve its objective without encountering opposition, but the precedent of the Spanish Civil War is not encouraging. A prudent assailant will not regard international approval as an adequate reinforcement of his own resources, though he may nevertheless be encouraged to embark on an otherwise hazardous operation by the comforting thought that, if the worst comes to the worst, he can always withdraw his ships as easily as he deployed them.

It is to be hoped that the Adriatic operation will not eventually illustrate the sharp rise, which takes place at the level of simple fleet operations, in the inherent defensive advantage of the victim. More precisely, it is much harder for an assailant to be sure that a fleet operation will be unopposed than to predict that a single warship will encounter no resistance that cannot easily be overcome. There are three reasons for this. First, a fleet necessarily operates over a much larger area of sea than a single warship, thus presenting a more extended and accessible target. Second, fleet operations usually last longer and, if their character is that of a blockade or patrol, the time needed to achieve the objective may not depend on the assailant alone. Finally, unless a fleet is actually deployed in readiness for an expected attack (which may impair its ability to discharge its original task), some of its component vessels are often more vulnerable than a single warship specifically chosen as a superior ship. Such a warship can dash into a harbour known to be inadequately defended, rescue a detained ship, and be out of reach before the victim can assemble his forces. Few victims can always manage to guard every point on their coast or each of their ships at sea. Even the United States has been the victim of superior ship operations. But, when a fleet must patrol an entire coastline for days or weeks, when it must be attended by lightly armed auxiliaries, when warships must oil at sea or stop to investigate a merchantman, then the victim needs only the scantiest of resources to raise the ante and deny the assailant the economies of a simple fleet operation. If he has a couple of submarines, some mines and a converted trawler to lay them, a few fast-attack craft or a bomber or two, then either the assailant must be completely convinced that the political will to resist is absent or else he must employ a superior fleet. In practice, therefore, the potential victims of simple fleet operations may well be as few in number as the potential assailants.

There is, however, one role in which the simple fleet might be immune from such vexatious impediments. Recent years have seen the revival of one variant of the expressive use of limited naval force, for which this type of operation is particularly well suited. Besides manifesting power in the form of an implied threat, warning or promise, warships can also veil impotence by a parting gesture of defiance. If troops must be withdrawn, colonies given up, allies abandoned, or injuries shrugged off, a naval demonstration may alleviate bitterness at home even if it does not always efface triumph or indignation abroad. However, whereas a single warship can symbolise an otherwise convincing power and resolve, a fleet may be necessary to cock a fugitive snook. Some governments, indeed, have employed more than a simple fleet for this purpose: five US carriers, with a greater strike power at their disposal than any other navy could deploy, dignified the final US evacuation from Saigon in 1975; the British squadron that palliated withdrawal from Aden in 1967 counted a strike carrier and a commando carrier among its eight warships and nine auxiliaries.

The 1967 episode, incidentally, was a good example of the flexibility of naval force in its political applications. The British squadron was originally conceived in the hope that its presence offshore might be welcome to a friendly post-independence regime in southern Arabia. Just what it – or the bomber force to be stationed on Masirah Island – might actually do was left conveniently vague. The one plausible military function was expressly excluded: 'there are, of course, to be some combat troops in the carrier-borne force. But there is no intention that these troops should be deployed on the shore'.[19] The purpose to be served by keeping this squadron offshore for six months after independence was thus essentially political and, in so far as it was intended to reassure conservative Arabs and deter revolutionaries, had evaporated before British troops completed their withdrawal on 29 November. Yet the squadron still assembled; it covered the evacuation; it stayed another two months in case British subjects still ashore needed rescue; and, when it finally dispersed, it may perhaps have alleviated some of the smarts and stings inflicted upon British public opinion.

In principle, however, this was a simple fleet operation, because landings were excluded (in the original concept of the fleet as a comfort for conservative sheiks, though perhaps not in the later role as a potential rescue force for British subjects) and there was no potential naval antagonist. If the need were to arise again, whether for Britain or for some other retreating nation, cost-effectiveness might demand a fleet that was simple in its composition as well as in its purpose. This would be particularly true of protracted operations. In 1967, for instance, the original conception envisaged keeping this fleet on station for six months, thus entailing constant reliefs for its component ships – a much more awkward and expensive process with carriers than with the lesser vessels that might have been considered symbolically adequate. Indeed, the political upheaval that produced the People's Republic of South Yemen may have disconcerted the British Foreign Office, but it must have had considerable compensations for the British naval staff. Moreover, even if these political developments further impaired the credibility of the entire project, as this was originally conceived, the fact that there was no one left ashore in a position to call on the fleet to do anything may well suggest future uses for this gambit. Other governments bent on disengagement from embarrassing involvements may reflect that the presence of a fleet initially softens the shock of abandoning a commitment, because these cruising warships suggest that, in circumstances and by methods left conveniently vague, the forces of the withdrawing government might still return. If political changes then take place ashore, these can at first be represented as insufficient to justify the intervention of the fleet and, when they subsequently go further, as having so altered the situation that the presence of the fleet no longer serves any useful purpose. The reader will have little difficulty in devising scenarios adaptable to several governments and more than one contingency that can already be foreseen for the years ahead.

The attractions of employing the simple fleet in the expressive mode are naturally increased by the extent to which the movements of warships can be improvised at short notice. If the fleet is not really intended to do anything except exercise 'a kind of vague menace',[20] its composition and readiness for war are relatively unimportant: any warships that are available might as well float in one sea as in another. They are easily despatched and still more easily withdrawn. And, although the symbolic rearguard seems the most likely purpose, it is not necessarily the only one. Japan, for instance, already has six destroyers and sixty frigates, more than enough to provide a simple fleet of respectable size.[21] The self-denying provisions of her constitution[22] have proved so insignificant an obstacle to the creation of this navy that they can scarcely be regarded as a serious impediment to its employment, though they have often furnished a convenient excuse. In the event of a further shift in Japanese attitudes – away from passive reliance on the US umbrella and from an exclusive preoccupation with economic development and commercial expansion – the formidable dynamism of the Japanese people, their outstanding naval tradition and their great industrial resources, particularly in shipbuilding, would enhance the impact of any demonstrative manoeuvre executed off an Asian coast by even a simple Japanese fleet. Naval analysts might sceptically inquire what such a fleet could actually do, and reinforce their doubts by arguing that, for many years to come, the US Pacific Fleet, the Chinese Navy and such fragments as may remain of the Soviet Far Eastern Fleet will offer naval arguments to reinforce Japanese political distaste for any reversion to the adventurism of the 1930s. To an Asian politician, however, the economic statistics of the 1990s and the naval memories of earlier decades might combine to invest the appearance of a Japanese fleet with far greater significance: to make it seem the first wave of an advancing tide rather than the last breaker of the ebb.

This is not an immediately plausible scenario and the political changes required to make it so are potential rather than inevitable or imminent. However, it is a reminder that the present state of international relations is no more immutable in its naval balance than in its political balance. It is easier to foresee the scope for simple fleet operations than to predict when, in what circumstances and by whom, they might be conducted.

Potential assailants are more easily identified when we enter the high-priced area of gunboat diplomacy: *superior fleet*, *simple amphibious*, and *opposed amphibious* operations. Although each of these categories differs from the other two and itself covers a wide range of magnitude, they have certain features in common that constitute a new threshold in the use of limited naval force. Politically there is a sharp rise in the level of risk and commitment. Even a *simple amphibious* operation – the disembarkation of marines or troops on a defenceless coast or one controlled by a government inviting the operation – usually represents a deeper and more uncertain involvement than the average superior ship operation. When HMS CENTAUR landed marines in Tanganyika, for instance, the carrier was in no danger and her helicopters reached their objective unopposed.[23] However, once they had arrived, there was no certainty that the mutinous Tanganyikan soldiers would be subdued without serious casualties, without widespread racial resentment, without snowballing popular and international resistance to this neo-colonialist intervention. The smoothness of the actual operation and its early conclusion should not blind us to the extent of the political risks run by the British government in responding to this Tanganyikan request – and to others in East Africa during that turbulent overture to 1964. Even in terms of naval resources, the commitment of three carriers between 20 January and 19 March was an undertaking that has long been beyond the power of the Royal Navy. It was the political gamble then that constituted the greater hazard. When one government invites the intervention of another, this usually implies the existence of a serious threat, whether external or internal, to the authority of the first government, a threat that the intervention is intended to neutralise, but that, failing swift success, it may actually exacerbate.

A striking example of this danger was provided by the US intervention in the Lebanon in 1983. This ought also to have been a simple amphibious operation, for it took place with some international support and at the invitation of the Lebanese government, who hoped it would facilitate the restoration of their authority, which had been challenged by armed dissidents. Instead, the contingent of US Marines, which had made a successful landing, became a focus for the hostility of the government's opponents and a target for terrorist attack. It had eventually to be withdrawn after failing to achieve its objective, and suffering more casualties than the Americans engaged in the simultaneous Operation Urgent Fury in Grenada.

The risks of involving soldiers in someone else's country are naturally even greater when opposition is expected to the actual landing, but even a *superior fleet* operation at sea implies a possibility of resistance politically much more significant than anything to be feared from a single ship. When two fleets are in contact, the possibilities of mistakes, of violence intended by neither government, are multiplied. Moreover, an inferior fleet is less easily, less gracefully, withdrawn than is a single ship. And, if a superior fleet has been assembled to enforce a blockade to which resistance is expected, the victim may only have to sink a single warship to expose the assailant government to demands for the use of less limited force. In all these types of operations the assailant is placing a stake on the board that he may have to increase before he can even retire it.

It follows, therefore, that these operations cannot prudently be undertaken by any assailant incapable of reinforcing his initial commitment or of withstanding the political repercussions of any resistance that may be encountered. In extreme cases, the assailant may have to be prepared to face a threat of war. In other instances, it may be only swelling international censure, growing domestic opposition or the expenses and casualties of an operation that lasts longer and meets more resistance than had originally been foreseen. Political stability at home, economic and military reserves, a capacity for defence of one's own country (or a strong and reliable protector), a readiness to run risks and some disposition to the exercise of power: most of these conditions ought to be met before naval resources are even considered.

In some ways they are even more important than naval resources. In 1935, when Britain reinforced the Mediterranean Fleet during the Abyssinian crisis, the shortage of anti-aircraft ammunition was a lesser impediment to a convincing threat of purposeful force against Italy than the obvious absence of political unity and determination in London. In 1956 British naval resources were adequate for an opposed amphibious operation against Egypt: the political resolve behind them was not. In both cases the really awkward answers to the prudent questions – what to do if the bluff is called or the initial attack repulsed – were political or economic rather than naval. Militarily, either operation (Suez doubtfully an act of limited force) might have succeeded, but only at the risk of a price Britain was not prepared to pay.

The 1970s and 1980s brought further examples of governments deploying warships, even ordering them into action, only to discover that success, if it could be achieved at all, would cost too much. Britain took years to concede her second defeat over Icelandic fishing limits; Colombia was quicker in the Gulf of Venezuela; France tried to help the Christian Lebanese with a show of naval force and some sporadic bombardment, but achieved little and did not persist. India did more for the Tamils in Sri Lanka, but gave up a task still unfinished. Iran and Iraq attacked a great many neutral ships in the Persian Gulf but, if either hoped to provoke outside intervention in their war, did not succeed; while the naval powers were half-hearted in their mostly ineffectual gestures of support for vessels flying their flag. Whether belligerent or neutral, everybody lost and there were no prizes.

In the conduct of international relations, even those governments who resort to force only when it can reasonably be expected to produce the desired terminal situation often get their sums wrong. Governments are even more likely to fail when they respond emotionally to what they see as an objectionable act. It is only against this discouraging background that it can possibly be argued that, when the conditions are just right, which seldom occurs, limited naval force can occasionally be an option worth considering. The risks inherent in gunboat diplomacy will outlive the Cold War and, particularly in the case of the higher-level operations, are likely to rise as technology proliferates and both ideology and organisation increase the number of the world's confidently assertive nations. Gunboat diplomacy would be a desperate choice – if war were not certain to be worse.

II CAPACITIES

The capacity to undertake the kind of operations we have been considering has two aspects: naval and political. The United States Navy, for instance, was not significantly stronger under President Reagan (1981–9), if measured against the yardstick of the Soviet Navy, than it had been under President Carter (1977–81). However, US use of limited naval force was much more frequent, much bolder and at a higher operational level under Reagan than under Carter. Argentina might have got away with her Operation Rosario in 1982 and kept the Falkland Islands if Britain had then had a different Prime Minister or even a less enterprising First Sea Lord. In a long war there may be time to build ships, change leaders, revolutionise tactics, allow the underlying strength of the nation and the navy to emerge in spite of initial disasters. In gunboat diplomacy there is seldom a second chance, naval or political. What decides the issue, for assailant and victim alike, is who and what is available when the need unexpectedly arises.

Political capacity for the use of limited naval force is of obvious importance at the lowest levels, for many navies can manage a simple ship or a superior ship operation if the circumstances are right – as they need to be even for the strongest navy. The specifically naval constraints of most importance are the location of the dispute and the likely duration of any naval intervention. To a small navy, distance and time, particularly in combination, can be serious deterrents, not least because the latter is often unpredictable. In October 1980, for instance, two British warships were diverted from a Far Eastern cruise to the Persian Gulf for the protection of shipping against the hazards arising from the outbreak of war between Iran and Iraq. This was the start of the Armilla Patrol, which was still being maintained twelve years later. Until Iraq invaded Kuwait in 1990, the Patrol normally comprised no more than two warships and a support vessel, but this meant, as we saw in the case of the Beira Patrol, six warships committed and, because of the taxing climate and the need for most of those years to maintain a high degree of readiness, frequent reliefs for the ships involved.

If we consider only total numbers of ocean-going warships and assume that support vessels could be chartered, ten navies might manage (some of them only just) a distant and protracted superior ship operation of this kind: Britain, China, France, Germany, India, Italy, Japan, Russia, Spain and the United States. If we take political factors into account, the picture looks different. China, India, Italy and Spain have not attempted anything of the kind since 1945; Germany and Japan are inhibited by their constitutions from considering any such ideas. In 1992 – though the passage of time could change both the naval and the political parameters – Britain, France, perhaps Russia, and certainly the United States were the only naval powers whose record suggested they would readily contemplate even a low-level use of limited naval force without regard to the constraints imposed by time and distance. Russia may now seem a doubtful starter, but the former Soviet Navy maintained a superior ship operation of similar size – sometimes called the West Africa Patrol – for many years after the abortive Portuguese raid on Conakry in 1970.[24] The British, French and US navies have longer and more extensive histories.

Many more navies, of course, can deploy a couple of ships in a distant sea for a brief period. Argentina, Australia, Belgium, Canada, Denmark, Greece, the Netherlands and Spain all sent one or two warships to the Middle East (although not all of them entered the Persian Gulf, let alone the combat zone) during the Gulf War.[25] This was a notable instance of the importance of political factors. Minesweepers apart, there was no naval requirement for these ships. The US Navy could have coped, but the US government expected an *acte de présence* from their friends, and sending a ship was a modest price for US goodwill. It would be stretching the terms of our definition to call it an expressive use of limited naval force, but it was undoubtedly a political gesture and, thanks to the endorsement of US policy by the United Nations, one less likely to raise sensitive hackles than other naval deployments.

The support for the United States that most of these navies offered was far less important, both navally and politically, than the help New Zealand gave Britain during the Falklands War, when HMNZS CANTERBURY relieved HMS CARDIFF on the Armilla Patrol, thus allowing the British destroyer to join the Task Force (already depleted by Argentine air attack) before the end of May 1982.[26]

More navies pass an easier test, which is readiness to contemplate superior ship operations in their own sea: Argentina,

Australia, Brazil, China, Egypt, Greece, India, Indonesia, Iran, Israel, both the Koreas, the Netherlands, Portugal, Turkey, Venezuela and Vietnam have all used or threatened limited naval force in this way. In terms of naval resources, Canada, Chile, Germany, Japan, the Netherlands, Pakistan, Spain, Sweden and Thailand are capable of it, if the circumstances are right. However, there are many political constraints. Sometimes these are primarily domestic, but other inhibitions may be related to the international situation or the local strategic balance. Neither Greece nor Turkey, for instance, can afford to commit their warships without regard to each other's reactions. Nor are these the only navies that must look over their shoulders, as even the US Navy sometimes had to while the Soviet Navy still flourished, before becoming involved in some sideshow.

At the higher levels of limited naval force the ranks of potential assailants are sharply thinned. Even a simple fleet operation at a reasonable distance demands – on the formula of three committed for one deployed – a substantial number of ocean-going warships. If the purpose is to patrol a coast against gun-runners, drug smugglers or illegal immigrants, even to mount a campaign against pirates (much needed in many seas), heavy weapons will not be required. Aerial reconnaissance can often be land-based, but numbers, sea-keeping and reliefs will be important. During the Anglo-Icelandic confrontation of 1958–61 over fishing limits, in which few shots were fired, thirty-six British destroyers and frigates had to be deployed (not all at once, of course) in Icelandic waters and, both then and in later confrontations, many sustained some damage from heavy seas and the deliberate collisions with Icelandic gunboats that became the main tactic of both sides.[27]

Not many navies have been able to find such a number of ships, and some of these have long been shrinking – a process the end of the Cold War is likely to hasten. The first edition of this book contained a list of middling navies with at least twenty ocean-going warships in 1963. The comparison with 1991 is instructive (see Table 4.1). For both years the figures shown are those of corvettes and larger surface warships and, for 1991, have been compiled from *The Military Balance*: IISS).

Only two of these middling navies – the Indian and the Japanese – have grown. The rest have all shrunk, some drastically. Only two other navies have joined the original ten:

Table 4.1   Ocean-going surface warships

	1963	*1991*
Argentina	20	14
Brazil	34	18
Britain	110	48
France	64	41
Germany	33	19
India	20	41
Italy	55	35
Japan	47	66
Spain	45	20

Source: IISS, *Military Balance*, 1990–1.

South Korea with thirty-nine ships and Turkey with twenty.[28] Of course, insistence on counting only ocean-going surface warships (corvettes and above) does produce a slightly misleading impression. For war and for coastal defence, some navies attach more importance to submarines. Moreover, those twenty-eight years saw the proliferation of fast attack craft, now prominent, for instance, in both the German and Swedish navies. When there are enough of them, their speed and missiles or torpedoes make them significant antagonists to larger warships unsupported by aircraft. In confined waters they ought usefully to strengthen the resistance of victims, but they are not really ocean-going. For short-range operations in coastal waters, assailants might nevertheless profit by their combination of speed and punch. The Iranian Revolutionary Guards made some use of fast motor-boats with hand-held rockets to harass merchant shipping in the Persian Gulf during the Iran–Iraq war; and fast attack craft played a part in the LIBERTY and PUEBLO incidents. Ideally – the principle cannot be too strictly applied in these days of specialisation – the warships one counts in estimating a navy's capacity for gunboat diplomacy ought to be not only ocean-going, but also versatile.

This is a criterion that restricts the scope of many smaller
navies, but the year 1992 saw a development that might conceivably modify some of the equations accepted in recent
decades. On 22 November 1992 there appeared in the Adriatic
twelve ocean-going warships engaged in a simple fleet operation.
These destroyers and frigates had been provided by Belgium,
Britain, France, Germany, Greece, Italy, the Netherlands, Spain,
Turkey and the United States. None of these countries would
have welcomed the political responsibility of deploying such a
fleet on their own and only the United States could have found
enough ships to keep the operation going for long enough. On a
co-operative basis, however, there was no problem. Italy, having
been accorded the privilege of command, furnished three ships,
and the others furnished one each. The task, when so widely
shared, was eminently suitable for a simple fleet:

> All ships trying to enter or leave the waters of the former
> Yugoslavia will be stopped. The provenance and destination
> of their cargo will be checked. If there is proof of non-
> observation of the United Nations resolutions, ships will be
> taken to an approved port or anchorage or to the port from
> where they came, *subject to agreement of the flag state*.

That last clause in the official statement made to *The Times*
(and quoted in their issue of 23 November 1992) by the spokesman of NATO Southern Command made it clear that this was
not an operation to which any opposition was expected, but the
German Defence Minister still found an *i* to dot and a *t* to cross:
'They can fire warning shots but they are not allowed to destroy
ships ... the HAMBURG is banned by the German constitution
from any hostile action.' A far cry from the German naval
bombardment of Almería in 1937,[29] but this was an operation
that began with very different preconceptions from those still
entertained by gunboat diplomacy's more traditional practitioners. Political considerations have always been important,
but these now demanded kid gloves as spotless as a naval
cadet's.

They also required the naval officers concerned to display
some suppleness in adapting to the special tastes of some of the
governments involved. Extra ships were only part of the price
Italy had to pay for the privilege of command. Two admirals had
to be found: one in charge of the seven warships representing

NATO (Operation Maritime Guard), the other heading the five that drew their inspiration from the Western European Union (Operation Sharp Fence). This division was reflected in the geography of their deployment and extended to the aircraft that supported them, though *The Times* reported, without explaining the apparent inconsistency, that France had, in the air, backed NATO as well as the Western European Union.

The eventual outcome of this unusual exercise of collective gunboat diplomacy – just begun at the time of writing – is hard to predict, but it could be of some importance in the future development of limited naval force. Many small and dwindling navies might attempt more in a co-operative undertaking than they would care to contemplate on their own. The operation launched in 1992, however, had some features that scarcely deserve to be imitated: the division of the fleet, for instance. This was not a case of naval heresy, but of political eccentricity. What in de Gaulle was a Roman *superbia* had later turned Byzantine, so France shunned the umbrella of NATO and recruited Belgium, Italy and Spain for a separate squadron free from any US taint. A somewhat similar pattern had emerged among the European warships sent to the Persian Gulf during the Iran–Iraq war and again after the invasion of Kuwait. Then it could be explained by differing attitudes towards the regional conflicts and by the reluctance of the French Navy (on land, the French Army seemed less inhibited) to come under US command. Its persistence in different circumstances casts some doubt on future European ability to achieve naval as well as economic unity, or even to develop the degree of naval co-operation that would make Europe a serious player at the higher levels of gunboat diplomacy. With over two hundred ocean-going warships (including six carriers, most of them small and some of them elderly), Europe is otherwise a passable candidate.

Of course, numbers alone will often not be enough for more demanding operations: superior fleet, simple amphibious, and opposed amphibious. There must be ships capable of overawing opponents, landing troops, smothering defences. Air cover will probably be needed and afloat support. We must not, however, be too rigid in our notions of minimum requirements. Much depends on who is using limited force, against whom, and in what circumstances. Operation Attila in 1974 encountered vigorous resistance from an armed, highly motivated Greek Cypriot population, many of them organised on a paramilitary basis and with some experience of guerrilla warfare. The Turkish landing was contested and there was much fighting between 20 July and 16 August.[30] If we call the operation 'limited', the reason is that it did not lead to war, though this option was briefly considered in Athens. However, casualties and the level of violence were high. Most of the fighting was done by soldiers, who were supported by land-based aircraft from Turkey. The function of the Turkish Navy was to escort the troopships, to protect them from the risk of interference by the Greek Navy, and to cover the actual landing by fire from destroyers. The operation was brutally effective and the slice of Cyprus it won remains Turkish to this day.

The 1975 Indonesian invasion of East Timor generated a literature as extensive as that devoted to the invasion of Cyprus, but, in each case, the military aspects have received much less attention than the political complications and the atrocity stories. All one can say is that both northern Cyprus and East Timor were the targets of an opposed amphibious operation involving the Turkish and Indonesian navies, though the seaborne invasion of East Timor was supplemented by an overland incursion. We know even less about the various seizures of the Spratly and Paracel Islands. These began as early as 1939 and have involved, at one time or another, the navies of China, France, Japan, the Philippines, Taiwan and Vietnam. One of the latest incidents (in 1988) led Chinese warships to shell a Vietnamese freighter off the Spratly Islands.[31] These were mostly exploits in the older tradition of gunboat diplomacy – as practised in China, for instance, before 1939. Nowadays a well-equipped navy, particularly one expecting a degree of military sophistication from the victim, would rather deploy in elaborate and even redundant strength, the better to cope with unforeseen kinds of resistance and, by swiftly overwhelming the defences, to minimise casualties. Against Grenada, where the resistance to be overcome was trifling compared to that offered by the Greeks in Cyprus, US warships, marines and soldiers had the assistance of one hundred helicopters and seventy combat aircraft, which flew 700 sorties.[32]

At a pinch, we can regard some of our middling navies as capable, in exceptionally favourable circumstances, of improvising one of these high-priced operations against a weaker and not too distant victim, though their post-1945 record makes it politically unlikely that Germany, Italy or Japan would consider the idea. That leaves Argentina, India, the Koreas, Spain and Turkey, each with some form and with potential victims within their naval range. Brazil is more of an enigma.

Britain and France still have the edge on other middling navies. Japan may have more ships, but lacks an aircraft-carrier, however small, adequate amphibious capability, afloat support and any recent operational experience. India's aircraft-carriers are elderly and less capable than the smaller British ships, her amphibious and logistic resources are scanty, and her sailors lack combat experience. However, the Indian Navy is growing, while the British and French are dwindling. Moreover, if Britain does not soon replace the veteran FEARLESS and the beached INTREPID, or if France does not quickly produce a new aircraft-carrier with better aircraft, some of their qualitative advantages over India and Japan will be lost.

History, prestige, recent experience, the quality of ships, weapons and sailors still put Britain and France in a category of their own when we assess the ability of middling navies to undertake the most demanding exertions of limited naval force. However, both navies are under pressure: the French from the financial burden of their independent nuclear deterrent; the British from the remorseless crumbling of their economic base. In the last decade of the twentieth century, there is nothing immutable about the ranking of middling navies. If political change were to occur in Japan – where the present, profit-oriented regime, however successful commercially, has broken with national tradition – it would not be difficult to expand and transform, in short order, the Japanese Navy. Japan could soon convert her shipyards and already has the cash to buy any aircraft-carriers or battle-cruisers that Russia may want to sell. None of that will necessarily happen, but it *could* – and in less time than Europe will probably need to get its political act together.

If we leave to the next chapter any analysis of the Soviet record and all speculation concerning the potential of the Russian Navy, there is one emerging trend that is worth noting. The higher priced applications of limited naval force occurred less frequently in the 1970s and 1980s than in the 1950s and 1960s. Britain and

France, in particular, took a smaller share, and a division may perhaps be discerned between the bold, classical, sometimes rough-and-ready approach adopted by Argentina, China, Indonesia, Turkey and Vietnam on the one hand, and US deployment of overwhelming power on the other. Britain and France, who share US concern to minimise their own casualties, but may increasingly lack the strength to be sure of dominating any conflict, are likely to be more wary than previously of the riskier operations of gunboat diplomacy, particularly those in which the victim's aircraft or soldiers may redress his naval disadvantage.

One navy of distinctly uncertain intentions is that of China. On paper it looks an imposing but predominantly defensive force, 'about 860 patrol and coastal combatants', seemingly out of all proportion to the fifty-four ocean-going surface warships, which do not include any kind of aircraft-carrier.[33] For a defensive posture, history provides ample justification: not only the century in which China's coasts were the hunting ground of naval predators, but the four decades that followed, in which the Cold War posed a double threat. Sometimes the United States seemed the likeliest enemy; at other times it was the Soviet Union; for a year or two, when the 1960s ended and the 1970s began, both could have figured in Chinese nightmares. Each had in the Pacific a stronger navy than China's and a well-armed Asian client. The altered balance resulting from the disintegration of the Soviet Union will not necessarily be to China's advantage. In the later 1970s and early 1980s, after all, those fleets tended to cancel one another out. And now there is the threat – still only potential but, in the light of Chinese experience, doubtless potent – of a resurgent Japanese Navy.

Even so, the Chinese Navy has not been inactive, clashing repeatedly with Vietnam and challenging Japan over fishing rights. Defence of that enormous coastline may be the priority, but Chinese warships have exercised as far as Chile. In the years ahead, political factors – what happens in China itself, but also in the East Asian balance – are likely to predominate. China has more than enough ocean-going warships to enable her to make use of limited naval force if the occasion arises and the political equation permits. Moreover, if the main trend of Chinese foreign policy in the last three decades has been coloured by increasing prudence, there is little indication of any fundamental decline in traditional Chinese arrogance or readiness to run occasionally unreasonable risks. Since HMS AMETHYST escaped by the skin of her teeth in 1949, China has not been, as she was in the 1920s and 1930s, the world's most regular victim of limited naval force. That no longer occurs in the rivers or on the coasts of China, and encounters further out to sea have not, in recent years, involved the major naval powers. The future of the Chinese Navy is as uncertain as that of China, but neither is likely to play a passive role.

After so many doubts and uncertainties it is a relief to turn one's attention to the *prima donna assoluta* of gunboat diplomacy. In the instances of limited naval force since 1945 listed in the Chronological Appendix, the US Navy was the assailant in 64 instances, the rest of the world in 134. The comparison is not mathematically exact, because the episodes mentioned in the Appendix are numerous and representative rather than complete. To have listed every trawler attacked by an Icelandic gunboat or every clash in the great rivers of China would have been tedious. However, the picture the Appendix paints of the dominant role of the US Navy since 1945 (Britain was more prominent before 1939) stands out more clearly still if one considers operational levels or compares the strength of the task forces habitually deployed by the US Navy for even minor operations with the scantier resources available to other navies. This is a luxury the Americans can permit themselves. Not only do they have half as many ocean-going surface warships as all the world's middling navies put together, but the quality of these ships and their equipment is not matched elsewhere. The twelve strike carriers or the forty-eight cruisers, to say nothing of sixty-five amphibious ships or over one hundred support vessels, have no equivalents among the middling navies. Numerically, the US Navy has greatly shrunk since this book was first published, but its statistics still inspire the same awe as the opening notes of the late Kirsten Flagstad: one wonders how anyone else could have the impertinence to sing on the same stage.

It can, of course, be argued that the US Navy do not always use their giant's strength with the same restraint, even delicacy, to which scarce resources constrain lesser navies. Some of the destruction unleashed on Libya or the level of civilian casualties in Grenada (many times higher than in the Falklands War) may seem to suggest a belligerent approach rather than a police operation. It is even debatable how far the concept of *limited* force commands acceptance in the US Navy. One cannot readily imagine a US parallel to the rescue of refugees from a Yemeni beach by the unarmed Royal Yacht BRITANNIA in 1986. On the other hand, would the Royal Navy have run such risks if they had been able to deploy as many helicopters and supporting aircraft as the US Navy managed at Mogadishu in 1991? The Americans play the game of gunboat diplomacy (as other navies might wish they more often could) to win. They can still proclaim: 'We've got the ships, we've got the men, we've got the money too.'[34] However, will they continue their long tradition of employing these ships in peacetime? Here prediction is more hazardous, for so much depends on US national resolve, on political developments within the United States, and on the international balance of power. At least, though, there is no doctrinal objection. On the contrary, US Navy Regulations are unusually explicit. Section 0614 on the *Use of Force Against Friendly States* covers most situations: 'The right of self-preservation ... is a right which belongs to states ... it includes the protection of the state, its honor, and its possessions, and the lives and property of its citizens.'[35]

Politically the case is different. The record of the past reveals seasons of intermittence in US naval activity. After the brisk business of the 1920s – not only in China and the Caribbean, but even in the Mediterranean – decline sets in with the 1930s and, before the middle of the decade, becomes inertia. The Spanish Civil War, that magnet to other navies, prompted the United States to withdraw their warships from European waters. Isolationism is a recurrent phenomenon in US politics, often associated with economic recession and the advent of a new President. It is one of the options for the United States in 1993: turning inwards to cope with the distressing problems of the inner cities and the underclass, instead of tackling the time of troubles that the end of the Cold War – and the eruption of all the festering sores neglected during the Cold War – have unleashed upon the world.

To US policy as a whole, that choice will be fundamental; but for the US Navy, for future US use of limited naval force, the consequences will not necessarily be set in concrete. Indeed, it is even arguable that the present US mood of disenchantment with the troubles of the outside world is more likely to lead to military withdrawals than to naval ones. As foreign garrisons are reduced, overseas bases abandoned, allies urged to cultivate

the virtues of self-reliance, the diplomatic and political functions of the US Navy may actually expand: those grey, restless,
innumerable ships will console Americans and reassure their
friends; they will constitute the universal, the flexible, the
removable reminder of US power and concern.

As might be expected, international capacity for the exercise
of limited naval force thus resembles a pyramid, with the
number of potential assailants dwindling as we rise from one
category to another, until the US Navy is left in solitary
occupation of the summit: the only navy with the sheer number
of ships, with enough aircraft-carriers, ocean-going surface
warships, amphibious craft and supply vessels to undertake
every class of operation, in any part of the oceans and for as
much of the future as can yet be foreseen. These are the tests
of capacity – the ability to spare enough ships at short notice, to
provide air cover without land bases, to show strength before it
need be used, to land where opposition is least, to stay long
enough at sea to achieve results – that must be met before a
navy can claim '*un caractère polyvalent ... pour toute mission*'.[36] Other
navies – the Russian has still to be examined – can occasionally
hope, in special circumstances, or in particular seas, to attempt
even the highest class of operation, but of those so far
considered only the US Navy can confidently expect to furnish
sufficient resources for most contingencies. Even the larger
navies of the rest of the world must usually expect to buy their
gunboat diplomacy in the bargain basement – a repository of
not always inconsiderable trifles that luck and good judgement
may sometimes render accessible to the thirty navies probably
capable of superior ship operations and to the few who might
manage a little more. Where the will exists, the world still
holds enough warships for some of them to find a way.

5 In the Absence of the Soviet Union

Change and decay in all around I see.

H.F. Lyte[1]

The world is always changing, but the pace is quickening. By Gibbon's reckoning, the decline and fall of the Roman empire lasted

> ... from the fortunate age of Trajan and the Antonines ... in the second century of the christian aera, [when] the empire of Rome comprehended the fairest part of the earth ... to its total extinction in the west, about five centuries after the christian aera.[2]

The full existence of the Soviet empire, on the other hand, spanned less than seventy-five years and, if we take 1980 as an approximate zenith, the end came a mere eleven years later – with Gorbachev's resignation speech on Christmas Day 1991. Perhaps it was the hectic pace of political development in the twentieth century that was the undoing of a Soviet empire born in revolution and the pangs of national defeat. Rotten before it was ripe, the new system of government never acquired enough maturity to tolerate reform or to survive without it.

When Mikhail Gorbachev became the last Secretary General of the Communist Party of the Soviet Union, and thus the empire's ruler, in March 1985, his accession speech promised a continuation of the cautious progress – 'acceleration of socio-economic development and the perfection of all aspects of social life' – begun in the brief reigns of his elderly predecessors.[3] Soon, however, he began to term this *perestroika* – restructuring – and to go further and faster, forgetting, or perhaps never having been told, that 'le moment le plus dangereux pour un mauvais gouvernement est d'ordinaire celui où il commence à se réformer'.[4]

Tocqueville thought only great genius could preserve the prince who tried to relieve his subjects after long years of oppression and, in half a decade, the avalanche of change in the Soviet Union triggered by reforms intended to be controlled and limited had altered for hundreds of millions the framework of their society, had transformed international relations, ended the Cold War, fragmented the Soviet empire, and cost Gorbachev his job.

Of course, the Soviet empire was much larger and more complicated than the Roman empire. Without counting all the satellites in Europe and other continents, the Soviet Union alone had inherited from the Tsars five times the area of the Roman empire and by 1991 had twice the population. Yet Moscow never commanded the ascendancy Rome long enjoyed: as the prime source of contemporary civilisation or as a power without an equal rival. The millennium and a half that divided the two empires imposed on the later of them a geopolitical environment too different to permit fair comparison. Even analogies are suspect, albeit occasionally tempting. Most of the inhabitants of the Roman empire, for instance, were slaves: some of the remainder were citizens and a handful were patricians. In the Soviet Union, the ruling class – the *nomenklatura* – was rather larger. Both empires were built by their soldiers, but communist doctrine taught its disciples to beware of Bonapartism and they avoided some Roman mistakes. Soviet generals, though spared civilian intrusion in most military matters, never controlled the state or the party they served. Even when both collapsed, the armed forces emerged from the dust and din of falling political masonry as victims, not victors.

Without being praetorians, they still had a good deal to lose. In 1985, so the *Military Balance* estimated, defence expenditure accounted for 16 per cent of Soviet Gross Domestic Product, compared with 6.5 per cent in the United States or 5.2 per cent in Britain.[5] What the armed forces lacked in political power, they (or at least, the officer corps) made up in privileges. Unlike their Western counterparts, Soviet naval officers, for instance, were better paid than most managerial civilians and enjoyed a social prestige to match. These advantages shrivelled as the artificial structure of the Soviet economy was distorted by the random fires of political change:

... the collapse of the USSR has transformed the former Soviet armed forces into an army without a state. Soldiers are badly paid and fed, if paid and fed at all, housed in overcrowded barracks, and have not the slightest idea what will become of them. They are led by hundreds of thousands of officers who, only a few years ago, were the elite of the nation and are now left with few professional prospects.[6]

Other accounts speak of widespread desertion, of conscripts failing to report or choosing for themselves which successor state to serve, of ethnic conflict within military units,[7] of indiscipline, and even of officers abandoning their units in search of more lucrative employment or simply of accommodation for their families (a particularly acute problem in units withdrawn from Eastern Europe). So far, however, no desperate commander has led his hungry soldiers to Moscow. Perhaps care has been taken to ensure that units within easy reach of the capital are still paid and fed.

What was once the Soviet Navy shares many of these problems and has worries of its own about allegiance, bases and vocation. The Strategic Rocket Forces still retain – at least for Russia – their role of last resort and, it is said, much of their discipline. The fighting that flares, subsides and revives across the struggling new republics of the old empire is a guarantee of employment for such soldiers as still want to serve – anybody. Soviet strategic submarines can strengthen Russia's deterrent, and in 1992 were thought to maintain their patrols. However, year by year since the spring tide of 1985, the surface warships have been spending progressively fewer days at sea, withdrawing from the Indian Ocean, leaving the Mediterranean, ending alongside at Severomorsk or Liepaja, rusting (so said Moscow Radio) at Petropavlovsk, exposed at Sevastopol to the rival claims of Russia, Georgia and the Ukraine. Some ships have been sold, and many paid off or scrapped. The results have not been surprising: disaffection in the Northern Fleet; rumours of private enterprise in the Baltic Fleet, and more plausible reports of fighting with Estonian soldiers in the naval base at Tallinn; a small mutiny and clashing loyalties in the Black Sea Fleet. And, if the Pacific Fleet managed to find enough fuel to send the ADMIRAL VINOGRADOV to the Persian Gulf – supposedly to help enforce sanctions against Iraq – conditions on board the destroyer did not impress the US,

British and French sailors, who were allowed, as never before, easy access to the ship at Bahrain.[8]

In Russia itself, as opposed to some of the southern republics, the death-throes of communism were less devastating (up to the summer of 1993 at least) than its birth-pangs in the years after 1917. Fewer people have died violent deaths; civil war has not swept the country, but only flickered on its borders; most of the successor governments in the former Soviet Union command some obedience; and many bureaucratic structures are still in place. Warships may be rusting at their wharves, but this time the sailors have neither killed their officers nor shelled the Winter Palace. *Perestroika* – that too potent fuel – stalled the machine it was meant to accelerate, but did not entirely destroy it. There could gradually, painfully, still be a fresh start or a new departure, even a crashing engagement of reverse gear. Unless, of course, there explodes the real revolution that has not, for all the upheavals, so far occurred.

Whatever the uncertain future may hold, it is political change within the borders of the former Soviet Union that is likely to matter most to the rest of the world. Many years must pass and several economic miracles be performed before China or Western Europe need again concern themselves with the risk of military invasion. Of course, if things get much worse in Russia and there seemed to be some risk of outside intervention, a more disquieting threat might emerge: a mad dog nuclear strike. If nuclear war has hitherto been avoided, this was because a rational opponent in full control of his own state and his own weapons was deterred from using the latter by his fear of retaliation. If the time comes when these conditions no longer obtain in Russia, we could be faced by the nightmare scenario, the extreme example of the potential impact of political change.

The future evolution of the Soviet Union's successor states is important not only because a bad enough outcome could produce a hideously larger conflict of the Yugoslav type, but because this evolution will take place in an increasingly turbulent world. In the last ten years, 36 countries have been involved in fighting with foreigners; 57 in internal conflicts; and 101 – among them such stable and tranquil countries as Switzerland – have suffered terrorist attacks.[9]

Nor should relief at the dissipation of the Soviet military threat that had been overhanging the West for forty years allow us to forget the survival of the hardware, a collection un-matched for size or sophistication outside the United States. These weapons, nuclear or conventional, are no longer con-trolled by a monolithic superpower: malevolent, but cautious, disciplined and with predictable patterns of behaviour. They are now unevenly distributed across the territory of fifteen unstable republics, whose governments are eager to profess good intentions and to proclaim reforms, but are plagued by every problem in the medical dictionary of politics. The English language weekly *Moscow News* estimated that, in March 1992, 7 million square miles of what had once been the Soviet Union, an area inhabited by 30 million people, were ravaged by 180 different conflicts, all of them violent.[10] Which states will survive, who will lead them, and in which direction? What will happen to those weapons?

These are the questions likely to matter most in the final years of the millennium. Less importance attaches to the future of the former Soviet Navy. That was one of the trappings of a superpower, the world's second largest and strongest fleet, a per-petual challenge to the otherwise unquestioned ascendancy of the US Navy. Its strategic role was the subject of much specu-lation, as usually happens when a continental power decides to supplement an army of overwhelming strength by a navy that is impressive, but no match for the obvious opponent at sea. One of the many partial answers to this puzzle, and one that seems to have had some attraction for Admiral Gorshkov himself, was that 'the fleet has always been an instrument of the policy of states, an important aid to diplomacy in peacetime'.[11]

Ranft and Till's magisterial work entitled *The Sea in Soviet Strategy* was mainly concerned with war, but included an in-teresting analysis of the peacetime missions of the Soviet Navy. They instanced the increasing frequency of naval visits, the evident importance attached to 'showing the flag', the political significance of selling ships (nearly 500 since 1956) and weapons to client states, actual or potential, and of providing training in their use. They argued, as have others, that some Soviet warships whose utility in war with the United States seemed doubtful – the rather small carriers or the battle-cruisers, for instance – might come in handy for limited operations. They concluded that, 'the Soviet Navy now appreciates and evidently intends to develop, maritime power as a general-purpose and multicapable instrument of state policy'.[12] When stated in those rather broad terms, the case that Ranft and Till argued was plausible.

A much more extended investigation, in greater depth and detail, was undertaken in *Soviet Naval Diplomacy*, edited by Dismukes and McConnell and with contributions from other writers. With its thorough analysis of relevant Soviet writing, its admirable case studies and the carefully constructed theories it advances, this book still provides the most comprehensive and illuminating treatment of its subject and has already been much quoted.[13] Its scope, however, is a good deal wider than

> ... the use or threat of limited naval force, otherwise than as an act of war, in order to secure advantage, or to avert loss, either in the furtherance of an international dispute or else against foreign nationals within the territory or the jurisdiction of their own state.[14]

Soviet Naval Diplomacy does not confine itself even to the concept of 'coercive naval diplomacy' as stated in its preface. Its range is wide and includes deployment patterns, diplomatic port visits, exercises, assistance with mine-clearing, foreign-base facilities and a variety of aids to diplomacy not involving the use of warships. This broad canvas, painted in meticulous detail, provides a striking background that lends extra emphasis to one rather significant omission. No example is given of the *use* of limited naval force by the Soviet Navy. Lesser navies, in the period (1967–76) covered by *Soviet Naval Diplomacy*, sank or captured ships on the high seas, mounted a blockade, bombarded the shore, or landed troops to conquer territory. The Soviet Navy did things of which the political significance was often a matter for conjecture: deployed ships, conducted manoeuvres, helped other governments to ferry soldiers.

Admittedly, other writers have gone further. Bruce Watson mentions reports that Soviet warships bombarded shore targets in Angola in 1976 and in Eritrea in 1978, but describes them as 'unsubstantiated'.[15] Ranft and Till describe incidents in 1985 when first a Norwegian vessel, then a Swedish one, was harassed by Soviet warships, but add that the Norwegians eventually received an apology.[16] As for threats, the most blatant example – the simulated attacks on the USS INDEPENDENCE during the Middle Eastern crisis of October 1973 – was so dangerously provocative as perhaps to be nearer a threat of war than one of limited naval force. Watson quotes Admiral Murphy, Commander of the US Sixth Fleet, as expressing the view that 'the stage for the hitherto unlikely "war at sea" scenario was set'.[17]

The record of Soviet naval activity is often clouded by this kind of ambiguity. Many writers, for instance, have been tempted to attribute a political purpose to the large Soviet naval manoeuvres of previous decades. Naturally anything on the scale of Okean 70 or Vesna 75 had to have a political impact on coastal states in the area affected and, in so far as the impression conveyed was one of Soviet strength and reach, this was doubtless welcome to the Soviet government. However, the object of gunboat diplomacy – unless this is purely expressive – is more narrowly focused: 'to secure advantage, or to avert loss ... in the furtherance of an international dispute'. It is by no means obvious that this was achieved – or always intended.

Norway is a case in point. As early as 1968, Exercise Sever featured a Soviet naval squadron sailing northwards along the Norwegian coast to carry out landing operations on the Rybachiy peninsula beyond the eastern extremity of Norway's Barents Sea coast, a procedure repeated in Exercise Okean of 1970. In 1968 a Soviet spokesman described Exercise Sever as the riposte to a provocative NATO naval manoeuvre (see the Chronological Appendix); the Norwegians thought it was intended to influence their policy; other writers linked it to the Czech crisis of that summer. However, it could have been just part of the long-term naval programme: another step in the westward extension of the Soviet Union's defensive perimeter. When some action has a result that is both obvious and politically advantageous, we may assume – though proof demands a prior declaration of intent – a political purpose. Where the outcome is uncertain, however, the assumption becomes distinctly dubious.

The result of these particular manoeuvres, as analysed in an interesting article by the Norwegian writer Arne Olav Brundtland, seems to have been that of reinforcing Norwegian support for NATO.[18] If such exercises continued, though on a declining scale – a landing on the Kola peninsula not far from the Norwegian border in 1987 included only five warships – the purpose was arguably more naval than political. In Scandinavia or elsewhere, it is difficult to find a convincing example of the Soviet Navy demonstrably securing advantage or averting loss by the use or threat of limited force in an international dispute. The repeated intrusion into Swedish territorial waters, for instance, of Soviet submarines could have been interpreted as a threat of force, but the purpose – and anything those submarines achieved – was obscure and arguably related to planning and training for war rather than to the furtherance of an international dispute.[19]

Until *glasnost* makes more progress, conjecture concerning Soviet policy and intentions is hazardous. Looking at the record as a whole, however, it does seem conceivable that the dominant motive of Soviet naval movements and dispositions could have been to enhance their readiness for war. In September 1981, for instance, a big landing exercise close to the Polish border was such an appropriate sequel to a hot summer of political unrest in Poland that Western observers assumed the manoeuvre to be politically motivated. Even in Moscow the naval staff must have been tempted to claim credit for good political judgement and even foresight. However, Zapad 81 was much more than a landing exercise. Planning was probably well advanced before the temperature began to rise in Poland; and the amphibious operation in which Zapad 81, in common with other large Soviet naval exercises, culminated could have been conceived as one more rehearsal of that wartime landing in Schleswig regarded by the West German and Danish navies as the likely role of the Baltic fleet. Taking political advantage, as opportunity serves, of the naval training programme and of normal naval movements provides an uncovenanted bonus that many navies are glad to earn, but it is not quite the same thing as gunboat diplomacy.

Another example of this approach is the voyage made by the aircraft-carrier MINSK on her way to join the Pacific Fleet in 1979. Starting from Nikolayev in the Black Sea, where she had been commissioned, she conducted manoeuvres in the Mediterranean with other Soviet warships. Then she sailed right round Africa, calling first for six days at Luanda, where the ship was visited by the President of Angola. In 1979 Angola was a Soviet client state beset by civil war, but it was no part of the mission assigned to MINSK to use or threaten force in that dispute. Many thousands of Cuban troops were already busily engaged in that task. The role of MINSK, and of the two modern cruisers, the amphibious warfare ship IVAN ROGOV and the tanker who accompanied her, was to provide an impressive reminder of the power and reach of

Angola's Soviet ally. The same moral would have been on offer when the MINSK, continuing her voyage, showed the flag at Mozambique, Mauritius and Aden. The visit to Aden lasted eight days and included an amphibious warfare demonstration by aircraft and helicopters from MINSK, as well as landing craft from IVAN ROGOV. In the Pacific the MINSK did not visit Vietnam, recently embroiled in hostilities with China, but attracted hostile comment from the Chinese press by conducting exercises in the East China Sea on the way to Vladivostok.

The Soviet Union thus turned the voyage of MINSK and her consorts to political purposes unrelated to the primary purpose of this naval movement: reinforcing the Pacific fleet. Even the unease caused in South Africa (on the other side in the Angolan civil war), when MINSK rounded the Cape and the South African government sent the destroyer PRESIDENT STEYN to shadow her (while trying to keep the news from the press), cannot have been unwelcome in Moscow. The Chinese, who had grounds for resenting the reinforcement of the Pacific fleet, found a subtler expression for their feelings. An article in the *Beijing Review*[20] compared the course followed by MINSK to the fatal voyage of Admiral Rozhestvensky and the Second Pacific Squadron to disaster at Tsushima in 1905.

There still remained a political bonus for Moscow, but none of this was gunboat diplomacy. MINSK never threatened to use limited force or sought to influence the outcome of an international dispute. Instead, the Soviet Navy profited from the transfer of some ships from the Black Sea to the Pacific Fleet to show the flag and remind a number of countries, friendly or otherwise, that the Soviet Union had an ocean-going navy and – ostensibly – a global reach.

In 1992, incidentally, MINSK was still in the Pacific, but laid up, in need of major overhaul, and seemingly in a deplorable condition. Indeed, reports in *United States Naval Institute Proceedings* suggested that most of the Russian aircraft-carriers were more or less unserviceable for want of the repairs and spares that might have been available from the shipyard where they were built – at Nikolayev (now in the Ukraine).[21]

Preoccupation with readiness for war and with the deployments this demanded, coupled with a degree of bureaucratic rigidity, might help to explain the contrast between the dangerous aggressiveness of Soviet anti-carrier forces in October 1973

– a programmed bellicosity – and the surprising caution displayed by Soviet warships on occasions when diplomatic encounters might have been conceivable. During the years when Soviet warships maintained a presence in distant seas, the threat they implied was seldom made manifest. A vague menace or the expressive mode was usually their nearest approach to gunboat diplomacy and, even when they went further, they could claim few concrete results.

This cautious approach fitted the general pattern of Soviet foreign policy, in which actions seldom matched the rough language of propagandists and, sometimes, even of diplomats. However, it contrasts sharply with the willingness to run risks and the ready resort to violence of lesser navies: those of Indonesia, Iran or Turkey, for instance. Nor does it reflect the ruthless use of force to defend Soviet interests *within* their own sphere of influence: shooting down US reconnaissance aircraft in 1960 or a Korean airliner in 1984; crushing revolts in the satellites; defending the shooting, by a Soviet sentry, of Major A.D. Nicholson, a member of the US military liaison mission in East Germany, near Ludwigslust on 24 March 1985;[22] intervening – in reckless defiance of the disastrous precedents – in Afghanistan. The prudent conduct of Soviet naval operations cannot altogether be explained by US superiority at sea, for US ships sometimes seemed to be the preferred targets for provocative behaviour by the Soviet Navy. The 1972 Agreement did not put an end to surveillance that was often harassing, to occasional collisions, or even to such exasperated gestures as the firing of flares, in April 1984, by the carrier MINSK at the closely shadowing US frigate HAROLD HOLT (which was hit three times) in the South China Sea.[23]

Perhaps what prevented the Soviet Navy from making greater use of gunboat diplomacy was the degree of open-ended risk that the practice so often entails. It is not that Russians are by nature reluctant to run risks. On the contrary, Soviet leaders have given frequent proof of their readiness to spurn compromise, to resort to violence and to incur losses, but only in situations they think they can control. When Khrushchev stuck his neck out in the Cuban missile crisis of 1962 and had to retreat with severe loss of face, his 'adventurism' led to his downfall. The 'dash' prized in the British and US navies – a characteristic of limited naval force since the days of the

Yangtse gunboats – might well be condemned as 'adventurism' in the Soviet Navy, if there was any likelihood that Soviet prestige could be endangered by failure to achieve swift success.

Forty years of Cold War conditioned the Soviet Union into a degree of understanding of US behavioural patterns. Other nations were less intensively studied and the ideological constraints on candid reports often meant that Soviet officers lacked the objective information needed for even rudimentary understanding of likely foreign reactions. Teasing US naval officers, the disciplined servants of a rational and fairly predict-able government, even teasing in the reckless fashion of October 1973, might perhaps be considered a finite risk, whereas opera-ting against Third World forces could be open-ended – as proved to be the case in Afghanistan, and as others had discovered before them. Afghanistan, however, was an unlucky departure from the sensible practice of doing the jungly jobs by proxy – Cuban or other – and the sailors were cautious. Perhaps the principle that governed the peacetime operations of the Soviet Navy bore some resemblance to the advice traditionally given to young barristers on their first appearance in court: never put a question to a witness unless you already know the answer.

All this is mere conjecture, but some explanation is needed for the low ranking among the exponents of gunboat diplomacy of the world's second strongest navy. That there is a tradition (whatever its doctrinal roots) of prudence and restraint seems obvious. It may well be inherited by the smaller Russian Navy, when this eventually returns to the high seas. However, nothing in the record of the Soviet Navy suggests that its eclipse or the emergence of a successor will have much direct impact on the statistics of limited naval force.

Indirectly, the repercussions might be greater. As previously suggested, the US Navy will be freer to act. The simple amphi-bious operation of December 1992, when US Marines and soldiers were landed in Somalia, might have seemed less attractive if a Soviet naval squadron had been hovering in the Indian Ocean, or if Somali war lords had been able to count on the Soviet Union as a source of clandestine support. Nor was it only the United States who felt the constraints – which were political and ideological as well as military – that a powerful Soviet Union could exercise on the conduct of international relations. Lesser countries who once sought the goodwill of one superpower as insurance against the displeasure of the other were constrained, if not to good behaviour, at least to observance of such restraint as Cold War priorities dictated. Some may now feel freer to pursue predatory ambitions of their own. If the Cold War fostered some conflicts (in Angola, for instance), a salutary fear of superpower intervention kept other conflicts from breaking out. Would Serbs and Croats, one wonders, have allowed themselves the savage luxury of civil war if there were still Soviet armoured divisions in Hungary, and if another Brezhnev, though one still in command of his faculties, reigned in Moscow?

It is easy, of course, to go too far in seeing the fall of the Soviet empire as the only trigger of the unexpected. Change is always with us and has many causes. However, it did give the unfolding of events a rattling jolt. The world, though granted a respite from the fear of general war, has entered a less predictable era, a time of troubles and of the likely proliferation of conflicts. When and where those conflicts might develop and what part might be played by any of the Soviet Union's successor states are questions to which it is too soon to attempt useful answers. If we look only at Russia, we cannot even guess who, in five years' time, will rule that country, and whose obedience, and how much of it, they will command or what purpose will inspire their efforts. Asking similar questions about the other fourteen republics or that flimsy umbrella, the Commonwealth of Independent States (poetically described by Yeltsin's biographers as 'a shroud over the abyss'[24]), engenders only an inflation of alternative futures.

It is safer to stick to the obvious. The future incidence of limited naval force will not be much affected by the beaching of the Soviet Navy, which made little use of that expedient. However, the fall of the Soviet empire has transformed the international environment in which others will exercise limited naval force. The world of the 1990s is likely to be less stable and predictable than the world of the 1970s. These are conditions conducive to conflict among nations and, if those conflicts take no worse a form than gunboat diplomacy, we shall have reason to be grateful, as well as surprised.

6 The Future of Gunboat Diplomacy

I shall sleep, and move with the moving ships.
Change as the winds change, veer in the tide.

Swinburne [1]

The seven decades sampled in this book have seen many changes in the practice of gunboat diplomacy. New assailants have emerged and some of the old ones now stay in home waters or play the role of victim. In an altered world, coastal states once reckoned as easy meat have acquired modern weapons and the knack of using them. So naval force nowadays often has to be less limited – demanding larger resources, more political commitment, and a higher level of command and control. The carefree days are over for dashing young naval officers, and in 1980 when helicopters launched from the USS NIMITZ abandoned their attempt to rescue US hostages from Tehran, the tactical decision had to be approved by the President of the United States in person. Revolutionary progress in radio communication had removed the need to delegate and the Cold War had provided an extra excuse for the centralising instinct few national leaders can resist.

Because the international environment, both political and military, has been changing during those seven decades, governments have had to take account of new factors when contemplating the use of limited naval force. The identification of disputes as amenable to resolution by gunboat diplomacy, the choice of methods, and the political precautions required have all become more complicated. Naturally the process has not developed at an equal pace or in the same manner across the whole range of assailants – nowadays a more diverse group than they used to be. Earlier chapters have illustrated the contrast between the US approach – assembling enough fire-power to minimise the risks of failure or prolonged combat – and the rough-and-ready, slug-it-out tactics of newer and less lavishly

140

equipped assailants. However, the general trend of the times has been to demand more effort from assailants in order to overcome greater resistance from their victims.

What is perhaps more surprising than the complications that change so often brings is the survival, in spite of unfamiliar political inhibitions and novel weapons, of so many of the old practices and purposes of gunboat diplomacy. On 17 January 1993, for instance, the US ships STAMP, HEWITT and COWPENS in the Gulf, together with the USS CARON in the Red Sea, launched forty Tomahawk cruise missiles against Baghdad.[2] The 1,000-lb warheads and the remarkable range of these missiles were far beyond the capacity of the German cruiser and four destroyers that fired 200 shells point blank into Almería on 31 May 1937, but the political purpose was the same. Each attack was a punitive bombardment in response to provocation by the victim, and also an act of purposeful force intended to deter the victim from repeating his offence.

In 1937 the Germans seem to have been successful in discouraging further attacks on their warships (the *Panzerschiff* DEUTSCHLAND had incurred twenty-two dead and eighty-three wounded when bombed on 29 May) by aircraft belonging to the Spanish Republican forces, but the Germans had a victim more sensitive to international opinion. Naturally the Germans did not escape foreign criticism, with the US Secretary of State expressing the pious hope that Germany might in future 'see its way to make peaceful adjustments', but Spanish proposals for retaliation were firmly vetoed by the Republic's principal backer: Joseph Stalin. 'The "incident" of Almería, therefore, was allowed to be forgotten.'[3]

In 1993, too, there was some murmuring against the United States, particularly from other Middle Eastern states, but the military and political strength of the United States was then more solid than Germany's in 1937. Moreover, the language of earlier resolutions by the Security Council of the United Nations could be interpreted as licensing US action. Saddam Hussein, being his own cynical master, was less easily deterred or excited than the divided government of the Spanish Republic. The small concessions he offered lost some of their significance amid the trumpetings of Iraqi defiance. Bluff tends to be easier for a self-confident dictator than for a democratic government dependent on the goodwill of voters and allies.

Bluff depends for its success on many factors, but perceived readiness for a fight is always important. That is one international league table which has changed considerably during a century that began with an exploit as remarkable as it has long been unrepeatable. In the summer of 1900, when the foreign legations in Peking were besieged by Chinese irregulars, the naval powers (US, European and Japanese) with warships in the Gulf of Pechili improvised a multinational relief force. Nine small and mostly obsolescent warships, with an assault force of 900 men, opened the road to Peking by capturing, in one night and at the cost of 172 casualties, the Taku forts (modernised and with Krupp guns) and the four brand-new, German-built destroyers that guarded the mouth of the Pei Ho river.

Two months later, after many battles on the way with Imperial Chinese troops as well as Boxer rebels, the multinational force, which a rather haphazard process of piecemeal reinforcement had raised to a strength of 14,000 men, made a triumphant entry to Peking. They relieved the legations (defended meanwhile by 400 sailors and marines introduced just before the siege began), caused the Dowager Empress of China to undertake a tour of inspection in the remoter provinces, successfully demanded the execution of some of her ministers, exacted an indemnity and, ably assisted by the aggrieved ladies of the *Corps Diplomatique*, enjoyed the usual spell of looting. These polyglot soldiers, sailors and marines had shown much courage, endurance and discipline in their battles with superior Chinese forces, but their success owed little to their generals, who were divided, or to their weapons, which were no better than those available to the forces of the Dowager Empress. The issue was mainly decided by the extraordinary incompetence – administrative, military and political – of their opponents.[4]

As previously argued, it is the subsequent proliferation of organised government that has been principally responsible for preventing the repetition of such exploits – in China or elsewhere. When on 22 August 1967 the British Embassy at Peking was burnt down, and its staff brutally maltreated, action could neither be taken nor contemplated. Since 1949, when HMS AMETHYST escaped by the skin of her teeth from an attack in the River Yangtse, the provision of an armed guard for the British Embassy had unfortunately had to be abandoned as no longer practicable. Even the United States has been unable to defend or rescue diplomats in capitals at all remote from the sea (for example Tehran in 1979).

This change has many causes. The civilised powers have become less concerned with the concept of prestige, no longer feel the same sense of responsibility for their servants overseas, have lost the old appetite for risk. Today's plethora of international organisations and alliances is no substitute for the instinctive solidarity that allowed the eight navies represented in the Gulf of Pechili to improvise their co-operation. However, there has also been a more material change: in the international balance of military power.

The contrast between the events of 1900 and those of 1990 is a measure of the transformation. On 28 May 1900, after the first attack by the Boxer rebels on the railway from Peking to Tientsin (the route to the sea), the *Corps Diplomatique* in Peking asked the admirals commanding the warships of various nations in the Gulf of Pechili to send guards for the Legations. Some 337 US, British, French, Italian, Japanese and Russian sailors and marines arrived by train on the evening of 31 May, followed on 3 June by fifty-two Germans and thirty-seven Austrians. The Chinese Foreign Ministry expressed disapproval, but were ignored. Under the command of the British Minister, Sir Claude Macdonald (a choice determined by his diplomatic precedence rather than by his youthful experience of active service as a regular soldier), this small force successfully defended the Legations against repeated attacks. Most of them were still alive when the arrival on 14 August of the international relief force ended the siege.[5]

On 2 August 1990 Iraq invaded Kuwait, crowning an easy conquest by making hostages of numerous European and US residents in Iraq and Kuwait and adopting an attitude of ambiguous menace towards their embassies. It took six months and twelve resolutions by the Security Council of the United Nations before the United States, feeling an acute political need for the physical presence of committed allies and demanding financial contributions from the shirkers (Germany and Japan had to pay 20 billion dollars between them), were ready to launch, from Saudi Arabian soil, an irresistible offensive of half a million men, with an overwhelming superiority in aircraft and missiles, against the Iraqis. That was a war and it cost a great

deal more to defeat this country of 20 million people in 1991
than it had for gunboat diplomacy to achieve a fuller and more
lasting triumph over 350 million Chinese in 1900.[6]

Those ninety years had brought many changes to the world
and the alteration in the relative military capacities of the
nations had been remarkable. Table 6.1 provides a simple illustration of the contemporary state of affairs. It shows how, in
crude military numbers, the traditional great powers had fallen
behind the less stable and less satisfied countries of the world.
In their haste to cash an illusory 'peace dividend', they have

Table 6.1   The balance of forces

The old guard	Soldiers	Tanks	Combat aircraft
Britain	153,000	1,330	538
France	289,000	1,340	597
Germany*	308,000	5,045	503
Italy	260,000	1,533	425
Japan*	156,000	1,222	387
New emerging forces			
Egypt	320,000	3,190	475
India	1,100,000	3,150	833
Iran	305,000§	500	185
Iraq	955,000	5,500	689
Israel	598,000+	4,288	553
Korea (North)	1,000,000	3,500	716
Korea (South)	650,000	1,550	469
Libya	55,000	2,000	513
Pakistan	500,000	1,850	470
Syria	300,000	4,000	558
Turkey	525,000	3,714	455
Vietnam	900,000	1,600	250
Yugoslavia	138,000	1,850	455

*Constitutionally inhibited from foreign deployment
Notes: § Add 150,000 Revolutionary Guards
         + On mobilisation
Source: IISS, *Military Balance*, 1990–1.

since fallen further still. Militarily speaking, these are all middling powers. The United States, China and what used to be the Soviet Union have been omitted at the top of the scale, together with many lesser lights at the bottom.

Naturally, these comparisons are oversimplified. Although supposedly civilised governments have been selling modern weapons to all comers on a scale beyond the wildest dreams of those *louche* traders once censured for peddling rum and rifles to the Red Indians, it would be misleading to suppose that all tanks are equivalent or all soldiers of equal value on the field of battle. Israel, for instance, has repeatedly shown that quality can beat quantity. Technological progress may have weakened the equation Napoleon formulated in 1808, but it has not yet destroyed it: 'A la guerre, les trois quarts sont des affaires morales, la balance des forces réelles n'est que pour un autre quart.'[7]

Qualitative advantage is of great importance in determining the outcome of a battle, but is hard to measure in advance with a persuasive degree of precision and objectivity. Many armies claim to be the best in the world, some may believe their own words, but very few can muster hard evidence. However, when generals and political leaders must decide whether to commit their forces, numbers can be rather daunting to the proudest. It is easy to forget, after the swift success gained by the United States and their allies in the Gulf War, just how much agonising there had been beforehand over Iraqi numbers, chemical weapons, missiles and defensive positions guarded by trenches filled with flammable petroleum. Iraqi strength, as magnified by Iraqi propaganda and the gullible Western media, created enough alarm to bring a steady stream of political personalities from Europe and the United States to Baghdad, where they pleaded with Saddam Hussein and were sent home with gift parcels of freed hostages. If the Iraqi dictator believed his bluff was working, he had been given some excuse for his error.

The arguments of arithmetic are reinforced by those of recent history. If the Soviet Union had to accept defeat in Afghanistan, as the United States had earlier done in Vietnam, a degree of dithering on the edge of the Yugoslav quagmire is at least understandable. And there are ten other middling countries, none of them particularly stable or satisfied, with larger ground and air forces than those of Yugoslavia.

So it is interesting to note that, among the world's turbulent warriors – the restless states with large armies and air forces – only three qualify for the list of middling navies in Chapter 4: India, South Korea and Turkey. Nor do any of these three yet pose a serious challenge (beyond the range of shore-based air cover) to the older naval powers. China, of course, is a different matter. No one will want to tangle with the Chinese Navy without US support. The same will be true of the Russian Navy, once they recover their sea legs. With those exceptions, however, there is a case for arguing that the satisfied powers have less to fear at sea than they do on land, if they wish to strengthen the influence of their diplomacy by a display of coercive potential. For that matter, the navies of China and India have intervened with some success in the Spratlys and Maldives, whereas Chinese soldiers left Vietnam in 1979 without achieving their political objective and, when India withdrew from Sri Lanka in 1990, the prestige of the Indian Army was among the casualties of the civil war that their intervention had failed to resolve.

It scarcely needs arguing that, in the future as in the past, coercive diplomacy will be less costly and less of a risk than war, or that navies will usually find it easier than armies or air forces to await (still uncommitted) the critical moment for intervention and, even then, if more resistance is encountered than was expected, to withdraw, relatively unscathed and with less loss of face. Fighting on or over the land has become a poker game demanding an ever-rising ante, as more nations acquire the latest weapons for their armies and air forces. It will be many years, even if the attempt is made, before such proliferation is matched at sea. Missiles and combat aircraft can be manned by an elite small enough to undergo advanced training. Warships need a larger crew. In 1950 the newly acquired Iranian frigate BABR was found drifting, powerless, in the Gulf, because the stokers had used the distilled water needed by the boilers for their own ablutions.[8]

The political application of limited naval force is likely to remain an economical expedient (for those naval powers willing to sustain their navies) and, by comparison with other forms of coercion, to seem an even better bargain in the years ahead. However, if it is cheap, will it also be effective? Can those nations with a clear naval advantage hope this will compensate for their relative – sometimes even absolute – decline in strength on the ground and in the air?

The reader persuaded by earlier arguments will know the answer: limited naval force is a specialised tool, a spanner that will turn a nut it happens to fit, not a hammer that will bang home any old nail. In 1991, once the Gulf War was over, navies played little part, often none at all, in most of the fighting that went on in Africa, Asia, Latin America, the Middle East, and even Europe. Some of these conflicts were in land-locked territory – Afghanistan, Chad, Kashmir, the Kurdish areas of Iran, Iraq and Turkey, Rwanda – but all were being fought out on the ground. Warships might once have made an entry in the dramas of Angola, Central America, East Timor, the Lebanon, Liberia and Sri Lanka, but soldiers had since assumed the burden of the action. They seemed unlikely to achieve a happy ending – either there, or in Yugoslavia, or in the many grumbling brawls of what used to be the Soviet Union – but navies had no more to offer or had already shot their bolt.

In the time of troubles so obviously ahead of us, disputes will clearly be frequent and enough of them will be accessible from the sea to provide occasional opportunities for the exercise of limited naval force. The types of operation noted as recurring – with different actors and in other theatres – over seven decades are likely to crop up again in the future. Some that have long been out of fashion – the naval rescue of deposed foreign rulers, for instance, frequent before 1939, but almost unknown after 1945 – might well be revived. As it is, one can think of defeated clients who might have tried a little longer if only they had been sure a warship was waiting to whisk them away before the worst could finally come to the worst. However, we must also expect changes, even novelties, in the new era of international relations inaugurated by the end of the Cold War.

The intense rivalry of the two superpowers and the general apprehension that this could erupt into open war long exercised a distorting influence by aggravating some disputes, but suppressing more. While it lasted it was felt as a burden, but its cessation has allowed many smouldering quarrels to flare into conflicts. Another result has been to attract attention to problems of a more general kind: some of them relatively novel, others familiar but hitherto neglected. Among those that may seem susceptible to treatment by the use of limited naval force

are illegal immigration, national encroachments on the freedom of the seas, piracy and terrorism, pollution and the smuggling of drugs and other unwelcome cargoes. Optimists may
wish to add: humanitarian relief to the innocent victims of
violence.

Fundamentally, of course, *illegal immigration* is a result of
excessive growth in the world's population. There are already
more people than the earth can comfortably support and too
few countries with the empty but habitable space that the
Americas once offered to desperate Europeans. The end of
empire, moreover, has made life harder for many millions, not
only in what used to be the Soviet Union, but also in former
colonies all over Africa and Asia. More people now starve and
suffer oppression, and therefore want to migrate, and fewer
countries are willing, even able, to receive them.

It is not the phenomenon that is novel – few problems in
international relations lack a precedent – but the likely scale of
it. Even the use of limited naval force to curb unwanted immigration has happened before. From the summer of 1946 to that
of 1948, cruisers, destroyers, frigates and minesweepers of the
British Mediterranean Fleet intercepted and boarded ships
carrying Jewish illegal immigrants bound for the British
Mandated Territory of Palestine, arrested their passengers, and
transferred them to detention camps.[9] This simple fleet
operation was largely successful, but the political objectives it
was intended to promote – reducing the violence of Arab resistance to Jewish immigration and preserving the possibility of a
binational state – were doomed to failure for other reasons.
Human beings have often tended to reject half a processed loaf
for the bitter bread that idealism bakes with blood and tears.

British attempts to control Jewish immigration to Palestine
were widely condemned at the time, particularly in the United
States, where much sympathy was felt for Jewish refugees
desperate to leave a Europe polluted by the stench of the
Holocaust. Forty-five years later, however, a different attitude
was adopted (President Clinton's campaign promises notwithstanding) towards the 200,000 Haitians expected to risk
turbulent seas in their flimsy boats to escape an island still
haunted by terrible memories from the reign of Papa Doc. In
January 1993 Admiral William Kime of the US Coast Guard
explained how he had deployed twelve large cutters, together

with twelve aircraft and helicopters, and had gratefully received further assistance from the US Navy, in order to intercept and repatriate the fleeing Haitians – as had happened with 40,000 of them since 1991 – before they could reach Florida.[10]

Circumstances do alter cases. The famous inscription on the Statue of Liberty in New York harbour –

> Give me your tired, your poor,
> your huddled masses yearning to breathe free,
> The wretched refuse of your teeming shore[11]

has long had more significance for historians than for immigrants. Nor is this merely a US phenomenon. All the richer countries of the world nowadays endeavour to restrict immigration in the face of increasing pressure from the 'huddled masses' of the poor and oppressed. The leaders of those richer countries have often been reluctant to adopt policies regarded as a departure from national traditions of affording asylum, but have had their hand democratically forced by the resentment uncontrolled immigration aroused, as once it did in Palestine, among the indigenous inhabitants. Since 1948, it must be remembered, global population has approximately doubled: from nearly 2,500 million to over 5,000 million. Whatever the resistance in the receiving countries, the incentives to mass migration are great and growing. Much of the movement that results, of course, is overland. The United States have had to fortify their frontier with Mexico, and Germany is one of the European countries that may need to follow the US example.

Some migration, however, is necessarily seaborne: for example, that of the Vietnamese fleeing the wretchedness of their own country for the fabled riches of Hong Kong. That colony being small and densely populated, it was easy enough to intercept those immigrants in territorial waters, but larger countries, where immigrants could vanish (perhaps with the help of compatriots already established as denizens) once they reached the coast, might have to operate naval patrols further out to sea. France, already regretting her fatal attraction for North Africans, is a case in point.

A recent survey by the International Institute for Strategic Studies of 'Mass Migration and International Security' emphasised the magnitude and the global diffusion of these pressures. Arguing that 'national security planners can no longer ignore the foreign policy issues raised by mass movements of peoples', it concluded, reasonably enough, that 'building barriers to deter such movements will not make the problem disappear' and, more optimistically, that 'in the long run, the only effective way of dealing with the problem is to address the conditions that create migrants'.[12] Perhaps the Ministers from thirty-five European countries who met at Budapest in February 1993 to discuss plans for reducing illegal immigration from Eastern Europe were able to make a start with ideas for improving life in 'the countries of origin'.[13] It is while awaiting the eventual outcome of such discussions that navies may be asked to undertake additional tasks, whether in the Mediterranean or the Narrow Seas, in the Caribbean or the Arafura Sea.

The *freedom of the seas* has attracted as many interpretations, all of them coloured by the interests of those employing the lawyers as any other concept. In the second half of the twentieth century a broad division has emerged, subject to various exceptions and qualifications, between those states with ocean-going navies who would like their ships to sail the seas without restriction, and most coastal states, who want their shores to remain inviolate and themselves to enjoy the exclusive right to exploit their offshore assets. With the proliferation of independence, the consensual trend has favoured the latter, creating what Ken Booth has called 'the threat of creeping jurisdiction',[14] a kind of oceanic arteriosclerosis, particularly noticeable in gulfs, straits and inland seas, as claims to territorial waters and exclusive economic zones extend ever further from the shore. This trend was meant to be codified in the 1982 Convention on the Law of the Sea, an instrument the nations of the world were quicker to sign than they were to ratify. Some have still not done so.

As always, there is a real divergence of interests behind the legal arguments. Many coastal states do not have an ocean-going navy, a wide-ranging merchant marine or a distant-water fishing fleet. So the farther out to sea they could erect a 'Trespassers will be Prosecuted' sign – particularly against oil tankers, warships with nuclear power or weapons, and foreign fishing boats – the better they would like it. Sometimes there is a political motive as well: the desire to keep outsiders, with their disturbing influence, at a safe distance. The United States, at the other extreme, has global interests – commercial as well as naval; and, by a curious geographical coincidence, its own coastal waters do not embrace any of the great arteries of international maritime trade. It has no Straits of Dover, Gibraltar or Malacca to flood its territorial waters with a dangerous stream of foreign traffic. Accordingly, the United States prefer a wider interpretation of the freedom of the seas.

Because rights not asserted may be lost, the use or threat of limited naval force in support of legal claims has been frequent in the past. Albania, Argentina, Brazil, China, Iceland, North Korea and Peru were some of the coastal states seeking to curb foreign incursions. Britain and France occasionally resorted to this expedient to uphold an opposite view, but it was naturally the US Navy, the world's most ocean-going one, that was foremost in demanding the utmost freedom of the seas. The forays made by the Sixth Fleet into the Gulf of Sirte had various motives, but one of them was to reject Libyan claims to control those waters; and, over the years, the US Coast Guard sent their vessels through the North West Passage in repeated denial of Canadian sovereignty over those Arctic waters. These were only dramatic incidents in a wider and more lasting campaign; the Annual Report for 1992 stated that:

... the Department of Defence conducts an active program of Freedom of Navigation operational asser- tions. [These] were conducted against the following countries [regarded as making excessive maritime claims] ... during the year from October 1 1990 to September 30 1991: Angola, Benin, Burma, Cameroon, Denmark, Dominican Republic, Ecuador, Haiti, Liberia, Nicaragua, Peru, Sierra Leone and Syria.[15]

Clearly, there is scope enough for disputes in the years ahead, but the pattern of the past suggests that the use or threat of limited naval force will be most likely when, as often happens, divergent legal opinions are reinforced by a conflict of more substantial interests. A serious attempt to tackle piracy, for instance, could easily encounter legal problems. In an interesting article, P.W. Birnie has drawn attention to the tendency of international law to exclude the seizure of ships for political motives from the definition of piracy, and to enlarge the area of territorial sea in which only the coastal state may act against pirates.[16] Where the pirates are based in the coastal state in question, acceptance of such a doctrine could prove a serious obstacle to their eradication. Conceivably, that could generate forceful pressure for change. We have it on the eminent authority of the late Professor O'Connell that, 'Governments in the matter of the Law of the Sea no longer act by reference to what they think the law is: they set out deliberately to break with the traditional rules in order to bring about the changes which they seek.'[17]

Whether or not they intend to change the law, governments have undoubtedly been willing to interpret it to suit themselves. In October 1985 Palestinian terrorists hijacked the Italian liner ACHILLE LAURO and murdered an American passenger. While the ship was 15 miles off Port Said, Egyptian officials struck a bargain with the terrorists: their freedom in exchange for the release of the ship. They were subsequently allowed by the Egyptian government to fly out of Cairo in an Egyptian air liner. Birnie believes that they were not pirates, but the US government disagreed, and four fighters from the carrier USS SARATOGA forced the air liner to land at the NATO air base of Sigonella in Sicily. President Mubarak of Egypt described this US action as 'piracy'. When the air liner landed at Sigonella, however, it was followed by a plane-load of US Special Forces under orders to arrest the terrorists and take them to the United States for trial as pirates. The Italians objected and, after a tense confrontation between US Special Forces and the Carabinieri, were allowed to take the terrorists to Rome and try them for murder.[18] This incident, in which the conflicting views taken by three governments of their rights and duties under international law were resolved by the threat or use of limited force, as well as the influence of political considerations, seems more likely to set a pattern for the future than the adoption of a deliberate strategy aimed at changing the law. However, the concept of the freedom of the seas could aggravate more disputes than it actually causes.

The Cold War and the decline of the colonial system operated in unintended conjunction to foster the revival of *piracy*, which, by the 1920s, more than a century of naval endeavour had managed to confine to Chinese waters. Writing in 1987 Birnie could quote substantial evidence of the incidence of piracy off the west coast of Africa, in the Caribbean and in the seas around South East Asia, particularly in the Straits of Malacca and Singapore. Most attacks, he argued, did not occur on the high seas but in territorial waters, and were probably perpetrated by nationals of the relevant coastal state: based in and operating from that state. Perhaps the most atrocious were the Thai pirates that were supposed between 1980 and 1985 to have killed 1,376 of the Vietnamese fleeing the economic collapse of their country in flimsy boats, and to have raped 2,283 of the Vietnamese women and kidnapped another 522.[19]

In any human calculus, this outweighs other maritime crimes, but consideration must also be given to those depredations to which the naval powers might have been supposed more susceptible. Many substantial merchant vessels, including some that flew the flags of superpowers, were attacked then and in later years. Among the more scandalous instances were: the 33,000-ton tanker seized in the South China Sea and taken to Singapore, where the cargo was sold;[20] the murder of Captain Bashforth and his First Officer, when the Danish ship BALTIMAR ZEPHIR was attacked off Indonesia;[21] and the tanker VALIANT CARRIER, also off Indonesia when she was boarded, robbed and left crippled, drifting, without lights, vulnerable to collision, and still dangerously full of flammable oil.[22]

The report in *The Times* of 28 December 1992 suggested that Indonesian pirates, who operated by night in fast, modern launches, included Indonesian servicemen and customs officers, sometimes still in uniform. Certain former colonies, particularly but not exclusively those where independence was won after much irregular fighting, have not yet succeeded in restoring respect for law and order. Nor are all governments equally anxious to combat piracy, as long as the victims are mainly foreigners. Thus press reports of piratical attacks on merchant vessels often mention that appeals for help, though broadcast by the ship's wireless, went unanswered. On paper it might seem that tackling piracy, if this is more than the coastal state can manage, ought to be a task for the appropriate regional organisation – the Association of South-East Asian Nations, for instance – but in practice this has not been effective. Nor does it

help that so many ships are owned in one country, but fly
another's flag of convenience and are officered and crewed
almost at random. Too many governments have an excuse for
shrugging off responsibility and no single country has inherited
the nineteenth-century role of Britain as the leading naval,
shipowning, seafaring, trading power with the strongest direct
national interest in fighting piracy.

The second half of the twentieth century has of course seen
the emergence of the United States as a superpower enjoying
friendly, and even co-operative, relations with most of the other
naval powers. However, while the Cold War lasted, the legal
obstacles to foreign warships entering territorial waters to
tackle pirates were reinforced by reluctance to divert ships from
their primary task or to alienate the states concerned, whether
these were clients or non-aligned. Piracy was one of several
problems that had to be subordinated to readiness for war.
Concentration on grand strategy has its price. Occasionally it
can threaten the mental flexibility so important to the naval
officer, and even impair his sense of proportion. In 1989, for
instance, Captain Balian of the USS DUBUQUE was court-
martialled for refusing, while on passage to the Persian Gulf, to
reduce his ship's combat-readiness by rescuing a boat-load of
distressed Vietnamese refugees.[23] Their perilous exodus had
continued throughout the 1980s – so had the piratical attacks.

Naturally it is conceivable, now that the end of the Cold War
has encouraged the United States to broaden the focus of US
international involvement, that attitudes will change. It is not
necessary to go back into history as far as the opening years of
the nineteenth century, when the US Navy smoked out a nest of
pirates at Tripoli, to find an instance of these enemies of the
human race being hunted in territorial waters. In October 1927
the British submarine *L4* sank a Chinese pirate ship in Chinese
territorial waters and took some of her crew to Hong Kong to
be tried and hung as pirates. It was only because of the involvement of a submarine that this was an unusual incident.[24] In
1962, before Confrontation with Indonesia pre-empted the
attention of the British Far East Fleet, several British warships
had conducted successful operations against pirates off Brunei.[25]
In later years, however, when naval powers have infringed the
legal rights of lesser states, they have seldom had the respectable excuse of endeavouring to eradicate that universal crime.

What, one wonders, would Captain Dalrymple Hay RN, whose squadron destroyed fifty-eight pirate junks and killed 1,700 Chinese pirates in the autumn of 1849, have thought of the advice given in the name of the British government to masters of British ships in 1992? Because there had been over eighty piratical attacks on ships in the first eight months of 1992, they were urged to have an anti-attack plan – but not to carry firearms, though the use of hoses might be considered. The sting was in the tail: 'There will be many circumstances when compliance with the attackers' demands will be the only safe alternative and when resistance or obstruction of any kind could be both futile and dangerous'. Towards the end of a long discussion concerning non-violent varieties of self-help, this passage (in paragraph 69) occurred:

> Ships from the Royal Navy will take all appropriate measures to respond to incidents of piracy on the high seas, and to provide humanitarian assistance to vessels attacked in territorial waters, whenever they are on hand to do so. However, the likelihood of a Royal Navy vessel being nearby when an incident occurs, particularly in distant waters, will not be great. British ships will therefore need to rely on their vigilance and resources to prevent attacks and on the capability of coastal States to suppress piracy and armed robbery.

Of course, Captain Dalrymple Hay's navy kept three times as many ships on foreign stations as there are ocean-going ships in the entire Royal Navy today. A century and a half ago, twenty-five of those ships were on the East India and China Station, where, the 1993 Merchant Shipping Notice tells us, 'attacks on ships when underway are most common'. Paragraph 67 points out that 'international law requires any warship or other government vessel to repress piracy on the high seas', but does not remedy the silence of the British media by naming any navy actually so engaged.[26] Things, one must conclude, are not what they were.

Much is tolerated nowadays – more, perhaps, than should be. *Pollution* is very much a contemporary problem, but the most vigorous naval response was an early one. In 1967 the 118,000-ton tanker the TORREY CANYON, a US-owned but Liberian-registered ship with an Italian crew and on charter to a British oil company, ran aground on the Seven Stones, a notoriously dangerous reef marked by a lightship in the busy shipping channel between the Scilly Isles and Land's End. Although the British government of the day initially seemed uncertain, the reef was arguably within British territorial waters. After some delay, while futile attempts were made at salvage and over 50,000 tons of oil escaped from the tanker, the Royal Navy patrolled a 20-mile exclusion zone around the tanker and, together with the Royal Air Force, sent aircraft to bomb the tanker. It took three days to burn the oil remaining in the tanks – a lesser amount, unfortunately, than that already polluting the beaches of Cornwall and Brittany.[27] Whether or not bombing might have been more successful if (with less tenderness for the property rights of the polluters) it had started earlier, this expedient has not since been employed.

Tankers, however, have continued, year after year, to lose power, to sink in storms, to run aground and to collide, spilling their dangerous cargo into the sea, to pollute beaches and to destroy wildlife. One day coastal states will lose patience and insist – as the United States are beginning to – on setting their own standards for the construction, seaworthiness, crewing and navigation of tankers allowed, though only on courses specified by the coastal state, to traverse their waters. Then navies will have a ticklish task – it is not always easy for a small warship to coerce a loaded supertanker with a convincing threat of limited force – in excluding not only tankers, but other ships carrying noxious or dangerous cargoes, if they fail to comply with the new rules.

The traffic in illegal *drugs*, on the other hand, may be less amenable to naval interference than was the smuggling of liquor in the days of American Prohibition (see the Chronological Appendix for 1929) or, in recent years, gun-running to Ireland. Naturally, navies have been involved when ships could be identified as targets for investigation. In 1988 the frigate HMS SCYLLA chased a suspect vessel in the English Channel and forced her into coastal waters for customs investigation.[28] However, the expedient can sometimes seem the use of a sledgehammer to crack a nut. The projected 'blockade' (the term used by the media, but disputed by the US government) of the Colombian coast, for which the carrier JOHN F. KENNEDY and other US warships were deployed in January 1990, had to be cancelled for political reasons (it had excited acute resentment in Colombia),[29] but it is difficult to regard it as a cost-effective method of intercepting goods that can be profitably consigned in small, light, easily concealed parcels. Limited naval force will never be an all-purpose tool.

Correctly targeted, however, and intelligently applied, gunboat diplomacy should have a future as varied and as rewarding as the recorded exploits of the last seven decades. It may seldom offer junior officers such scope for independent initiative as the Yangtse could provide in the 1920s, but it will occasionally manage a rescue or a capture, achieve what negotiation could not, contrive a middle way between war and acquiescence. When the conditions are right – which does not often happen – this is a tool that anyone with warships can grasp. Using it to advantage demands a degree of gumption, political even more than naval. Neither virtue nor resources are enough. That may be why the dimmer politicians, professors and media pundits, who prefer problems to be simply black and white, continue to patter the cliché 'the days of gunboat diplomacy are over'. They were wrong twenty years ago, they are wrong today, and they will be wrong in twenty years' time. While ships can float, limited naval force will sometimes find a way through reef and shoal.

Chronological Appendix: Seventy Years of Gunboat Diplomacy

This Chronological Appendix is not a complete list of all the examples of the application of limited naval force during the last seventy years; that would need a separate book. The instances listed below have been chosen to show the different ways in which, year by year, many governments have employed this expedient in various parts of the world. Because it is meant to illustrate the range of gunboat diplomacy, and to avoid tedious repetition, the choice made does not reflect the actual distribution of gunboat diplomacy in particular years or geographical areas. The number of incidents in China during the late 1920s, for instance, was far larger than the selection included here. This chronology does not, therefore, present a historically or geographically representative cross-section of the actual employment of gunboat diplomacy during the last seventy years, and cannot be used as a basis for mathematical conjectures.

The choice of examples has been guided by the definition reached in Chapter 1:

> gunboat diplomacy is the use or threat of limited naval force, otherwise than as an act of war, in order to secure advantage or to avert loss, either in the furtherance of an international dispute or else against foreign nationals within the territory or the jurisdiction of their own state.

Naval action in time of war has been excluded, unless this took place against allies or neutrals, and actions resulting in war (whether declared or not) have only been quoted as examples of failure – and on the assumption that only limited force was originally intended.

The description 'assailant' is given to the government that initiated the use or threat of naval force. Assailants are not necessarily aggressors. Similarly, the 'victim' is the other party to the dispute or, in the absence of a specific dispute, the government whose sovereignty was infringed, whether or not this government invited or acquiesced in the action taken. Victims are not necessarily innocent.

The classification of incidents is in accordance with Chapter 2: D stands for definitive force, P for purposeful, C for catalytic, and E for expressive.

Finally, an attempt has been made in the summary of each incident to indicate whether the action taken was successful or not. The only judgement implied is whether or not the results achieved corresponded with the intention of the assailant, and no attempt has been made to take account of wider considerations. For instance, the Turkish invasion of Cyprus in July 1974 is described as successful because it secured the slice of Cyprus sought by the Turkish government. The adjective 'successful' does not imply any

158

judgement that Turkish acquisition of this territory was in the long term advantageous either to Turkey or to anyone else, or that the decision to take it by force was necessarily correct. The whole of this chronology is intended only to illustrate the uses of gunboat diplomacy as an instrument of governments, and the merits of the foreign policies that promoted its employment are beyond the scope of this book.

1919

Date	Assailant	Victim	Incident	Type
1918–21	Britain	Russia German forces in area	After the armistice with Germany in November 1918, a British squadron was sent to the Baltic to support British policy. When withdrawn in 1921 it had failed to overthrow the Soviet regime, but had helped to secure independence for Estonia, Latvia and Lithuania (see Chapter 2). Partly successful.	C

Note: French, US and Italian warships were involved to a lesser extent, and limited naval force was much used by various powers at this time in the seas around Russia.

| 14 May 1919 | United States | Greece/ Turkey | USS ARIZONA lands marines to guard US Consulate at Constantinople during Greek occupation of that city.[1] | P |

1920

| 14 May | United States | Mexico | 'Bandits in charge Manzanillo since 11 a.m. 14th. Destroyer THORNTON, Commander Stirling, arrived 4 p.m. and saved town from violence. Standing by.'[2] | P |
| 18 May | Soviet Union | Iran/ Britain | Bolshevik destroyer and motor-boats seize White Russian ships in Enzeli harbour, bombard and occupy town, and expel small British contingent. | C |

1920

Date	Assailant	Victim	Incident	Type
			Although Persian territory occupied has later to be given up and attempted conversion to communism fails, operation later enables Soviet Union to improve its political position in Persia at British expense. Partly successful.[3]	
17 November	Britain	Greece	After the electoral defeat of the pro-British Greek Prime Minister, Venizelos, he leaves the country hurriedly on a yacht that was escorted by HMS CENTAUR to prevent any attempt by the new Greek government to arrest Venizelos. Successful.[4]	D

Note: British naval activities in the Baltic and the use of limited naval force against the Bolsheviks continued.

1921

Date	Assailant	Victim	Incident	Type
28 February –19 March	Britain	Soviet Union	British warships evacuate British subjects and sympathisers from Batum before this capital of the ephemeral (now renascent) state of Georgia falls to the Bolsheviks. Successful.[5]	D
5 August	United States	China	The US Navy establish a Yangtse river patrol 'to protect US interests, lives and property and to maintain and improve friendly relations with the Chinese people'. The success achieved in the first objective was more conspicuous than in the second.[6]	P
18 August	United States	Panama	400 US Marines embarked by USS PENNSYLVANIA to induce Panama to conform to	P

1921

Date	Assailant	Victim	Incident	Type
			US decision regarding her border dispute with Costa Rica.[7] Successful.	
1 November	Britain	Austria/ Hungary	HMS GLOWWORM and other British ships of the Danube Flotilla collect the ex-Emperor Karl of Austria-Hungary after the failure of his attempt to regain the throne and convey him to Rumania, whence HMS CARDIFF takes him to Madeira. This intervention by the Royal Navy was approved by the principal European governments and the use of naval force was needed only to prevent the ex-Emperor being rescued by his partisans, or kidnapped by his opponents, while on his way to exile.[8]	D

1922

Date	Assailant	Victim	Incident	Type
14 August	Britain	China	President Sun Yat Sen rescued from Canton after his defeat by Chinese rebels and taken to Shanghai in British gunboat. Successful.[9]	D
September	Britain United States France Italy	Turkey	British and other warships (including HMS IRON DUKE) sent to Smyrna (being evacuated by Greeks and occupied by Turks after their war) to maintain order and protect foreign nationals and property until Turkish authority established. Warships also gave some help with the evacuation of over 200,000 mainly Greek civilians. Partly successful.[10]	P
September/ November	Britain	Turkey	British fleet sent to the Dardanelles and Bosphorus	P

1922

Date	Assailant	Victim	Incident	Type
			to help prevent Turkish forces from crossing into Europe. Successful.[11]	
18 November	Britain	Turkey	The Sultan of Turkey rescued from his rebellious subjects by HMS MALAYA and taken to Malta. Successful.[12]	D

1923

Date	Assailant	Victim	Incident	Type
January	Britain/ France	Lithuania	British cruiser and French gunboat sent to Memel after Lithuanian seizure of that port (then under temporary French control). French garrison was rescued and face saved, but Lithuania kept Memel. Only partly a success.[13]	P
27 August	Italy	Greece	Italian fleet bombarded and occupied Greek island of Corfu in order to extract concessions from Greek government (see Chapter 2). Successful.	P
6 December	Britain France Italy Japan Portugal United States	China	Warships sent by these governments to Canton to protect Customs House (then under foreign control for recovery of debt) against seizure by Chinese government. Warships withdrawn the following April. Successful.[14]	P

1924

Date	Assailant	Victim	Incident	Type
11 January	Britain	Mexico	HMS CAPETOWN sent to Minatitlau to protect a British oil refinery during a Mexican revolution.	P
			She was successively relieved by other British cruisers, and it was the commander of HMS	P

1924

Date	Assailant	Victim	Incident	Type
			CONSTANCE who, after the arrival of various Mexican gunboats, informed the belligerents that he could not approve of the firing of the ships' guns in his vicinity, so he suggested their battle should take place elsewhere. Successful.[15]	
27 February	United States	Honduras	US Marines landed at Puerta Ceiba to protect US interests in civil disturbances. Successful, but US warships had again to intervene in later months.[16]	P
18 December	Italy	Albania/ Yugoslavia	Three Italian destroyers sent to Albanian ports when the Albanian government was threatened by insurrection that was allegedly sponsored by Yugoslavia. Unsuccessful.[17]	P

1925

Date	Assailant	Victim	Incident	Type
23 June	Britain	China	An armed detachment landed by HMS TARANTULA to protect the British concession at Shameen opens fire when the bridge is attacked by Chinese troops. Successful.[18]	P
4 August	United States	Nicaragua	US Marines withdrawn from many areas, but trouble soon prompts Nicaraguan government to solicit help, and USS DENVER sent to Corinto and USS TULSA to Bluefields, both on 13 September. Their presence did not prevent a *coup d'état*. Unsuccessful.[19]	P
12 October	United States	Panama	US Marines land in Panama at the request of the	P

1925

Date	Assailant	Victim	Incident	Type
			President of Panama to restore order after rioting. Successful.[20]	
5 November	United States	France	Two US destroyers sent to Beirut for the reassurance of US nationals endangered by disturbances in the French mandated territory of Syria and the Lebanon. They stayed one month. Successful.[21]	P

1926

Date	Assailant	Victim	Incident	Type
6 May	United States	Nicaragua	Cruiser USS CLEVELAND lands marines at Bluefields to protect US nationals and property from civil war. This was the first of many instances and the marines were not finally withdrawn until 1933. Although successful in its immediate objective, this intervention developed into military occupation of the entire country.[22]	P
4 September	Britain	China	British gunboats break an anti-British boycott at Canton and Swatow by clearing the harbour of the picket-boats maintained by the strike committee, and landing marines to clear pickets from British-owned wharves. Successful.[23]	D
5 September	Britain	China	After persuasion by HM Consul had failed, HM ships WIDGEON and COCKCHAFER rescue British Merchant Navy officers from two ships captured by the Chinese, and inflict severe damage on the city of	P

1926

Date	Assailant	Victim	Incident	Type
			Wanhsien. Subsequent negotiations lead to recovery of ships as well. Successful, but substantial casualties.[24]	

Note: In 1926 fifteen British, nine US, ten Japanese and six French gunboats regularly patrolled the Yangtse river. These and other warships were constantly in action throughout 1926.

1927

Date	Assailant	Victim	Incident	Type
January/ February	Britain France Italy Japan The Netherlands Portugal Spain United States	China	British expeditionary force and US Marines land at Shanghai to protect International Concession after the British concession at Hankow had been seized (the intervention of a British cruiser enables the foreign community to be evacuated). Other powers sent warships to Shanghai. Altogether, thirty-five warships (nine of them British) were concentrated off this Chinese port and 40,000 troops and marines (half of them British and Indian) were landed or held in readiness offshore. Most of them were withdrawn when the immediate threat was over, but small garrisons were retained for many years. No serious fighting took place and the threatened attack by the Chinese revolutionary armies was successfully deterred.[25]	P
23 February	Britain	Nicaragua/ United States	Having received no satisfactory reply to their request for US protection of British subjects in Nicaragua, the British government announce the despatch of	P

1927

Date	Assailant	Victim	Incident	Type
			the cruiser COLOMBO to Corinto. This elicits the desired undertaking and COLOMBO leaves again a few days later. Successful.[26]	
24 March	Britain United States	China	British and US warships bombard Nanking to cover the evacuation of foreign nationals after attacks by Chinese troops on foreign consulates and nationals in Nanking. Successful, and Chinese apologies later received.[27]	

Note: The year 1927 saw too many interventions in China to be listed, but one unusual incident deserves mention. On 20 October the British submarine *L4* sank a Chinese pirate ship in Chinese waters. The Chinese government complained that excessive force had been used and that victims as well as pirates had died. This illustrates the relative clumsiness of the submarine as an instrument of limited naval force. Nevertheless, enough pirates were rescued to be taken to Hong Kong and hung.[28]

Date	Assailant	Victim	Incident	Type
30 May	Britain	Egypt	Battleships sent to Alexandria and Port Said to reinforce diplomatic representations to Egyptian Government. Latter eventually give satisfaction on 14 June. Successful.[29]	P

1928

Date	Assailant	Victim	Incident	Type
5 January –30 June	Britain	China	Royal Navy operate a weekly convoy system for British shipping using the Yangtse. Successful.[30]	P
10 April	Japan	China	Japanese warships, which had already assembled at Tsingtao, land marines to protect Japanese interests threatened by Chinese invasion of Shantung province in course of civil	C

1928

Date	Assailant	Victim	Incident	Type
			war. Landing soon develops into full-scale expeditionary force, much fighting takes place, and original objective is lost sight of. Japanese forces eventually withdrawn. Unsuccessful.[31]	
30 April	Britain	Egypt	To speed compliance with an earlier request for an objectionable Bill to be withdrawn from the Egyptian Parliament, five warships are demonstratively despatched from Malta. Successful.[32]	P

1929

Date	Assailant	Victim	Incident	Type
March	United States	Canada	US Coast Guard cutter DEXTER sinks Canadian ship I'M ALONE (a rum smuggler) by gunfire in international waters. A long legal wrangle ensued.[33]	D
23 April	United States	Mexico	'Commander [of US destroyer ROBERT SMITH] and Consul have conferred with officers of the Federal gunboat BRAVO and have obtained promises not to bombard Guayamas.' One of many naval interventions in 1929 to protect US nationals and property during an insurrection in Mexico.[34]	P

Note: Because of the rarity of incidents involving the Soviet Navy, it is worth recording that, on 12 October, the Soviet gunboats LIEBKNECHT, KALMUK, BATRAK, ARACHANIN and LENIN sank three Chinese gunboats and captured another, and thus enabled Soviet troops to take the town of Tungkiang at the confluence of the Amur and Sungari rivers. This was not, however, an act of limited naval force, but part of an undeclared war that lasted months and involved many thousands of troops.[35]

1930

Date	Assailant	Victim	Incident	Type
January	Soviet Union	Turkey	The unobserved entry to the Black Sea of the battleship PARIZHSKAYA COMMUNA and the cruiser PROFINTERN alters the naval position to the advantage of the Soviet Union 'and to this may be traced the acceptance by Turkey of the protocol on naval armaments concluded between the two countries on 7 March 1931'.[36]	C
16 July	Britain	Egypt	Warships sent to Alexandria, Port Said and Suez to protect foreign nationals and interests after rioting (the Italians had said they would send ships if the British did not). Warships withdrawn 29 July. Successful.[37]	P
27 July –2 August	Britain Italy Japan United States	China	Gunboats evacuate foreign nationals from Changsha during fighting in course of civil war. Successful.[38]	D

1931

Date	Assailant	Victim	Incident	Type
11 April	United States	Nicaragua	USS ASHEVILLE sent to Puerto Cabezas to protect US (and British) nationals endangered by local disturbances that had arisen after the reduction of the US Marine occupying force. Successful.[39]	P

1932

Date	Assailant	Victim	Incident	Type
29 January	Japan	China	Japanese warships (including aircraft-carrier) bombard Chapei and land sailors after attacks on Japanese subjects and a boycott. The Japanese said they had taken 'drastic measures in a possible	C

1932

Date	Assailant	Victim	Incident	Type
			minimum degree'.[40] The incident led to weeks of serious fighting before Japanese forces were largely withdrawn. Unsuccessful.	
February	Britain United States	Japan/ China	A British cruiser squadron and the US Asiatic Fleet are sent to Shanghai to protect the International Concession, to secure ceasefire, and the withdrawal of Chinese and Japanese forces from vicinity (see above). Soon after arriving, Admiral Sir H. Kelly 'told the Japanese Admiral he was to give orders forthwith to stop his aircraft flying over my ships and that I would open fire if they did so ... he has promised to help me in every way to obtain peace'.[41] British and US writers differ in their attribution of national credit for the ceasefire signed aboard HMS KENT and made effective on 3 March.[42] Successful.	C

1933

Date	Assailant	Victim	Incident	Type
13 August	United States	Cuba	Two US warships sent to Havana (others, with marines embarked, hovering offshore), so that 'moral effect' would help President Roosevelt's special envoy to change the Cuban government to US advantage. Successful, but not for long.[43]	P
5 September	United States	Cuba	*A coup d'état* having toppled the pro-US government, the US Atlantic Fleet (including the battleship MISSOURI) is concentrated in Cuban	P

1933

Date	Assailant	Victim	Incident	Type
			waters. An acceptable Cuban government having been achieved, naval withdrawal begins on 23 January 1934. Successful.[44]	

Note: On 2 January the last US Marines were withdrawn from Nicaragua after many years of US occupation of that country.[45]

1934

Date	Assailant	Victim	Incident	Type
January	United States	China	USS TULSA lands marines to protect US Consulate at Foochow. Successful.[46]	P
23 June	Italy	Albania	Nineteen Italian warships sent to make a demonstration at Durazzo to induce the Albanian government to make concessions to Italy. Only partly successful.[47]	P

Note: On 15 August US Marines were finally withdrawn from Haiti after many years of occupation.

1935

Date	Assailant	Victim	Incident	Type
March	Britain	Greece	Battleship HMS ROYAL SOVEREIGN sent to Phaleron Bay to protect British interests after Greek Monarchist revolt. No action required.[48]	C
20 September	Britain	Italy	The British government formally notified the Italian government of the reinforcement of the British Mediterranean Fleet (by much of the Home Fleet and some ships from the China Station). The British had no intention of going to war, so this was either expressive or meant to be a threat that might influence Italian conduct in the Abyssinian crisis. The Italians treated	E or P

1935

Date	Assailant	Victim	Incident	Type
			it as a bluff and countered with an equally demonstrative reinforcement of their troops in Libya. This led to Italian proposals for mutual de-escalation that were eventually tacitly accepted. The British move thus failed – an example of the difficulty often experienced by democratic governments in bluffing.[49]	

Note: During the mid-1930s the Royal Navy kept a cruiser, eighteen gunboats and some destroyers in Chinese rivers and waters as well as the British China Fleet.

1936

Date	Assailant	Victim	Incident	Type
4 May	Britain	Italy	HMS ENTERPRISE manifested British sympathy for the defeated Emperor of Abyssinia by taking him to safety in Palestine. HMS CAPETOWN subsequently took him to London.[50] No such kindness was shown, forty-three years later, to the deposed Shah of Iran.	E
3 August	Germany	Spain	The *Panzerschiff* DEUTSCHLAND and torpedo boat LUCHS visit Ceuta in Spanish Morocco to show Hitler's support for Franco's rising (see Chapter 2).	E
19 August	Spain	Britain and others	Interference with foreign shipping in the seas around Spain begins and is continued by Spanish warships on both sides in the Civil War. British and other foreign warships intervened on many occasions, both protectively and for other purposes.[51]	P
1 December	United States	Argentina and others	President Roosevelt arrives at Buenos Aires in the	E

1936

Date	Assailant	Victim	Incident	Type
			cruiser INDIANAPOLIS escorted by the USS CHESTER to attend the first session of the Inter-American Conference for the Maintenance of Peace, where one of the main points at issue was US reluctance to accept the Argentinian doctrine prohibiting intervention in other countries. On paper, it was Argentina who was successful.[52]	

Note: The Spanish Civil War (1936–9) saw gunboat diplomacy on a scale (in terms of frequency of incidents, number of assailants and victims, variety and importance of warships involved, potential gravity of political implications) that surpassed even the decade of the 1920s in China. The few references in this chronology cannot do justice to an episode equally noteworthy for two novel features: humanitarianism as a motive for limited naval force, and the gathering storm clouds of imminent world war as a conditioning factor. See J. Cable, *The Royal Navy and the Siege of Bilbao* and other books in the Bibliography.

1937

Date	Assailant	Victim	Incident	Type
January –March	Britain	Spain	British destroyers, having completed the evacuation of British subjects, start rescuing foreigners, including many Spaniards stranded in ports controlled by the opposing faction in the Civil War. Successful.	D
April –October	Britain France	Spain	After Spanish Nationalists launch offensive against the Basque Republic, the Royal Navy are drawn into protecting British ships bringing food to Bilbao and a variety of ships taking refugees to France and Britain. Some help in the latter task, which involves many confrontations with Spanish Nationalist warships,	D

1937

Date	Assailant	Victim	Incident	Type
			is received from the French Navy. Usually successful.	

Note: See J. Cable, *The Royal Navy and the Siege of Bilbao* (see Bibliography).

Date	Assailant	Victim	Incident	Type
31 May	Germany	Spain	A German cruiser and four destroyers bombard Almería in retaliation for a Spanish air attack on the DEUTSCHLAND (see Chapter 6). No German warships seem to have been bombed subsequently, though this happened to several British warships and there were 150 air attacks on British merchant vessels. As the British government confined themselves to protests, these attacks continued throughout the war. A German success.[53]	P

1937

Date	Assailant	Victim	Incident	Type
August	Italy	Spain Britain France and others	'Unknown' (actually Italian) submarines start sinking ships bound for Spanish Republican ports. On 1 September HMS HAVOCK was unsuccessfully attacked and the tanker WOODFORD was sunk the next day (see below).[54]	P

Note: On 30 June Soviet gunboats were again in action on the Amur, this time against the Japanese, who sank one.[55]

Date	Assailant	Victim	Incident	Type
14 September	Britain France	Italy	At the Nyon Conference Britain and France agreed that their warships would attack and destroy unidentified submarines in areas where merchant ships had been attacked. This threat was temporarily successful and submarine attacks were suspended.[56]	P

1938

Date	Assailant	Victim	Incident	Type
11 January	Italy	Spain and others	Italian submarines resume the sinking of merchant ships bound for ports in Republican Spain (see below).[57]	P
1 February	Britain	Italy	After the sinking by an 'unknown' submarine of the British ship ENDYMION off Cartagena, the Italian ambassador was told that the Royal Navy reserved the right to destroy all submerged submarines in its patrol zone. No further sinkings by submarines. Successful.[58]	P
December	Argentina	United States and others	Imitating President Roosevelt (see 1936), the Argentinian Foreign Minister arrives at Lima aboard the cruiser LA ARGENTINA to attend the Pan-American Conference, a gesture that symbolised an increasingly independent policy followed by Argentina both on this occasion and in subsequent years.[59]	E

1939

Date	Assailant	Victim	Incident	Type
9 February	Britain	Spain Germany Italy	HMS DEVONSHIRE evacuates 450 Spanish Republicans from Minorca as part of a deal (negotiated on board this cruiser) whereby this Republican island was surrendered to the Nationalists on condition that no German or Italian forces were allowed to occupy it. Successful.[60]	P
23 March	Germany	Lithuania	Having successfully demanded the cession of Memel, Hitler emphasises the forceful character of this transaction by sailing into the harbour that very	E

1939

Date	Assailant	Victim	Incident	Type
			day in DEUTSCHLAND. Successful.[61]	
17 May	Britain France United States	Japan	Warships land sailors at Kulangsu to protect international settlement against incursion by Japanese forces. Although British and French contingents are withdrawn on outbreak of European war (3 September), US sailors do not leave until Japanese do so simultaneously on 18 October. Successful.[62]	P

1940

Date	Assailant	Victim	Incident	Type
21 January	Britain	Japan	HMS LIVERPOOL stops Japanese ship ASAMU MARA 35 miles off Tokyo and removes twenty-one German passengers. In spite of strong Japanese protests, this results in Japanese agreement to refuse passage on Japanese ships to German reservists bound for Germany.[63]	D
6 February	Britain	Norway	HMS COSSACK enters Norwegian territorial waters and, in defiance of Norwegian protests, liberates 299 British prisoners from the German ship ALTMARK (see Chapter 2). Successful.	D
10 May	Britain	Iceland	British cruisers BERWICK and GLASGOW, with destroyers FEARLESS and FORTUNE, land troops to occupy Iceland in case the Germans might otherwise be tempted to do so. Icelandic Prime Minister protested that neutrality and independence of Iceland had been violated, but changed his mind and made a broadcast that evening asking his people	C

1940

Date	Assailant	Victim	Incident	Type
			to treat British soldiers as their guests. Successful.[64]	

1941

Date	Assailant	Victim	Incident	Type
19 January	Britain	United States	'In order to clothe the arrival of our new Ambassador, Lord Halifax, in the United States with every circumstance of importance, I arranged that our newest and strongest battleship, the KING GEORGE V, with a proper escort of destroyers, should carry him and his wife across the ocean.'[65] From a nation in Britain's desperate straits, this was indeed an expressive gesture.	E
12 April	United States	Denmark	The Governor of South Greenland 'greatly disturbed and resentful' at the agreement concluded by the US government with the Danish Minister in Washington (who was disavowed and dismissed by his government) for the establishment of US defence facilities in Greenland, informs the US Consul at Godthaab that he would only be prepared to admit it as inevitable 'when faced with the *fait accompli*'. This is provided by the US Coast Guard cutters CAYUGA, NORTHLAND and MODOC (the last of which was to be twice mistaken, a month later, by the Royal Navy for the German battleship BISMARCK).[66] On 19 April the US Consul was to report that the Governor 'has exhibited	P

1941

Date	Assailant	Victim	Incident	Type
			a very co-operative attitude and a very realistic understanding'. Successful.[67]	
19 July	United States	Germany	US Navy ordered to escort ships of any nationality to and from Iceland. When US warships engaged in this un-neutral practice came into conflict with German submarines, President Roosevelt denounced German action as 'piracy', described their warships as 'the rattlesnakes of the Atlantic' and declared 'we have wished to avoid shooting. But the shooting has started and history has recorded who fired the first shot.'[68] Historians may also deduce a dual motive for the President's original intervention, which was purposeful in helping Britain, and catalytic in bringing the United States nearer to war with Germany.	P and C

1942

Date	Assailant	Victim	Incident	Type
6 November	United States	France	A British submarine HMS SERAPH under nominal US command picks up General Giraud (who had escaped from German captivity) from La Fosette on the French coast and takes him to Gibraltar so that his influence can be used to reconcile his compatriots to the Allied landing in French North Africa. The General was duly collected, but his influence did not come up to US expectations.[69]	D

1943

Date	Assailant	Victim	Incident	Type
8/9 September	Italy	Germany	Italian Fleet sails for Malta to surrender, attracting German air attack, but earning British diplomatic support: '... when the Italian fleet loyally and courageously joined the Allies, I felt myself bound to work with the King of Italy and Marshal Badoglio ...'[70]	E and P

1945

Date	Assailant	Victim	Incident	Type
October	United States	Soviet Union China	In an effort to help the Chinese Nationalists gain control of Manchuria before the communists do, the US Navy transport nationalist troops to Dairen and other ports but, when refused permission to land by local Soviet commanders and fired on by communist Chinese, Vice-Admiral Bailey did not persist and the communists had time to gain control. Unsuccessful.[71]	D

1946

Date	Assailant	Victim	Incident	Type
5 March	United States	Soviet Union	To encourage the Turkish government to resist Soviet territorial demands, the body of the deceased Turkish Ambassador to Washington is sent home in the battleship MISSOURI.[72] The US Secretary of State thought this gesture persuaded the Soviet Union to relax their pressure on Turkey.[73]	E
6 March	France	China	In the course of a dispute over the withdrawal from North Vietnam of the Chinese troops who had entered this French	P

1946

Date	Assailant	Victim	Incident	Type
			territory in the aftermath of war with Japan, the French cruiser EMILE BERTIN opens fire on troops at Haiphong. Results uncertain, but Chinese do go.[74]	
18 July	Britain	Iran Soviet Union	HMS NORFOLK and HMS WILD GOOSE sent to nearby Basra (Iraq) after rioting at the British oil refinery at Abadan (Iran) had been fomented by the Soviet-backed Tudeh party. Intervention in Iran was not needed (though British troops were landed at Basra in August), but outcome was salutary for British interests and a setback setback to Soviet influence.[75]	P
30 September	United States	Soviet Union Limitrophe Countries	US government announce that units of the US Navy will be permanently stationed in the Mediterranean to carry out US policy and diplomacy. They are still there and their presence has usually been to US advantage. Successful.[76]	C
22 October	Britain	Albania	An attempt to override Albanian objections and assert the right of innocent passage through the Corfu Straits (where HMS ORION and HMS SUPERB had been shelled by Albanian coastal batteries in May of that year) results in severe damage and loss of life to the British destroyers SAUMAREZ and VOLAGE in a freshly laid minefield. Although most of the mines were later removed by heavily escorted British	P

1946

Date	Assailant	Victim	Incident	Type
			minesweepers, the October venture was a costly fiasco.[77]	

1947

Date	Assailant	Victim	Incident	Type
	Britain	The future Israel and others	For most of the year British naval patrols in the Mediterranean intercepted and seized ships carrying Jewish illegal immigrants to Palestine, thereby hoping to placate Arabs and facilitate an agreed solution of the Palestine problem. Most ships were intercepted, but politically the operation was a complete failure (see Chapter 6).	P
18 March	United States	Soviet Union Satellites Greece	On the day that Congressional authorisation was sought for President Truman's programme of aid to Greece against communism, the US government announced that a strong naval squadron (including the carrier LEYTE) would visit Greek ports.[78]	E

1948

Date	Assailant	Victim	Incident	Type
28 February	Britain	Guatemala	Cruisers SHEFFIELD and DEVONSHIRE sent to Belize to deter Guatemala from prosecuting by force her claim to British Honduras. Successful.[79]	P
24 June	United States	Israel and Arab States	Three US destroyers assigned to Count Folke Bernadotte, UN Mediator for Palestine, 'to maintain peace between Arab and Israeli forces'. They did not succeed in this impossible task, but they did evacuate the UN team from Haifa in July 1948.[80]	C

1948

Date	Assailant	Victim	Incident	Type
November	United States	China	Some 1500 marines landed to reinforce US naval base at Tsingtao (abandoned in February 1949). Temporarily successful.[81]	P
November	Britain United States	China	Two US cruisers and British destroyer sent to Shanghai to protect nationals. Temporarily successful.[82]	P

1949

Date	Assailant	Victim	Incident	Type
19 April	Britain	China	HMS AMETHYST tries to ascend Yangtse to relieve the guard on HM Embassy at Nanking, but is driven aground by Communist artillery fire. Attempts at rescue, first by HMS CONSORT, later by HMS LONDON and BLACK SWAN, failed, but AMETHYST finally escaped to join the fleet on 31 July. A failure which presaged the end of gunboat diplomacy in the great rivers of China.[83]	P
April	Britain United States	China	Additional British and US cruisers sent to Shanghai for protection of their nationals. Temporarily successful.[84]	P
26 June	China	Britain United States	During Chinese civil war, Nationalists proclaim a blockade of the Chinese coast and, in spite of British and US protests, attack and capture British and US vessels. No lasting success.[85]	P

1950

Date	Assailant	Victim	Incident	Type
March	United States	Vietnam	Two US destroyers sent to Saigon to demonstrate US support for Bao Dai, but protest against visit led to	E

1950

Date	Assailant	Victim	Incident	Type
			serious rioting on 19 March. No great success.[86]	
27 June	United States	China	US Seventh Fleet patrols Taiwan Straits to prevent communists from invading Formosa or Nationalists from invading China. Successful.[87]	P
7 December	China	Japan	Japanese fishing vessel DAI-ICHI-UNZEN MARU seized by communist Chinese warship – the first of 158 vessels captured during the next four years before Japanese fishermen agreed to respect Chinese prohibited zones. Successful.[88]	D and P

1951

Date	Assailant	Victim	Incident	Type
June–October	Britain	Iran	During prolonged dispute with Iran about nationalisation of a British oil company, British warships are deployed as a standing threat of armed intervention to protect the oil refinery on the Iranian island of Abadan. The Iranians call the British bluff and the ships are eventually withdrawn.[89]	P
1 July	Egypt	Britain Israel	Egyptian corvette stops, plunders and damages British merchant ship in Gulf of Akaba as part of an attempted Egyptian blockade of Israel. Protests and resort to Security Council unavailing.[90]	P
14 July	Britain	Egypt	British destroyer flotilla sent to Red Sea to prevent further incidents. Agreement on procedures for British ships using the Gulf of Akaba reached on 26 July.[91]	P

1951

Date	Assailant	Victim	Incident	Type
24 October– 31 December	Britain	Egypt	British warships (altogether twenty-seven, but usually two cruisers at a time) employed to keep the Suez Canal open to shipping when Egyptian labour was withdrawn and clearance denied to British merchant ships. The cruisers protected an imported labour force and the Egyptians resumed normal working in February–March 1952. Successful.[92]	P and D

1952

Date	Assailant	Victim	Incident	Type
January	Britain	Egypt	After a *coup d'état* in Egypt, a large British naval force (including carrier HMS OCEAN) assembles off the Egyptian coast in case intervention is needed to protect British nationals in Egypt.[93]	C
12 September	United States	Soviet Union	President Tito goes to sea in the USS CORAL SEA to observe a fire-power demonstration during the visit to Split of this carrier with the cruiser SALEM and four destroyers.[94] Showing that US help was available – and acceptable – to Yugoslavia carried an obvious message for Marshal Stalin.[95]	E

1953

Date	Assailant	Victim	Incident	Type
January	Argentina	Britain	Argentine naval vessel lands a party and erects buildings to signify occupation of the disputed British territory of Deception Island. On 16 February the buildings are demolished and the intruders arrested and expelled by	E and D

1953

Date	Assailant	Victim	Incident	Type
			HMS SNIPE. Not a success for Argentina.[96]	
September	South Korea	Japan	South Korean naval vessels start seizing Japanese fishing boats crossing the so-called 'Rhee Line', which nobody else recognised.[97] This continued for two years, with the captive fishermen being exploited as hostages to gain concessions from Japan on other issues.[98]	E and D

1954

Date	Assailant	Victim	Incident	Type
May	United States	Britain Guatemala Others	In order to prevent the Guatemalan government from importing arms to resist a revolution got up by the CIA, the US government threaten a naval blockade and establish air-sea patrols in the Gulf of Honduras from 20 May to 7 June.[99] The British government are induced to discourage British ships from carrying arms.[100] Successful.	P
July	South Korea	Japan	A South Korean force is landed on the Takeshima Islands, long disputed between South Korea and Japan. A Japanese patrol boat that was later sent to investigate withdraws when fired on. A success for South Korea, by whom islands are henceforth occupied.[101]	D
26 July	United States	China	After six US nationals are killed on a British airliner shot down by Chinese fighters, two US aircraft-carriers (HORNET and PHILIPPINE SEA) are deployed and the C-in-C of the US	C

1954

Date	Assailant	Victim	Incident	Type
			Pacific Fleet announces that all his ships and aircraft have orders to be 'quick on the trigger'. Two Chinese aircraft were shot down, but the US government (unlike the British, who confined themselves to negotiations) got no apology from the Chinese, nor compensation. Unsuccessful.[102]	
16 November	Peru	Panama and others	Peruvian warships seized five Panamanian-registered whalers in unrecognised 200-mile zone. Other powers are victims in similar incidents. Successful.[103]	D

1955

Date	Assailant	Victim	Incident	Type
6–13 February	United States	China	US Seventh Fleet (with five carriers) evacuate Chinese nationalists from Tachen Islands, successfully deterring communist interference.[104]	D and P
18 May	United States	North Vietnam	US Navy complete the evacuation (begun on 16 August 1954) of 300,000 refugees from North Vietnam, a provision of the 1954 Geneva Agreements that might have been less fully implemented without naval intervention.[105]	D
3–9 August	South Korea	Japan	South Korean warships capture eleven Japanese fishing vessels, the crews being kept as hostages (see for 1953). Successful.[106]	P and C

1956

Date	Assailant	Victim	Incident	Type
October	United States	Britain France	Harassing tactics used by US Sixth Fleet against British	E

1956

Date	Assailant	Victim	Incident	Type
			and French warships to show US disapproval of Anglo-French intervention at Suez. Point made, but with less impact than US-sponsored run on the pound.[107]	
18 October	France	Germany	French warships arrest in international waters German freighter HELGA BODE carrying arms to Algerian rebels – one of many.[108]	D
31 October	United States	Egypt Britain France	US Sixth Fleet lands marines at Alexandria and elsewhere to protect evacuation of US citizens during Suez crisis. Successful.[109]	D

1957

Date	Assailant	Victim	Incident	Type
20 April	United States	Egypt Jordan Soviet Union[110] Syria	US naval transports with 1,800 marines aboard anchor off Beirut in readiness for intervention in Jordan (whose independence and integrity were regarded as threatened by Nasserist subversion) while the Sixth Fleet carried out manoeuvres in the Eastern Mediterranean. King Hussein succeeded in re-establishing his authority.	C
February–April	United States	Egypt	US destroyers patrol Straits of Tiran and Gulf of Akaba to prevent Egyptian interference with US merchant vessels bound for Israel. Successful.[111]	P

1958

Date	Assailant	Victim	Incident	Type
12–17 January	United States	Indonesia	Destroyer Division 31 asserts right of innocent passage through Lombok and Mahassai Straits after these	E

1958

Date	Assailant	Victim	Incident	Type
			had been claimed as territorial waters by Indonesia. Successful.[112]	
18 January	France	Yugoslavia	Yugoslav ship carrying arms to Algerian insurgents intercepted on high seas by French Navy. Arms seized. Successful.[113]	D
15 July	United States	Lebanon Syria Egypt Soviet Union	US Sixth Fleet lands marines in the Lebanon (see Chapter 2).	C
1 September	Britain	Iceland	Royal Navy protect British trawlers defying Icelandic ban on fishing within 12-mile limit. From 1 September 1958 to 14 March 1959, RN ships foiled sixty-five Icelandic attempts to arrest trawlers, but in the end the Icelandic case had to be conceded.[114]	P and C
7 September	United States	China	US Seventh Fleet ordered to escort Chinese Nationalist convoys to within 3 miles of Quemoy, so as to prevent Chinese Communist Navy from making their blockade effective. Successful, and no fighting involving US Navy. One of the aircraft-carriers employed was the USS ESSEX, sent via the Suez Canal after taking part in the Lebanon operation.[115]	P

1959

Date	Assailant	Victim	Incident	Type
12 February	South Korea	Japan	Aggrieved by Japanese repatriation of certain Koreans to the North, the South Koreans threaten to resume seizure of Japanese	P

1959

Date	Assailant	Victim	Incident	Type
			fishing vessels (see 1953). Partly successful.[116]	
26 February	United States	Soviet Union	USS R.O. HALE sends a party aboard the Soviet trawler NOVOROSSISK on the high seas after repeated breaks in the Atlantic submarine cables. No admissions, but no more breaks.[117]	P
7 April	France	Morocco Czecho-slovakia	French Navy intercept Czech freighter carrying arms to Morocco and confiscate arms as really destined for the Algerian rebels. Successful.[118]	D
24 April– 4 May	United States Colombia	Cuba	US and Colombian warships patrol coast of Panama to prevent any further landing of Cuban guerrillas, but the first group surrender and are disavowed by Cuban government.[119]	P

1960

Date	Assailant	Victim	Incident	Type
5 April	Nether-lands	Indonesia	To deter attacks by Indonesia on New Guinea, the Netherlands government announce despatch of carrier KAREL DOORMAN and two destroyers. No attacks are made, but reactions from Indonesia are damaging and those from third parties are adverse.[120]	P
July	United States	Congo	US carrier WASP arrives off coast ready to evacuate US citizens and, while there, delivers petrol to UN forces.[121]	P
17 November	United States	Cuba	After armed uprisings allegedly inspired by Cuba against the governments of Guatemala and Nicaragua, the carrier USS SHANGRI-LA	P

1960

Date	Assailant	Victim	Incident	Type
			and US destroyers patrolled the Caribbean coasts of these countries until 10 December 'to prevent intervention on the part of Communist-directed elements'. Successful.[122]	

1961

Date	Assailant	Victim	Incident	Type
15 April	United States	Cuba	Visible presence offshore of US fleet encourages a group of Cuban exiles organised by the CIA to attempt a landing meant to lead to the overthrow of Castro. Receiving no actual naval support, the bid fails.[123]	C
1 July	Britain	Iraq	After Iraqis claim sovereignty over Kuwait on 25 June and make menacing troop movements, Britain responds to Kuwaiti appeal for help by landing marines from HMS BULWARK. These are reinforced by tanks, troops and, ultimately, forty-five warships (including two aircraft-carriers). Ground forces replaced by Arab League troops on 19 October and Iraq recognises Kuwaiti independence on 4 October 1963. Iraqi aggression successfully deterred by quick British response.[124]	P
21 July	France	Tunisia	After an initial bombardment by aircraft from the carrier ARROMANCHES, the cruisers COLBERT, BOUVET and CHEVALIER-PAUL force the entrance to the Lake of Bizerta and, with the help of French troops, break the Tunisian blockade of the	P

1961

Date	Assailant	Victim	Incident	Type
			Bizerta naval base complex and re-establish French control. Successful in its immediate objectives, though France later made concessions.[125]	
19 November	United States	Dominican Republic	Visible presence offshore of US fleet(including carriers FRANKLIN D. ROOSEVELT and VALLEY FORGE with 1800 marines aboard) enables President Kennedy's representative to secure the expulsion of the Trujillos (the family of the late dictator) and the establishment of a government acceptable to the United States. Successful.[126]	P

1962

Date	Assailant	Victim	Incident	Type
15 January	Indonesia	Netherlands	Indonesian motor-torpedo-boats try to land infiltrators in New Guinea, but are caught by Netherlands Navy, who sink one and put rest to flight. Failure.[127]	C
16 May	United States	North Vietnam Laos Thailand	Carrier covers landing of US marines in Thailand, an operation intended to demonstrate US readiness to intervene if communists push their military success in Laos too far. Successful.[128]	E and P

1963

Date	Assailant	Victim	Incident	Type
21 February	France	Brazil	French destroyer TARTU sent to fishing grounds off north-east coast of Brazil after three French lobster boats had been seized by Brazilian warships 60 miles off the coast. Brazil	C and E

1963

Date	Assailant	Victim	Incident	Type
			countered with a cruiser, five destroyers and two corvettes, TARTU was soon withdrawn, and the effect of these moves (in which the two navies took it in turns to play the part of assailant) is open to question (see Chapter 4).	
26 February	United States	Dominican Republic	US aircraft-carrier BOXER anchors off Santo Domingo ready to send helicopters to rescue Vice-President Johnson in case of trouble during the latter's visit. Nothing happens.[129]	P and D
27 April	United States Britain	Haiti	US task force (with BOXER and 2000 marines) cruises off Haiti to protect US nationals in case of conflict between Haiti and Dominican Republic, perhaps also to intervene if government of Haiti is overthrown, but crisis blows over.[130] A British destroyer and frigate also stand by. US, but not British, nationals subsequently evacuated.	C
13 August	Cuba	Britain	Two Cuban warships land a party on a British island in the Bahamas to seize nineteen Cuban refugees and two fishing boats. Investigation by HMS LONDONDERRY reveals that the normally uninhabited island had been used by Cuban exiles based in the United States as a launching pad for their attacks on Cuba. Steps were taken to discourage the use of British territory for this purpose. A success for Cuba.[131]	D and P

1964

Date	Assailant	Victim	Incident	Type
12–20 January	Britain United States	Zanzibar	After Zanzibar government is overthrown by *coup d'état*, USS MANLEY, HMS OWEN and RHYL and RFA HEBE with one company of infantry evacuate US and some British nationals. Successful.[132]	D
20 January –19 March	Britain	Kenya Tanganyika Uganda	These three African governments having sought British assistance in subduing mutinies in their armies, three carriers (ALBION, CENTAUR and VICTORIOUS) are deployed with other warships and RFAs as well as two Marine Commandos and army units. Successful.[133]	P
	Turkey	Cyprus Britain	To reinforce their threat of armed intervention, failing the adoption of satisfactory measures for the protection of the Turkish minority in Cyprus:	P
29 January			Turkish fleet assembles off Iskanderun.	
15 February			The fleet sails.	
13 March			The fleet embarks troops. These threats brought a concession, but a lasting solution had to await actual intervention (see 1974).[134]	
2–5 August	North Vietnam	United States	US destroyers on patrol in the Gulf of Tongking are attacked by Northern Vietnames torpedo-boats.[135] Much about this incident is still obscure, but, if the attack was meant to discourage US naval interference, it failed, and US retaliation can be regarded as marking the moment when the conflict in	P

1964

Date	Assailant	Victim	Incident	Type
			Vietnam first assumed the character of war between the United States and North Vietnam.[136]	

1965

Date	Assailant	Victim	Incident	Type
28 April	United States	Dominican Republic	US Marines landed from aircraft-carrier to protect US citizens during civil war. Mission later extended to eradication of communist influence from Dominican government. By 6 May, the United States had 22,000 men ashore and 9000 afloat. By 3 September a provisional government acceptable to the United States had been established, but the final withdrawal of US forces took place only on 20 September 1966. Although its objectives were achieved, this protracted operation was both controversial and expensive ($150 million, but low casualties). Forty ships of the US Navy were involved.[137]	C
23 November –7 December	Britain	Rhodesia	Pending the arrival of British troops and military aircraft, the carrier HMS EAGLE cruises off the coast of Tanzania to allay the anxiety of Zambian government about the risk of air attacks from Rhodesia. Successful.[138]	C

1966

Date	Assailant	Victim	Incident	Type
10 April ·	Britain	Rhodesia	As authorised by the Security Council resolution of 9 April 1966, HMS BERWICK boards the Greek tanker MANUELA and persuades her not to continue her voyage to Beira. British naval patrol continues	P and E

1966

Date	Assailant	Victim	Incident	Type
			throughout the year to turn back tankers believed to be carrying oil for Rhodesia. Apparently successful in its limited objective (see Chapter 4).	
September –October	Britain	Argentina	HMS PUMA sent from Simonstown to Port Stanley after a 'symbolic' invasion of the Falklands by a group of private Argentine citizens and anti-British demonstrations in Argentina itself. PUMA stayed until 17 October, but the problem was solved by negotiation.[139]	E

1967

Date	Assailant	Victim	Incident	Type
24 May	Britain	Egypt	In response to Egyptian declaration of blockade of Straits of Tiran, British Prime Minister threatens joint action to assert rights of passage. British warships are held ready at Malta (including carrier VICTORIOUS) and in Red Sea (including carrier HERMES). United States (who have two carriers near Crete) are not keen, and nothing comes of this threat of purposeful force (denounced by the Egyptian Foreign Minister as gunboat diplomacy). But this loose talk later gives Nasser a pretext for his 'big lie' attributing the destruction on the ground of his air force to the British and US carriers rather than the Israeli air force. Widely believed, this triggers attacks on British and US nationals and interests. More than a failure for Britain: a damaging fiasco.[140]	P and C

1967

Date	Assailant	Victim	Incident	Type
8 June	Israel	United States	Israeli torpedo-boats and aircraft attack and cripple (34 dead, 171 wounded) the USS LIBERTY while this 'spy ship', on the high seas, was monitoring radio transmissions during the Six Day War. US Navy do not believe Israeli claim that ship was wrongly identified, but are not allowed to retaliate.[141]	D
10 July	Soviet Union	Israel	Soviet naval squadron visits Port Said (eight ships) and Alexandria (four ships) and its commander declares 'we are ready to cooperate with Egyptian forces to repel any aggression'.[142] Whether or not this had any impact on Israel, the gesture may have alleviated Arab disappointment at Soviet inaction in the Six Day War.	E
11 October– 25 January 1968	Britain	South Yemen	Task Force 318, with ten warships and more auxiliaries, though planned for other purposes, deploys off Aden to cover British withdrawal and, if need be, to protect or evacuate British civilians (see Chapter 4).	C

Note: 1967 was a year far richer in gunboat diplomacy than these few examples would suggest. The Royal Navy alone were involved in a dozen more incidents throughout the year and from the West Indies to Hong Kong.

1968

Date	Assailant	Victim	Incident	Type
23 January	North Korea	United States	North Korean naval craft put a stop to the use of spy ships for close electronic surveillance of their coast by capturing the USS PUEBLO and bringing the ship and her crew into port before	D and P

1968

Date	Assailant	Victim	Incident	Type
			US forces could intervene. US government later have to make humiliating concessions to obtain release of crew (see Chapter 2). Successful.	
24 January	United States	North Korea	US naval task force, including three carriers, assembles in Sea of Japan as part of US response to seizure of PUEBLO. It begins to disperse, without doing anything, on 6 February.[143] Probably unsuccessful.	C
6 February	Soviet Union	United States	Two Soviet cruisers and four destroyers enter Sea of Japan in a rather unconvincing show of support for North Korea.[144]	E
July	Soviet Union	Norway	In Exercise Sever, a large amphibious force sailed along the Norwegian coast from the Baltic to the Kola peninsula.[145] This was explained by the Soviet press as a reply to the NATO naval exercises of the previous month – 'needless to say, such a show of bellicosity in the immediate vicinity of our frontiers could not be ignored'.[146] (see Chapter 5.)	E

1969

Date	Assailant	Victim	Incident	Type
22 April	Iran	Iraq	Iranian warships escort Iranian merchant ship from Khorramshahr to the Persian Gulf in successful defiance of an Iraqi threat to stop any ships flying the Iranian flag from sailing through waters claimed by Iraq. For want of warships, Iran had yielded to a similar threat in 1961.[147]	P

1969

Date	Assailant	Victim	Incident	Type
22 April	United States	North Korea	Large US task force with four carriers sent to Sea of Japan after North Korean fighters shoot down a US surveillance aircraft on 15 April. Carriers provide fighter escorts for further reconnaissance flights. There was no reaction from North Korea, and Soviet Navy merely keep US ships under observation. Task force withdraw on 26 April.[148]	E and P
13 June	South Korea	North Korea	An armed North Korean vessel sent to pick up a spy from the South Korean island of Huksando is intercepted at sea and sunk by a South Korean destroyer.[149]	D
29 November	Spain	Britain	After changes in the Spanish government had prompted newspaper speculation that Spanish claims to Gibraltar might now no longer be pressed so vigorously, the Spanish helicopter carrier DEDALO and twelve other Spanish warships were sent to Algeciras Bay, apparently to demonstrate continued Spanish determination (see Chapter 2).	E

1970

Date	Assailant	Victim	Incident	Type
9 September onwards	United States	Syria Soviet Union	Sixth Fleet deployed in Eastern Mediterranean and subsequently reinforced in response to revolt in Jordan and invasion of that country by Syria. Successful.[150]	P
September–October	Soviet Union	United States	Soviet Mediterranean Squadron is reinforced to pose threat to Sixth Fleet, including occasional training of guns in response to vigorous US manoeuvres.	P

1970

Date	Assailant	Victim	Incident	Type
			Raises temperature, but does not deter.[151]	
22 November	Portugal	Guinea	Unsuccessful seaborne attack on Conakry.[152]	D
December	Soviet Union	Portugal	At request of Guinea, Soviet Navy begin coastal patrol to deter any repetition. Successful, but patrol continues for years after threat has vanished.[153]	P

1971

Date	Assailant	Victim	Incident	Type
11–16 January	Ecuador	United States	Ecuadorean warships seize eight US fishing vessels in unrecognised 200-mile zone. Vessels only released on payment of $500,000. Successful.[154]	D
29 November	Iran	Ras al Khaimah Iraq Britain	Iranian Navy seize Greater and Lesser Tumb islands at mouth of Persian Gulf, encountering resistance and inflicting casualties. Britain, about to relinquish her protectorate in the Gulf, did not intervene. Indignation aroused in Arab countries causes Iraq to retaliate against Iranian interests, and Libya to retaliate against British ones. But Iran keeps the islands.[155]	D
10 December	United States	India	Apparently to deter India from pushing to extremes her military victory over Pakistan, United States form task force centred on carrier ENTERPRISE and later send it into Bay of Bengal 'to insure the protection of US interests in the area'. The move certainly attracted attention, but the influence it exercised is open to question.[156]	E and C

1971

Date	Assailant	Victim	Incident	Type
			Much the same might be said of the Soviet response: deploying an anti-carrier group.	

Note: Meanwhile, the Royal Navy tried to get some diplomatic advantage out of their withdrawal from the Far East, forming a task force that, on the way home, could also beat an imperial retreat from the Gulf.

1972

Date	Assailant	Victim	Incident	Type
26 January– 7 February	Britain	Guatemala	HMS ARK ROYAL and PHOEBE sent to Belize to deter Guatemalan threat. Seemingly successful.[157]	P
5 September	Iceland	Britain	Icelandic gunboat cuts trawl wires of British fishing boat PETER SCOTT. Further incidents follow. British frigate deployed outside disputed zone on 7 September, but not yet involved.[158]	P ·
25 November	Iceland	West Germany	Gunboat AEGIR cuts trawl wires of German fishing boat. None of these incidents was intrinsically decisive, but, over the years, their constant repetition did the trick.[159]	P

1973

Date	Assailant	Victim	Incident	Type
21 February	Israel	Lebanon	Israeli missile boats land commandos to attack Palestinian guerrilla bases in the Lebanon. Tactical success, but deterrence not achieved.[160]	P
April	Spain	Morocco	Exchange of gunfire between Spanish and Moroccan warships over fishing rights. Incidents continue.[161]	P
20 May	Britain	Iceland	After continued Icelandic harassment of British fishing vessels, British warships enter exclusive zone claimed	P

1973

Date	Assailant	Victim	Incident	Type
			by Iceland to protect trawlers. Even before this happened, eighteen British frigates had been needed over the previous six months. Incidents and fishing continue.[162]	
28 June– 6 August	New Zealand Australia	France	New Zealand frigate OTAGO (relieved by CANTERBURY) supported by Australian naval auxiliary enters French nuclear-test danger zone off Mururoa to reinforce protests against French nuclear tests. As French eventually agree to conduct future tests underground, this may be considered a partial success.[163]	E
13 August	Iceland	Britain	Icelandic gunboat chases British trawler for 150 miles, but, owing to presence of British frigate, fails to make an arrest. One of many incidents between May and September.[164]	P
15 October	United States	Egypt Syria Soviet Union	Sixth Fleet establish a chain of communication and support across the Mediterranean to permit the airborne reinforcement of Israel. A success not otherwise achievable.[165]	D
25 October	United States	Soviet Union	Sixth Fleet reinforced and concentrated south of Crete as part of US response to threats of Soviet military intervention in Middle East. Successful.[166]	P
October	Soviet Union	United States Israel	Soviet Mediterranean Squadron steadily reinforced and aggressive Soviet surveillance of Sixth Fleet, as well as naval escort for seaborne supplies to the Arab states. Only the latter is successful.[167]	P

1974

Date	Assailant	Victim	Incident	Type
15–21 January	China	South Vietnam North Vietnam	Chinese warships do battle with South Vietnamese and land troops to occupy Paracel Islands, which are also claimed by North Vietnam.[168]	D
31 January	South Vietnam	China Philippines Taiwan	Troops landed to occupy Spratly Islands, which several countries claim. Successful.[169]	D
15 February	North Korea	South Korea	Gunboats sink alleged South Korean spy ship. Successful. Four similar incidents during rest of year.[170]	D
20 July	Turkey	Cyprus Greece Britain	Seaborne invasion and seizure of part of island. Successful.[171]	D
23 July	Britain	Turkey	After Turkish invasion, HMS HERMES and other British warships evacuate 2500 mainly British civilians from Kyrenia beach and reinforce British base at Dhekelia. Successful in its limited objectives.[172]	D
25 November	United States	Arab oil producers	US carrier CONSTELLATION enters Persian Gulf as a gesture intended to emphasise US objections to any interruption of oil supplies. Outcome uncertain.[173]	E

1975

Date	Assailant	Victim	Incident	Type
8–9 February	Spain	Morocco	Spanish naval task force sent to Ceuta and Melilla in response to Moroccan pressure against these enclaves. Outcome uncertain.[174]	P
12 April	United States	Cambodia	After US withdrawal from Indochina war, US carriers OKINAWA and HANCOCK send helicopters and marines to	D

1975

Date	Assailant	Victim	Incident	Type
			evacuate US citizens from Phnom Penh. Successful.[175]	
20 April	United States	North Vietnam	Five US carriers in similar operation in South Vietnam. Successful.[176]	D
12 May	Cambodia	United States	Cambodian patrol boat captures US merchant ship MAYAGUEZ.[177]	D
	United States	Cambodia	Rescue operations subsequently undertaken by carrier CORAL SEA assisted by destroyers and land-based aircraft. Crew released, but US marines incur needless casualties by attacking wrong island.[178]	D
5–8 November	Britain	Guatemala	HMS ZULU sent to patrol off coast of Belize (plus air and army reinforcements) in response to threatening Guatemalan concentration. Successful.[179]	P
15 November	Iceland	Britain	Harassment of British trawlers resumed after extension to 200 miles of Iceland's EEZ.[180]	P
25 November	Britain	Iceland	With the arrival of HMS LEOPARD and other ships, the Third Cod War begins.[181]	P
7 December	Indonesia	Fretilin	When Portuguese withdrawal from East Timor leads to the emergence of independence movement Fretilin, Indonesia undertakes naval bombardment and invasion as prelude to annexation. More of a military success than a political one.[182]	P

1976

Date	Assailant	Victim	Incident	Type
2 February	Iceland	Britain	After a brief truce for fruitless talks, Icelandic	P

1976

Date	Assailant	Victim	Incident	Type
			gunboats resume harassment and British frigates return. Incidents continue until May, when Britain finally has to concede the success of Iceland's gunboat diplomacy.[183]	
14–29 April	Vietnam	China Philippines Taiwan	Vietnamese Liberation Navy occupy Spratley Islands. China protests. Successful.[184]	D
18 July	Soviet Union	Signatories of Montreux Convention	Soviet aircraft-carrier KIEV transits Bosphorus and Dardanelles to assert Soviet interpretation of Montreux Convention.[185] Successful; and Soviet Union continued to send carriers through the Straits.	E
29 July	Greece Turkey	Turkey Greece	Both countries threaten use of naval force over despatch of Turkish seismic research vessel to disputed waters of Aegean. Nothing happens, though Greece mobilises Aegean Fleet on 1 September. Probably a success for Turkey.[186]	P
September	Israel	Lebanon Syria PLO	Israeli naval vessels patrolling in Lebanese waters intercept ships carrying arms to PLO forces in the Lebanon. Successful.[187]	D

1977

Date	Assailant	Victim	Incident	Type
April–May	France	Djibouti	In the run up to independence, eighteen French warships are deployed off Djibouti to provide reassurance and, if the need arose, evacuate French nationals. As France still had bases in Djibouti a dozen years later, success may be assumed.[188]	C

1977

Date	*Assailant*	*Victim*	*Incident*	*Type*
6 July	Britain	Guatemala	HMS ACHILLES sent to Belize, where occasional presence of a frigate had been needed for much of the year in response to threatening attitude of Guatemala. Successful.[189]	P
21 September– 1 October	Argentina	Soviet Union Bulgaria	Argentine Navy arrest (after firing and casualties) seven Soviet and two Bulgarian trawlers inside 200-mile zone. An incident noted in London as well as Moscow.[190]	P
12 October	Burma	Thailand	Burmese gunboat sinks Thai fishing boat and captures another, allegedly in Thai territorial waters. Outcome obscure.[191]	D
25 November– 19 December	Britain	Argentina	After signs of growing Argentine militance on Falklands issue, nuclear submarine DREADNOUGHT is deployed to Falklands waters with two frigates in distant support. It is still not clear whether Argentina had any inkling, but the crisis passed without trouble.[192]	C

1978

Date	*Assailant*	*Victim*	*Incident*	*Type*
6 January	Argentina	Chile	Twenty-five Argentine warships sail for Beagle Channel (in which ownership of certain islands is disputed with Chile) and later carry out exercises, C. in C. stating that navy is ready for action. This threat exercises an advantageous influence on subsequent negotiations.[193]	C
17 January	Soviet Union	Eritrea	Soviet warship alleged to have opened fire to assist defence of port of Massawa against Eritrean Liberation	C

1978

Date	Assailant	Victim	Incident	Type
			Front. If true, a rare instance.[194]	
January	Surinam	Guyana	Surinam allegedly uses gunboats to harass Guyanese nationals in a fisheries dispute eventually settled by negotiation.[195]	E
April	Britain France United States	Ethiopia Soviet Union	Warships of the three countries hold joint exercises off the Horn of Africa, which are denounced by Ethiopia and the Soviet Union as provocative.[196]	E
13 April	China	Japan	After Japanese repeat their claim to the Senkaku islands, China reacts by sending a flotilla of armed fishing vessels to manifest their disagreement. No Japanese naval reaction or clear result.[197]	E
29 December	United States	Iran Soviet Union	In response to chaos in Iran, CONSTELLATION task force is despatched to manifest US concern, but move is cancelled a few days later after Soviet complaints of 'gunboat diplomacy'. Outcome damaging to US prestige.[198]	E

1979

Date	Assailant	Victim	Incident	Type
21 July	South Korea	North Korea	Spy boat sunk on high seas.[199]	D
August	Canada	United States	Canadian ships seize nineteen US tuna boats in 200-mile zone off Pacific oast. US retaliate by embargoing Canadian tuna. Dispute continues.[200]	D
17 October	United States	Cuba	To manifest displeasure at presence of Soviet troops in Cuba, US navy carry out	E

1979

Date	Assailant	Victim	Incident	Type
			landing exercise in US enclave at Guantanamo Bay.[201]	
November	United States	Iran Soviet Union	After the US Embassy in Tehran is attacked and staff made hostages, two carrier battle groups are deployed in Indian Ocean. This long-lasting operation strains the resources of the US Navy, but has little discernible impact.[202]	C

1980

Date	Assailant	Victim	Incident	Type
24–25 April	United States	Iran	US Navy helicopters from USS NIMITZ in Arabian Sea attempt to rescue US hostages from US Embassy in Tehran. Mechanical failures cause the operation to be abandoned. An embarrassing failure.[203]	D
August	Libya	Italy	Libyan submarine and frigate drive Italian floating oil rig SAIPEM II away from disputed waters of Medina Bank.[204]	P
7 October	Britain	Iran Iraq	HMS COVENTRY and another British warship diverted to Gulf to start Armilla Patrol for 'protection of merchant shipping' during war between Iran and Iraq. Continued in later years with limited success.[205]	P

1981

Date	Assailant	Victim	Incident	Type
19 August	United States	Libya	Aircraft from carrier USS NIMITZ shoot down two oncoming Libyan aircraft while task force is in Gulf of Sirte to emphasise US rejection of Libyan claim that Gulf is in their territorial waters. Dispute persists.[206]	P

1981

Date	Assailant	Victim	Incident	Type
August	Iran	Denmark	Iranian Navy seize Danish ship carrying explosives to Iraq. The start of a long campaign against neutral shipping in the Gulf.[207]	D
September	Soviet Union	Poland	During a period of political disaffection in Poland, the Soviet naval exercise Zapad culminates in the landing of 6000 troops and marines on the Baltic coast close to the Polish border.[208]	E

1982

Date	Assailant	Victim	Incident	Type
2 April	Argentina	Britain	Argentine Naval Task Force 40 lands troops to seize Port Stanley, capital of the Falkland Islands. Initially successful, but leads to war and defeat of Argentina.[209]	D
3 May	United States	Cuba	In Exercise Ocean Ventura, US Navy land 400 marines at their enclave in Guantanamo Bay and evacuate 300 Americans. Cubans call it 'intimidating show of strength'.[210]	E
December	United States	Arab states Soviet Union	Fourteen warships of US Task Force 60 deployed off Lebanese coast carry out exercises, including bombing practice, to demonstrate US resolve.[211]	E

1983

Date	Assailant	Victim	Incident	Type
January	Argentina	Brazil	Argentine patrol boat turns back Brazilian naval survey vessel from Beagle Channel in assertion of disputed territorial claim.[212]	P
April	Spain	Britain	Three Spanish warships arrive in Algeciras Bay to express Spanish indignation	E

1983

Date	Assailant	Victim	Incident	Type
			at visit to Gibraltar of HMS INVINCIBLE in which HRH the Duke of York is serving.[213]	
August	South Korea	North Korea	South Korean warships sink a North Korean ship allegedly engaged in spying.[214]	D
September –December	France United States	Lebanon	Aircraft from French carrier bomb shore targets and USS NEW JERSEY bombards them to support peace-keeping force landed in 1982, but this is later withdrawn after terrorist attacks.[215]	C
25 October	United States	Grenada Cuba Britain	In Operation Urgent Fury, a US naval task force lands troops, in spite of indignant protest by British Prime Minister, to occupy island and replace left-wing government by one more acceptable to the United States.[216]	D

1984

Date	Assailant	Victim	Incident	Type
March	France	Spain	French patrol vessel attacks and captures two Spanish trawlers in Bay of Biscay, causing casualties.[217]	D
April	Soviet Union	United States	Carrier MINSK fires flare at US destroyer HAROLD HOLT, trailing her in South China Sea.[218]	E
June	United States Soviet Union Britain France	Iran Iraq	The naval powers manifest their continued concern at the maritime repercussions of the Iran–Iraq war by keeping warships in the Persian Gulf.[219]	C

1985

Date	Assailant	Victim	Incident	Type
August	United States	Canada	US Coast Guard send icebreaker POLAR SEA through North West Passage to dispute Canadian claim to territorial rights. Since 1957 there had been nine similar transits.[220]	E
10 October	United States	Egypt Libya PLO	Fighters from carrier USS SARATOGA intercept Egyptian airliner carrying Palestinian terrorists (who had hijacked cruise liner ACHILLE LAURO, murdering an American passenger) and force it to land at NATO air base in Sicily. Would have been more successful with greater Italian co-operation.[221]	P

1986

Date	Assailant	Victim	Incident	Type
January	Britain	South Yemen	Royal Yacht BRITANNIA, with discreet cover from British warships, evacuates civilians threatened by civil war.[222]	D
March	United States	Libya	Aircraft from carriers of the US Sixth Fleet sink Libyan patrol boats and attack anti-aircraft batteries after Libyan missiles are fired at US aircraft. One of several incidents in 1986 during a dispute over access to the Gulf of Sirte that lasted for most of the 1980s.[223]	P
September	Turkey	Greece	Turkish warships fire across bows of Greek patrol vessel off Lesbos.[224]	E
October	France	Panama	French fishery protection vessel ALBATROS sinks trawler SOUTHERN RAIDER off Réunion on personal orders	D

1986

Date	Assailant	Victim	Incident	Type
			of French Prime Minister. May have been mistaken for ship engaged in gunrunning.[225]	

1987

Date	Assailant	Victim	Incident	Type
May	New Zealand Australia	Fiji	Two New Zealand frigates and five Australian warships stand by to evacuate their nationals after civil disturbances.[226]	P
July–August	France	Iran	After Iranian attacks on French merchant ships, the French carrier CLEMENCEAU is sent to the Gulf and French Prime Minister declares: 'We have no aggressive intentions, but we want to be respected and we will be respected.'[227]	E
August	Colombia	Venezuela	Colombian frigate CALDAS tries to assert Colombian claims to sovereignty in the disputed waters of the Gulf of Venezuela, but eventually withdraws when confronted by superior Venezuelan force.[228]	P
August	India	Sri Lanka	Two Indian frigates lie off Colombo ready to evacuate Indian High Commission endangered by civil war.[229]	P
21 September	United States	Iran	After ships flying US flag are mined in the Gulf, naval commandos from frigate USS JARRETT seize the minelayer IRAN AJR.[230]	P
December	Britain	Iran	British warships SCYLLA and YORK protect merchant ships from attack by Iranian speedboats in the Gulf.[231]	P

Note: In spite of the efforts made by the naval powers (which did *not* include a proper system of convoy and escort), 178 merchant ships were attacked by Iran or Iraq in the Gulf during 1987.[232]

1987

Date	Assailant	Victim	Incident	Type
January	Canada	Haiti	Two destroyers sent to Caribbean in case Canadians are endangered by disturbances in Haiti.[233]	P
12 February	Soviet Union	United States	Frigate BEZZAVETNY and her consort try to 'shoulder' the inquisitive USS YORKTOWN and CARON out of Soviet territorial waters in the Black Sea. Diplomatic protests are exchanged.[234]	P
March	China	Vietnam	Chinese warships shell Vietnamese ships (sinking two) in running dispute over Spratlys.[235]	P
April	United States	Iran	After the frigate USS SAMUEL B. ROBERTS is mined in the Gulf, US Navy carry out reprisal attacks, sinking Iranian frigate SAHAND and other warships.[236]	P

1988

Date	Assailant	Victim	Incident	Type
April	Canada	France	Canadian fishery protection vessel seizes French trawler CROIX DE LORRAINE, arresting crew and passengers (including four French politicians). French Ambassador recalled.[237]	P
May	Australia	Vanuatu	Two Australian warships with 900 troops on board stand by to evacuate nationals endangered by riots and threaten intervention.[238]	P
November	India	Maldives	Indian frigate GODAVERI foils *coup d'état*, rescues hostages, and sinks ship carrying mercenaries.[239]	D

1989

Date	Assailant	Victim	Incident	Type
January	United States	Libya	Fighters from carrier USS KENNEDY shoot down two approaching Libyan aircraft 100 miles north of Tobruk.[240]	P

1989

Date	Assailant	Victim	Incident	Type
July	India	Sri Lanka	Indian carrier VIRAT sent to cruise off Colombo after Sri Lanka demands withdrawal of Indian troops. Probably had little impact.[241]	P
August	France	Lebanon	To support French efforts at mediation in civil war, carrier FOCH and other warships are deployed off the coast. Unsuccessful.[242]	P

1990

Date	Assailant	Victim	Incident	Type
January	United States	Colombia	Carrier USS KENNEDY and support ships sailed from US port to monitor Colombian coast for airborne drug traffic. Operation abandoned after Colombian protests.[243]	E
February	United States	Cuba Panama	Cuban government protest after US Coast Guard cutter fires on, and attempts to board, Panamanian-registered freighter HERMANN when she sails from Cuba for Mexico with a cargo of chromium. She was suspected of carrying drugs. Seemingly a fiasco.[244]	D
June	Britain France United States	Liberia	British, French and US warships deployed off Monrovia in readiness to evacuate nationals endangered by civil war. US ships evacuate 1600 in August and stand by until November. Successful.[245]	D and P
July	Britain	Trinidad	HMS BIRMINGHAM deployed to Trinidad in case her help was needed during attempted *coup d'état* by Islamic fundamentalists.[246]	P

1990

Date	Assailant	Victim	Incident	Type
September	West African Peace-keeping Force	Liberia	Five West African states land a peace-keeping force in Liberia to deal with civil war. Fighting, including action by warships, still continuing two years later.[247]	P

1991

Date	Assailant	Victim	Incident	Type
January	United States	Somalia	After attacks on US Embassy in Mogadishu, armed helicopters from USS GUAM and TRENTON carry out opposed evacuation of 281 people of thirty different nationalities. Successful.[248]	D
July	Britain	Grenada	HMS AMBUSCADE diverted to Grenada to reassure the island's Prime Minister, who feared civil unrest.[249]	P

Notes and References

INTRODUCTION

1. T.B. Millar, *The Indian and Pacific Oceans: Some Strategic Considerations*, Adelphi Paper no. 57 (London: Institute for Strategic Studies, May 1969).
2. See A. Preston and J. Major, *Send a Gunboat* (London: Longman, 1967), for the earlier history.
3. See also the Chronological Appendix.
4. See, for instance, M. Small and J.D. Singer, *Resort to Arms: International and Civil Wars 1816–1980* (Beverly Hills: Sage Publications, 1982).
5. To enforce the claims of Don Pacifico, a British subject (just) resident in Athens.
6. R.D. Colvin, 'Aftermath of the Eilath', *United States Naval Institute Proceedings*, October 1969.
7. A German aircraft had bombed and damaged the Russian battleship SLAVA as early as 1915; see M.G. Saunders (ed.), *The Soviet Navy* (London: Weidenfeld & Nicolson, 1958) p. 50.
8. Admiral J.D. Watkins USN, *The Maritime Strategy* (Annapolis: US Naval Institute, January 1986), and H.L. Garrett, Admiral F.B. Kelso, General Gray, article in *United States Naval Institute Proceedings*, April 1991.
9. Sir Isaac Newton, *The Mathematical Principles of Natural Philosophy, Definition III*, trans. from the Latin by A. Motte and published by Benjamin Motte at the Middle Temple Gate in 1729.

1 DEFINITIONS

1. Lewis Carroll, *Alice Through the Looking Glass* (London: Nonesuch Press, 1963).
2. On 25 October 1917, when the threat of bombardment and the use of her sailors ashore led to the capitulation of the Kerensky government to the Bolsheviks. Historians cannot agree as to whether the cruiser fired live rounds or not.
3. J. Symons, *The General Strike* (London: Cresset Press, 1957) p. 53.
4. Vice-Admiral Muselier has written his own first-hand account: chapters 22–24 of *De Gaulle Contre le Gaullisme* (Paris: Editions du Chêne, 1946). See also the Bibliography.
5. C. von Clausewitz, *On War*, trans. J.J. Graham (Harmondsworth: Penguin Books, 1968) p. 101.
6. A. Buchan, *War in Modern Society* (London: Watts, 1966).
7. See J. Barlow Martin, *Overtaken by Events* (New York: Doubleday, 1966) *passim*.

2 PRINCIPLES AND PRECEDENTS

1. *Fowler's Modern English Usage* (Oxford: Oxford University Press, 2nd edn 1965).
2. Use of local force to create or remove a *fait accompli*. See G. Hugo, *Britain in Tomorrow's World* (London: Chatto & Windus, 1969) chapter 5.
3. *Instilling Fra Undersøkelsekommisjonen av 1945* (Oslo, 1947) Bilag I.
4. R. Omang, *Altmark-Saken 1940* (Oslo: Gyldendal Norsk Forlag, 1953).
5. The whole of this section is based on, and the quotations taken from Omang, op. cit., and the *Instilling* of 1945.
6. Intelligence reports from Bergen, confirmed later by aircraft of Coastal Command RAF, were the first definite reports of her location since the previous December and these reached C-in-C Home Fleet at 1710 on 15 February. See S.W. Roskill, *The War at Sea* (London: HMSO, 1954) vol. I, pp. 151–3.
7. Sir P. Vian, *Action This Day* (London: Frederick Muller, 1960) *passim*.
8. Ibid.
9. Norwegian time.
10. He may have been stretching a point here, as he does not appear to have received specific instructions at this stage, but Admiral Forbes was doubtless rightly confident that a generous and informed interpretation would be given to his order: 'ALTMARK your objective'.
11. Vian, op. cit.
12. It was one of the incidental Anglo-Norwegian controversies arising from this incident as to whether or not Captain Vian had ever uttered the first clause of his instructions. See *Correspondence Respecting the German Steamer* ALTMARK (London: HMSO, 1950) Command 8012.
13. Captain Halvorsen's report in Omang, op. cit.
14. Captain Halvorsen asked Captain Vian: 'If there are no prisoners on board ALTMARK – what then?' and received the reply, 'That will be a mistake from my government's side' (Doc. 89 in Omang, op. cit.).
15. In the latter case, army officers were also involved, though the commander of the Norwegian patrol vessel POL III was the first to take action and shore-based naval torpedoes dealt the *coup de grâce*. See J.L. Moulton, *The Norwegian Campaign of 1940* (London: Eyre & Spottiswoode, 1966) *passim*.
16. Article 17 of *Alminnelig Instruks for Sjøforsvarets Sjefer under Nøytralitetsvern*. See Omang, op. cit.
17. Omang, op. cit., Doc. 26.
18. 'The US imperialist aggressors have lately gone so far as to infiltrate boats carrying espionage and subversive elements' (*New York Times*, 25 January 1968).
19. Statement by Major-General Pak Chung Kook, the North Korean delegate, at the meeting of the Military Armistice Commission at Panmunjon on 24 January 1968 (*New York Times*, 26 January). The document finally signed by Major-General Gilbert H. Woodward on 23 December 1968 admitted 'the validity of the confessions of the crew of the USS PUEBLO' and that the ship 'had illegally intruded' into North

Korean territorial waters, apologised for espionage, and promised not to do it again. By a procedure of which Mr Rusk said, 'I know of no precedent', signature was preceded by Woodward's oral statement that its contents were untrue (*Washington Post*, 23 December 1968).

20. In testimony to the House Foreign Affairs Committee on 24 January 1968 (*Keesing's Contemporary Archives*).

21. 'At the 260th meeting of this commission held four days ago, I again registered a strong protest with your side against having infiltrated a number of armed spy boats ... and repeatedly demanded that you immediately stop such criminal acts' (General Pak on 24 January, *New York Times*, 26 January 1968).

22. Televised address on 26 January as reported by *International Herald Tribune*, 27 January 1968.

23. By a curious coincidence, one of the most extended examples of the use of this technique had been given by the government of South Korea, which had exploited many hundreds of Japanese hostages to secure concessions from the government of Japan between 1953 and 1959 (see the Chronological Appendix). The government of South Korea did not, however, venture to extend this technique to their relations with the Soviet union and denied that their naval vessels had, as charged by the Soviet Union, made an unsuccessful attack on the Soviet survey ship UNGO off the Korean coast on 28 December 1959.

24. *The Times*, 1 February 1968.

25. In the statement of 24 January previously quoted.

26. 'The Pentagon never admitted it publicly until the plane was lost, but all ship surveillance of the North Korean coast was discontinued after the PUEBLO was seized' (*Christian Science Monitor*, 21 April 1969).

27. Lt Murphy's account in *Christian Science Monitor*, 17 June 1969.

28. See the Chronological Appendix.

29. For an analysis of US problems in the PUEBLO affair, see G. Hugo, *Appearance and Reality in International Relations* (London: Chatto & Windus, 1970) chapter 2.

30. See the Chronological Appendix.

31. See J. Cable, *Navies in Violent Peace* (London: Macmillan, 1989) pp. 49–56, and M. Adkin, *Urgent Fury: The Battle for Grenada* (London: Leo Cooper, 1989) *passim*.

32. *Keesing's Record of World Events*.

33. C.A. Macartney, *October Fifteenth: A History of Modern Hungary 1929–1945* (Edinburgh: Edinburgh University Press, 1956) part II, chapter XVIII.

34. C.M. Woodhouse, *Something Ventured* (London: Granada Publishing, 1982) *passim*.

35. Governments engaged in disputes may proclaim that their quarrel is only with the leaders, not the people, of the opposing state, but tend in practice to regard ordinary people as more legitimate victims of violence than politicians. The British government, for instance, rejected proposals for the assassination of Hitler, and Saddam Hussein, unlike thousands of his subjects, survived for years after the Gulf War.

36. See the Chronological Appendix.

37. See Chapter 4.

38. See J. Barros, *The Corfu Incident of 1923* (Princeton University Press, 1965), where it is argued that the unknown assassins operated without the knowledge or complicity of the Greek government, who did their unavailing best to clear up the crime.
39. Quoted in Barros, op. cit. The last paragraph referring to the Conference of Ambassadors has been omitted.
40. See Barros, to whose book, which is by no means partial to Italy, this account is heavily indebted.
41. Barros, op. cit.
42. For all these instances, see the Chronological Appendix.
43. Barros, op. cit.
44. G.V. McClanahan, *Diplomatic Immunity* (London: Hurst, 1989) pp. 147–53.
45. Jane Austen, *Northanger Abbey* (London: J.M. Dent, 1936) (first pub. 1818) p. 211.
46. See Lt F.C. Miller USN, 'Those Storm-Beaten Ships upon which the Arab Armies Never Looked', *United States Naval Institute Proceedings*, March 1975.
47. S.S. Roberts, 'Superpower Naval Confrontations', in B. Dismukes and J. McConnell (eds), *Soviet Naval Diplomacy* (New York: Pergamon Press, 1979) p. 204.
48. Roberts, op. cit., and H. Kissinger, *Years of Upheaval* (London: Weidenfeld & Nicolson/Michael Joseph, 1982) *passim*.
49. Roberts, op. cit., p. 210. It is in describing this crisis that Roberts takes issue with the author's view that submarines are ill-suited to the use of limited naval force, arguing (his p. 212) that the US Navy would have taken it for granted that Soviet submarines were present. This begs the question. Could a submerged submarine have done anything but *sink* a carrier – or some other US warship – and would anyone have regarded this as *limited* force? See, however, Lt Brent A. Ditzler USN, 'Naval Diplomacy Beneath the Waves' (unpublished thesis) for a more generalised defence of the submarine's role.
50. See Article III (6) of the *Agreement* in J. Goldblat (ed.), *Agreements for Arms Control* (London: Taylor & Francis, 1982) p. 196. The 1893 incident, on the other hand, was swiftly and decently resolved, not by any treaty but by the principles of gentlemanly behaviour then customary among naval officers. The French Admiral, on his own initiative, sent his offending captain to apologise (Viscount Grey of Fallodon, *Twenty-five Years* (London: Hodder & Stoughton, 1925) p. 14).
51. Quoted in B. Ranft and G. Till, *The Sea in Soviet Strategy* (Basingstoke: Macmillan, 2nd edn 1989) p. 178.
52. Kissinger, op. cit., pp. 602–13.
53. Quoted in A. Dowty, *Middle East Crisis* (University of California Press, 1984) p. 260.
54. See G. Bennet, *Cowan's War* (London: Collins, 1963); S.W. Page, *The Formation of the Baltic States* (Harvard University Press, 1959); R.H. Ullman, *Britain and the Russian Civil War* (Princeton University Press, 1968) vol. 2; S. Roskill, *Naval Policy Between the Wars* (London: Collins, 1968) vol. I, p. 144.

55. Ibid., pp. 144–5.
56. D.M. Mercer, 'The Baltic Sea Campaign', *United States Naval Institute Proceedings*, September 1962.
57. Roskill, op. cit., p. 147.
58. Ullman, op. cit., pp. 259–60.
59. Page, op. cit., *passim*.
60. Though Finnish representatives in London explained to Lord Curzon as late as 7 May 1919 the apprehensions entertained by the Finnish government of a Russian naval attack. See S. Jägerskiöld, *Riksföreståndaren Gustaf Mannerheim 1919* (Helsingfors: Holger Schildts Förlag, 1969) p. 170.
61. 'We must be ready, in the last resort, to use force to bring Nasser to his senses' (Eden to Eisenhower, 27 July 1956; quoted in A. Eden, *Full Circle* (London: Cassell, 1960) p. 428).
62. This authorised the President 'to employ the armed forces of the US as he deems necessary to protect the territorial integrity and political independence of any such nation or group of nations requesting such aid against overt armed aggression from any nation controlled by international Communism'.
63. F. Qubain, *Crisis in Lebanon* (Washington: Middle East Institute, 1961).
64. These unhappy victims thus paid for their zeal in intercepting a consignment of arms on the previous day.
65. Although most Muslims tended to support one side and most Christians the other, this was not a straightforward religious conflict. President Chamoun retained the loyalty of his Muslim Prime Minister and of Kamal Jumblatt's principal Druze rival, while a number of Christians initially co-operated with the rebels.
66. C. Chamoun, *Crise au Moyen-Orient* (Paris: Gallimard, 1963) p. 414.
67. See Marine Corps Historical Branch G3, *Marines in Lebanon 1958* (Washington, 1966).
68. Though the US Ambassador had told Chamoun on the 14th that he should appeal to the Security Council and seek diplomatic support from other Arab governments. R. McClintock, 'The American Landing in Lebanon', *United States Naval Institute Proceedings*, October 1962.
69. Robert Murphy, President Eisenhower's special envoy to the Lebanon, says the UN observers operated only in the daytime, leaving the frontier open at night (R. Murphy, *Diplomat Among Warriors* (New York: Doubleday, 1964) p. 448).
70. Chamoun, op. cit., p. 423: [in total contrast with the rejoicing in Baghdad] 'a great fear gripped every supporter of a peaceful and independent Lebanon. Their morale, long sorely tried, suddenly plumbed the depths of disaster.'
71. Formally, this request was addressed, as that of 11 May had been, to Britain and France as well, but it was understood that the effective response would be American, with British forces being earmarked for Jordan and the French committed in Algeria. Chamoun himself, however, thought the Sixth Fleet to be so far away that they would need forty-eight hours, and thus asked for interim British and French help within twenty-four hours. See McClintock, op. cit.

72. As C-in-C Specified Command, Middle East.
73. D. Heinl, *Soldiers of the Sea* (Annapolis: US Naval Institute, 1962). When the transport planes did arrive, they landed at an airport first secured by seaborne marines. The same was true of the British operation at Kuwait in 1961.
74. Murphy, op. cit., p. 455.
75. Murphy, op. cit., p. 433.
76. So have some Americans, notably Miles Copeland in his interesting book *The Game of Nations* (London: Weidenfeld & Nicolson, 1969). The US government probably could have imposed a settlement more favourable to US interests, but could they then have withdrawn and avoided further intervention?
77. Soviet statement of 17 July 1958, Tass.
78. *Documents on German Foreign Policy*, Series D, vol. III, Doc. 27 (London: HMSO, 1951).
79. On 26 July; see H. Thomas, *The Spanish Civil War* (London: Eyre & Spottiswoode, 1961) p. 228.
80. It has been suggested that the presence of DEUTSCHLAND also prevented the Republican battleship JAIME I from bombarding Ceuta, but this may have been no more than a coincidence. See D.A. Puzzo, *Spain and the Great Powers 1936–1941* (Columbia University Press, 1962).
81. See Chapter 4.
82. *The Observer*, 30 November 1969.
83. *Keesing's Contemporary Archives.*

3   THE ALTERED ENVIRONMENT

1. Captain First Rank K. Penzin, 'The Changing Methods and Forms of Warfare at Sea', *Soviet Military Review*, March 1967.
2. Even the Koreans, though newcomers to gunboat diplomacy in the twentieth century, have a naval tradition as ancient as that of Britain and much older than that of the United States.
3. See Chapter 2.
4. When the bombs were dropped on Hiroshima and Nagasaki, it is arguable that neither side realised what was at stake.
5. Even in the extreme case of the Cuban Missile Crisis, enormous effort and expenditure were needed to demonstrate the serious intent of President Kennedy's words about treating 'any nuclear missile launched from Cuba against any nation in the Western Hemisphere as an attack by the Soviet Union on the United States, requiring a full retaliatory response upon the Soviet Union', (Broadcast of 22 October 1962, quoted in R. Kennedy, *13 Days* (London: Macmillan, 1969) pp. 134–5).
6. See Chapter 2.
7. To whom the Soviet Union had supplied not only aircraft, but also a dozen motor-torpedo-boats, then at Basra.
8. They were all three sunk in succession on 21 September 1914 by the same German submarine.

9. See the Chronological Appendix.
10. In 1946. See the Chronological Appendix.
11. Admiral D.E. Jeremiah, 'Beyond the Cold War', *United States Naval Institute Proceedings*, May 1992.
12. Admiral E. Zumwalt, *On Watch* (New York: Quadrangle, 1976) pp. 72–3.
13. See, for instance, Lt E.J. Rogers USN, 'Mines Wait but We Can't', *United States Naval Institute Proceedings*, August 1982.
14. J. Cable, *Navies in Violent Peace* (Basingstoke: Macmillan, 1989) p. 64.
15. Lt E. Fortin USN, 'Those Damned Mines', *United States Naval Institute Proceedings*, July 1992.
16. In 1941 an hour's steady shelling by two battleships at close range failed to sink the already crippled BISMARCK, which had to be finished off with torpedoes. Today, one hit could destroy the mightiest of US carriers.
17. *The Times*, 2 July 1992.
18. *The Times*, 10 November 1992, and L. Barrett, article in *West Africa*, no. 3923, of 23 November 1992.
19. Isaac Newton, *The Mathematical Principles of Natural Philosophy*; see n. 9 in Introduction.
20. Efforts to condemn Indian seizure of Goa or US intervention in Cuba or Grenada failed to secure the requisite support in the United Nations.
21. This is an over-statement where Germany is concerned, but it was the implication of the Locarno Agreement.
22. See the Chronological Appendix (1924) for an interesting exception to this rule.
23. This island quarrel had much earlier origins and, at one time or another, many more parties. See M.S. Samuels, *Contest for the South China Sea* (London: Methuen, 1982) *passim*.
24. Quoted in *United States Naval Institute Proceedings*, February 1981.
25. B. Urquhart, 'United Nations Diplomacy in 1990', in D.D. Newsom (ed.), *The Diplomatic Record 1990–1991* (Boulder, Colorado: Westview Press, 1992).
26. A. Waley, *The Opium War Through Chinese Eyes* (London: George Allen & Unwin, 1958) p. 33.
27. Cable, op. cit., p. 100, and *The Times*, 5 October 1989.

4 OPERATIONS AND CAPACITIES

1. The then US Secretary of the Navy in a speech of 7 May 1925 to the Connecticut Chamber of Commerce. Quoted in L.T. Beman, *Intervention in Latin America* (New York: H.W. Wilson, 1928).
2. The International Institute for Strategic Studies, *The Military Balance 1991–1992* (London: Brassey's, 1991).
3. Secretary of State for Defence, *Statement on the Defence Estimates 1966*, Part I: *The Defence Review* (London: HMSO) Cmnd 2901, p. 10.
4. *Statement on the Defence Estimates 1971* (London: HMSO) Cmnd 4592, p. 12.

5. See Chapter 2.
6. See Chapter 3.
7. See the Chronological Appendix.
8. *Le Monde*, 25 February 1963. In the context, this ambivalent phrase may be rendered as 'to express resentment'.
9. The particulars are to be found in an interesting scrap-book, entitled HMS ROYAL OAK *1936–1938 Commission: Executive Officer's Log*, in the National Maritime Museum at Greenwich. Quoted by kind permission of the Trustees.
10. *File ADM 116 3679* in Public Record Office, Kew.
11. H. Thomas, *The Spanish Civil War* (London: Eyre & Spottiswoode, 1964) pp. 456–7, and 475–6.
12. C.E. Hernandez Gonzalez, 'The CALDAS Incident', *United States Naval Institute Proceedings*, March 1988.
13. L. Freedman and V. Gamba-Stonehouse, *Signals of War* (London: Faber & Faber, 1990) pp. 117–20.
14. *Le Monde*, 18 and 22 April 1967.
15. Admiral Cabanier, 'Evolution de la Marine Française', *Revue de Défense Nationale*, July 1965.
16. See F.C. Gregory, 'The Beira Patrol', *RUSI Journal*, December 1969, for an interesting analysis.
17. E.J. Grove, *Vanguard to Trident: British Naval Policy since World War II* (London: Bodley Head, 1987) p. 301.
18. Hansard, vol. 789, col. 299.
19. Minister of State, Foreign Office, in the House of Commons, 19 June 1967. Hansard, cols 1256–7.
20. This was the objective assigned by Sir Winston Churchill to HMS PRINCE OF WALES and REPULSE on their brief incursion into Far Eastern waters in 1941, but the disastrous outcome of that venture in the face of superior Japanese forces about to launch their planned offensive need seldom be feared in the ordinary crises of peacetime. See W.S. Churchill, *The Grand Alliance* (London: Cassell, 1950) chapter 32.
21. IISS, op. cit.
22. Article 9: '... the Japanese people forever renounce war as a sovereign right of the nation and the threat or use of force as a means of settling international disputes. ... land, sea and air forces, as well as other war potential will never be maintained'.
23. But see Lt Col. T.M.P. Stevens, 'A Joint Operation in Tanganyika', *RUSI Journal*, February 1965, for an interesting analysis of the military problems that might have arisen.
24. A.N. Shulsky, 'Coercive Diplomacy', in B. Dismukes and J. McConnell (eds), *Soviet Naval Diplomacy* (New York: Pergamon Press, 1979) pp. 130–3.
25. See P. Gilchrist, *Sea Power: The Coalition and Iraqui Navies* (London: Osprey Publishing, 1991).
26. M. Middlebrook, *Task Force: The Falklands War 1982*, (Harmondsworth: Penguin Books, 1987) pp. 182–3.
27. Grove, op. cit., pp. 330–3.
28. IISS, op. cit.

29. In retaliation for the bombing by Spanish Republican aircraft of the German pocket battleship DEUTSCHLAND (Thomas, op. cit., pp. 440–1).
30. 'Operation Attila', *Armies and Weapons*, no. 14, November/December 1974.
31. M.S. Samuels, *Contest for the South China Sea* (London: Methuen, 1982) and *The Times*, 4 June 1988.
32. J. Cable, *Navies in Violent Peace* (Basingstoke: Macmillan, 1989) p. 52.
33. IISS, op. cit. Repeated reports of the sale of the uncompleted ex-Soviet aircraft-carrier VARYAG to China were contradicted in *Jane's Defence Weekly*, vol. 18, no. 2, of 21 November 1992.
34. G.W. Hunt, British music hall song, 1878.
35. Quoted in Lt Com. Bruce Harlow USN, 'The Legal Use of Force – Short of War', *United States Naval Institute Proceedings*, November 1966.
36. 'La Défense: la Politique Militaire Française et Ses Réalisations', *Notes et Etudes Documentaires*, no. 3343 of 6 December 1966 (Paris: Secrétariat Général du Gouvernement).

5 IN THE ABSENCE OF THE SOVIET UNION

1. H.F. Lyte, *Hymns Ancient and Modern*.
2. E. Gibbon, *The History of the Decline and Fall of the Roman Empire* (London: Chatto & Windus, 1875) (first pub. 1783) pp. 1 and 641.
3. S. White, *Gorbachev and After* (Cambridge: Cambridge University Press, 1992) p. 15.
4. 'For a bad government the most dangerous moment usually comes when it starts to reform itself' (A. de Tocqueville, *L'Ancien Régime* (Paris, 1856) Book III, chapter IV).
5. IISS, *The Military Balance 1992–1993* (London: Brassey's, Autumn 1992) p. 218.
6. IISS, *Strategic Survey 1991–1992* (London: Brassey's, May 1992) pp. 25–26.
7. T. Rakowska-Harmstone, 'Warsaw Pact Cohesion and the Crisis of 1989–90: Demographic Trends and Ethnic Conflict', in L. Freedman and J. Saunders (eds), *Population Change and European Security* (London: Brassey's, 1991) pp. 249–50.
8. *Current Digest of the Post-Soviet Press*, 26 August 1992; *Moscow News*, no. 16, 19–26 April 1992; *The Times*, 20 October 1992.
9. E.F. Mickolus, T. Sandler and J.M. Murdoch, *International Terrorism in the 1980s* (Iowa State University Press, 1989).
10. *Moscow News*, no. 14, 5–12 April 1992.
11. Admiral Sergei Gorshkov, quoted in B. Ranft and G. Till, *The Sea in Soviet Strategy* (Basingstoke: Macmillan, 2nd edn., 1989) p. 222.
12. Ibid., pp. 236–7.
13. B. Dismukes and J. McConnell (eds), *Soviet Naval Diplomacy* (New York: Pergamon Press, 1979).
14. See Chapter 1.

15. B. Watson, *Red Navy at Sea: Soviet Naval Operations on the High Seas 1956–1980* (Boulder, Colorado: Westview Press, 1982) pp. 62 and 156.
16. Ranft and Till, op. cit., pp. 228–9.
17. Watson, op. cit., p. 116.
18. 'The Impact on Norway of the Growth of the Soviet Navy', in J. Skogan and A.O. Brundtland (eds), *Soviet Seapower in Northern Waters* (London: Pinter Publishers, 1990).
19. See W. Agrell, 'The Impact of "Alien Underwater Activity": Swedish Security Policy and Soviet War Planning in the Baltic Area 1972–88', in ibid.
20. Watson, op. cit., p. 142 and *passim* for the whole voyage of MINSK.
21. According to *Jane's Defence Weekly* (vol. 18, no. 21) of 21 November 1992, MINSK has since been sold for scrap, other ships were likely to follow, and the only Russian carriers still in commission were the ADMIRAL KUZNETSOV and the ADMIRAL GORSHKOV in the Northern Fleet. However, the notion that China might buy an ex-Soviet carrier was not quite dead even in 1993, when *The Observer* of 16 April suggested NOVOROSSIYSK as the chosen vessel.
22. David R. Jones (ed.), *Soviet Armed Forces Review Annual Vol 9 1984–1985* (Gulf Breeze: Academic International Press, 1986) pp. 87–8.
23. *The Times*, 4 April 1984.
24. V. Solvyov and E. Klepikova, *Boris Yeltsin: A Political Biography* (London: Weidenfeld & Nicolson, 1992) p. 275.

6 THE FUTURE OF GUNBOAT DIPLOMACY

1. A.C. Swinburne, *'The Triumph of Time'* in *Selected Poems* (London: Macmillan, 1950) p. 35.
2. *The Times*, 19 January 1993.
3. H. Thomas, *The Spanish Civil War* (London: Eyre & Spottiswoode, 1964) pp. 440–2.
4. P. Fleming, *The Siege at Peking* (London: Rupert Hart-Davis, 1959) *passim*.
5. Ibid.
6. IISS, *Strategic Survey 1990–1991* (London: Brassey's 1991) *passim*.
7. *Correspondence Militaire de Napoléon Ier, publiée par ordre du Ministère de la Guerre tome cinquième* (Paris: E. Plon et Cie, 1876) p. 451: 'In war, three-quarters of the business is determined by morale, only a quarter by the physical balance of forces.'
8. J. Cable, *Intervention at Abadan* (Basingstoke: Macmillan, 1991) p. 28.
9. E.J. Grove, *Vanguard to Trident* (London: Bodley Head, 1987) pp. 155–8.
10. *The Times*, 16 January 1993.
11. C. Blanchet and B. Dard, *Statue of Liberty*, trans. Bernard A. Weisberger (New York: American Heritage, 1985) p. 118.
12. IISS, op. cit., pp. 37–48.
13. *The Times*, 16 February 1993.

14. K. Booth, *Law, Force and Diplomacy at Sea* (London: George Allen & Unwin, 1985) p. 208.
15. D. Cheney, Secretary of Defense, *Annual Report to the President and Congress, February 1992* (Washington: US Govt Printing Office) p. 78. Since 1979 US military ships and aircraft have exercised their rights and freedoms in all oceans against the objectionable claims of more than thirty-five countries at the rate of some thirty to forty per year. See Captain G.V. Galdorisi USN, 'Who Needs the Law of the Sea?', *United States Naval Institute Proceedings*, July 1993.
16. P.W. Birnie, 'Piracy, Past, Present and Future', *Marine Policy*, vol. II, no. 3, July 1987.
17. D.P. O'Connell, *The International Law of the Sea* (Oxford: Clarendon Press, 1982) p. ix.
18. Birnie, op. cit., and J. Adams, *Secret Armies* (London: Hutchinson, 1987) pp. 274–90.
19. Birnie, op. cit.
20. *The Naval Review*, October 1991. Cited by kind permission of the editor.
21. *The Times*, 14 and 28 December 1992.
22. The Naval Review, October 1992. Cited by kind permission of the editor.
23. The Times, 11 and 16 February 1989.
24. See the Chronological Appendix. Even today, a few governments are prepared to take drastic action. In 1993 a court in the United Arab Emirates sentenced two convicted pirates to the amputation of an arm and a leg (*The Times*, 12 March 1993).
25. Grove, op. cit. p. 262. An article entitled 'Piracy and Armed Robbery at Sea' by M.C. Pugh (*Low Intensity Conflict and Law Enforcement*, vol. 2, Summer 1993) suggests such a robust approach would get little support from today's international lawyers.
26. *The Times*, 10 February 1993: Department of Transport, *Merchant Shipping Notice No. 1517*; P.M. Kennedy, *The Rise and Fall of British Naval Mastery* (London: Allen Lane, 1976) p. 171.
27. C. Gill, F. Booker and T. Soper, *The Wreck of the Torrey Canyon* (Newton Abbot: David & Charles, 1967) *passim*.
28. *The Times*, 6 October 1988.
29. *The Times*, 8 and 10 January 1990.

NOTES TO CHRONOLOGICAL APPENDIX

1. D.M. Cooney, *A Chronology of the United States Navy 1775–1965* (New York: Franklin Watt, 1965). This source lists seven other US naval interventions in various parts of the world during 1919.
2. Telegram from US Consul at Manzanillo, *Papers Relating to the Foreign Relations of the United States* (henceforth *US Doc.*) 1920, vol. III (Washington: US Govt Printing Office, 1936) p. 153.
3. *Documents on British Foreign Policy 1919–1939* (henceforth *Brit. Doc.*) First Series, vol. XIII (London: HMSO, 1963) pp. 488 747.

4. *Brit. Doc.*, vol. XII (London: HMSO, 1962) pp. 504 and 510.
5. Ibid., pp. 675–8.
6. S. Roskill, *Naval Policy Between the Wars*, vol. I (London: Collins, 1968) p. 271, note 5.
7. Council on Foreign Relations, *American Relations in the Caribbean* (Yale University Press, 1929) chapter 5.
8. 'The Exiling of the Late Ex-Emperor Karl of Austria-Hungary', *Naval Review*, vol. XI, 1923.
9. A.J. Toynbee, *Survey of International Affairs* (henceforth cited as Toynbee, irrespective of editor for particular year) (Oxford: Oxford University Press, 1925) Supplement, p. 41.
10. See series of articles 'Smyrna and After' in *Naval Review*, vols XI and XII, 1923 and 1924.
11. Britain had not yet concluded a peace treaty with Turkey after the Great War of 1914–18, but had been neutral in the later Greco-Turkish war, which Turkey had just won. The genuineness of British neutrality – as readiness to fight either belligerent – is attested by an Admiralty telegram of 29 July 1922 to the C-in-C Mediterranean instructing him to be prepared to bombard the Piraeus, to seize Greek shipping, and to blockade Greece. The purpose was to dissuade Greece from occupying Constantinople. Fortunately, threats sufficed. Roskill, op. cit., pp. 195–6.
12. D. Walder, *The Chanak Affair* (London: Hutchinson, 1969) p. 334.
13. Toynbee, 1920–23, p. 259.
14. Toynbee, 1925, vol. II, p. 313.
15. Paymaster Lt H.R.H. Vaughan, 'Some Notes upon a Visit to Mexico', *Naval Review*, vol. XII, 1924.
16. US Doc., 1924, vol. II, pp. 300–24.
17. Toynbee, 1925, vol. II, p. 286.
18. See Command 2636 (China No. 1) of 1926 (London: HMSO). This was only one of many similar incidents in 1925.
19. W. Kamman, *A Search for Stability* (University of Notre Dame Press, 1968) *passim*.
20. Toynbee, 1925, vol. II, p. 412.
21. Toynbee, 1925, vol. I, p. 431.
22. Kamman, op. cit., p. 58.
23. Toynbee, 1926, p. 289.
24. Toynbee, 1926, pp. 307–14. See also P.D. Coates, *The China Consuls* (Hong Kong University Press, 1988) pp. 467–9.
25. Toynbee, 1928, p. 240.
26. Kamman, op. cit., pp. 92–4.
27. *The China Year Book 1929–30* (Tientsin Press) pp. 843–7. See also Coates, op. cit., pp. 474–6.
28. Ibid., pp. 795–8.
29. Toynbee, 1928, pp. 240–1.
30. Other countries did much the same (*The China Year Book*, op. cit., pp. 771–803).
31. Toynbee, 1928, pp. 407–13.
32. Ibid., p. 273.

33. H.R. Kaplan, 'A Toast to the Rum Fleet', *United States Naval Institute Proceedings*, May 1968.
34. US Doc., 1929, vol. III, p. 400.
35. P.S.H. Tang, *Russian and Soviet Policy in Manchuria and Outer Mongolia* (Duke University Press, 1959) chapter 5.
36. M. Beloff, *The Foreign Policy of Soviet Russia* (Oxford: Oxford University Press, 1949) vol. 2, chapter 3.
37. Toynbee, 1930, pp. 217–18.
38. Article entitled 'Communism on the Yangtse', *RUSI Journal*, vol. LXXVI, 1931.
39. Kamman, op. cit., pp. 201–2.
40. *Brit. Doc.*, Second Series, vol. 9, Doc. 143.
41. After discussions in Geneva and elsewhere, as well as in Shanghai itself, a ceasefire was negotiated on board Admiral Kelly's flagship by Chinese and Japanese representatives. Ibid., p. 371.
42. Mr Stimson, US Secretary of State, subsequently declared that the decisive factor had been the concentration of the US Main Fleet at Hawaii (R.H. Ferrell, *American Diplomacy in the Great Depression*, Yale University Press, 1957). French and Italian warships were also sent to Shanghai, but were not involved in the settlement of the Sino-Japanese dispute.
43. R.F. Smith, *The United States and Cuba* (New Haven: C.S.V. Press, 1960) chapter 10.
44. Toynbee, 1933, pp. 380–90.
45. Kamman, op. cit., p. 217.
46. Cooney, op. cit.
47. Toynbee, 1934, p. 536.
48. K. Edwards, *The Grey Diplomatists* (London: Rich & Cowan, 1938) chapter 8.
49. A.J. Marder, *From the Dardanelles to Oran* (Oxford: Oxford University Press, 1974) chapter III – 'The Royal Navy and the Ethiopian Crisis of 1935–1936'.
50. Toynbee, 1935, vol. II, p. 357.
51. See Appendix to N.J. Padelford, *International Law and Diplomacy in the Spanish Civil Strife* (New York: Macmillan, 1939) for a useful list of incidents.
52. *Franklin D. Roosevelt and Foreign Affairs*, vol. III (Harvard University Press, 1969).
53. For this and other Spanish Civil War incidents, see H. Thomas, *The Spanish Civil War* (London: Eyre & Spottiswoode, 1961) *passim*.
54. See note 53.
55. Beloff, op. cit., p. 167.
56. See note 53.
57. See note 53.
58. See note 53.
59. A. Paz and G. Ferrari, *Argentina's Foreign Policy 1930–1962* (University of Notre Dame Press, 1966).
60. Thomas, op. cit., p. 580

61. L. Mosely, *On Borrowed Time* (London: Weidenfeld & Nicolson, 1969) chapter 7.
62. A.J. Toynbee, *The Eve of War 1939*, pp. 634–6.
63. N.R. Clifford, *Retreat from China* (London: Longmans, Green & Co., 1967).
64. D.E. Nuechterlein, *Iceland: Reluctant Ally* (Cornell University Press, 1961) chapter 2.
65. W.S. Churchill, *The Grand Alliance* (London: Cassell, 1950) p. 22.
66. Captain R. Grenfell, *The Bismarck Episode* (London: Faber & Faber, 1958) pp. 93–4.
67. *Foreign Relations of the United States Vol. 2* (Washington: US Govt Printing Office, 1959) pp. 46–54.
68. J. Pratt, *The American Secretaries of State and their Diplomacy* (New York: Cooper Square, 1964) chapter 13.
69. A. Heckstall-Smith, *The Fleet that Faced Both Ways* (London: Anthony Blond, 1963) chapter 28.
70. W.S. Churchill, *Closing the Ring* (London: Cassell, 1952) pp. 101–3 and 167. This view also has Italian support. See M.A. Bragadin, *The Italian Navy in World War II* (Annapolis: US Naval Institute, 1957).
71. M. Beloff, *Soviet Foreign Policy in the Far East 1944–51* (Oxford: Oxford University Press, 1953) p. 42.
72. Rear-Admiral J.D. Hayes, 'The Sea 1956–1967', *Naval Review*, 1969 (Annapolis: US Naval Institute).
73. In fact, the pressure continued and menacing manoeuvres by the Soviet Black Sea Fleet had to be countered by US and British visits to Istanbul. See G. Kirk, *The Middle East 1945–1950* (Oxford: Oxford University Press, 1954).
74. *Keesing's Contemporary Archives.*
75. Ibid.
76. Ibid.
77. L. Gardiner, *The Eagle Spreads His Claws* (Edinburgh: William Blackwood & Sons, 1966) *passim.*
78. *Keesing's Contemporary Archives.*
79. Ibid.
80. Cooney, op. cit.
81. *Keesing's Contemporary Archives.*
82. Ibid.
83. Toynbee, 1949–50, pp. 322–4, and C.E. Lucas-Phillips, *Escape of the Amethyst* (London: Heinemann, 1957) *passim.*
84. *Keesing's Contemporary Archives.*
85. Ibid.
86. Ibid.
87. Cooney, op. cit.
88. Z. Ohira and T. Kuwahara, 'Fishing Problems between Japan and the People's Republic of China', *The Japanese Annual of International Law*, no. 3, 1959.
89. J. Cable, *Intervention at Abadan* (Bassingstoke: Macmillan, 1991) *passim.*

90. *Keesing's Contemporary Archives*.
91. Ibid.
92. Ibid.
93. J. Cable, *Navies in Violent Peace* (Basingstoke: Macmillan, 1989) p. 43.
94. Information kindly supplied by the US Naval Attaché in London.
95. A similar demonstration had been arranged for the Spanish government in January and was followed by fleet visits and the negotiation of an agreement for US bases in Spain. Cooney, op. cit.
96. *Keesing's Contemporary Archives*.
97. Ibid.
98. Even larger numbers of Japanese vessels and fishermen were seized by Soviet patrol ships from 1945 to 1969, but the extent to which Japanese fishermen were excluded from the Sea of Okhotsk and even parts of the Sea of Japan cannot be attributed to Soviet naval superiority alone. Other factors, including the prolonged retention in the Soviet Union of Japanese prisoners of war, played an important part in the protracted Soviet–Japanese negotiations. See Z. Ohira, 'Fishing Problems between Soviet Russia and Japan', *The Japanese Annual of International Law*, no. 2, 1958.
99. Cooney, op. cit.
100. A. Eden, *Full Circle* (London: Cassell, 1960) chapter 6.
101. *Keesing's Contemporary Archives*.
102. Ibid.
103. Ibid.
104. Cooney, op. cit.
105. Ibid.
106. *Keesing's Contemporary Archives*.
107. A.J. Barker, *Suez: The Seven Day War* (London: Faber & Faber, 1964) pp. 90–91.
108. J. Bernigaud, 'Les Aspects Maritimes de la Guerre d'Algérie', *Revue de Défense Nationale*, October 1968.
109. Captain D.J. Carrison, *The United States Navy* (New York: Praeger, 1968) p. 39.
110. The US government regarded the opposition in Jordan as Soviet inspired, a view that later received some support from the Soviet protest, on 29 April, against the movement of the Sixth Fleet as 'an open military demonstration against the countries of the Arab East' (*Keesing's Contemporary Archives*).
111. Cooney, op. cit.
112. Ibid.
113. *Keesing's Contemporary Archives*.
114. Ibid., and F. Galsworthy, 'More Fun than Fury in the Fish War', *United States Naval Institute Proceedings*, February 1961.
115. E.F. Baldridge, 'Lebanon and Quemoy', *United States Naval Institute Proceedings*, February 1969.
116. *Keesing's Contemporary Archives*.
117. Cooney, op. cit.
118. During the Algerian War, the French Navy also stopped and searched on the high seas (even outside the Mediterranean) British, Bulgarian,

Danish, German, Italian, Panamanian, Polish, Rumanian, Swedish and Yugoslav vessels. See Bernigaud, op. cit.

119. Cooney, op. cit., and *Keesing's Contemporary Archives.*
120. *Keesing's Contemporary Archives.*
121. Cooney, op. cit.
122. *Keesing's Contemporary Archives.*
123. H. Johnson, *The Bay of Pigs* (London: Hutchinson, 1965) *passim.*
124. Lt Commander J. Stewart, 'East of Suez', *United States Naval Institute Proceedings*, March 1966, and E.J. Grove, *Vanguard to Trident* (London: Bodley Head, 1981) pp. 246–9.
125. *Keesing's Contemporary Archives.*
126. J. Barlow Martin, *Overtaken by Events* (New York: Doubleday, 1966) chapter 4.
127. *Keesing's Contemporary Archives.*
128. *Naval Review*, 1964 (Annapolis: US Naval Institute).
129. Martin, op. cit., chapter 13.
130. Ibid., chapter 18.
131. *The Times*, 16, 17 and 21 August.
132. *Keesing's Contemporary Archives.*
133. Lt Col. T.M.P. Stevens, 'A Joint Operation in Tanganyika', *RUSI Journal*, February 1965, and Grove, op. cit., p. 263.
134. P. Windsor, *NATO and the Cyprus Crisis*, Adelphi Paper no. 14 (London, IISS, November 1964).
135. *Keesing's Contemporary Archives.*
136. J.C. Goulden, *Truth is the First Casualty* (Chicago: Rand McNally, 1969) *passim.*
137. Captain J.A. Dare, 'Dominican Diary', *United States Naval Institute Proceedings*, December 1965.
138. *Keesing's Contemporary Archives.*
139. Ibid.
140. Grove, op. cit., p. 290; H. Wilson, *The Labour Government 1964–1970* (London: Weidenfeld & Nicolson, 1971) p. 397; B. Dismukes and J. McConnell, *Soviet Naval Diplomacy* (New York: Pergamon Press, 1979) p. 162–4.
141. Cable, *Navies in Violent Peace*, op. cit., pp. 45–6.
142. *The Times*, 11 July 1967.
143. *Keesing's Contemporary Archives.*
144. Dismukes and McConnell, op. cit., pp. 122–3
145. Statement of Norwegian Minister of Defence. Quoted in *NATO Letter* of January 1969.
146. Major-General B. Tephinsky, 'NATO: Northern Flank', in the Soviet weekly *New Times*, no. 36 of 11 September 1968.
147. *Keesing's Contemporary Archives.*
148. *The Times*, 23 April 1969, and Dismukes and McConnell, op. cit., pp. 126–7.
149. *The Times*, 14 June 1969 (similar incidents took place in September and October of the same year).
150. Dismukes and McConnell, op. cit., chapter 5.
151. Ibid.

152. Op. cit., chapter 4
153. Ibid.
154. *Keesing's Contemporary Archives.*
155. Ibid., and IISS, *Strategic Survey 1971* (London: IISS, 1972) pp. 40–2.
156. Dismukes and McConnell, op. cit., pp. 178–92.
157. *Daily Telegraph*, 31 January 1972.
158. *Keesing's Contemporary Archives.*
159. Ibid.
160. Ibid.
161. Ibid.
162. Ibid.
163. Ibid.
164. Ibid.
165. See Chapter 2.
166. See Chapter 2.
167. See Chapter 2.
168. D.P. O'Connell, *The Influence of Law on Sea Power* (Manchester: Manchester University Press, 1975) pp. 10–11.
169. M.S. Samuels, *Contest for the South China Sea* (London: Methuen, 1982) pp. 101–3.
170. *Keesing's Contemporary Archives.*
171. The best short account is in IISS, *Strategic Survey 1974* (London: IISS, 1975). See also Chapter 4.
172. *Army Quarterly*, January 1975, and J. Winton, *For Those in Peril* (London: Robert Hale, 1992) pp. 129–39.
173. I. Ahmad and D. Caploe, 'The Logic of Military Intervention', *Race and Class*, vol. XVII, no. 3, 1976.
174. *Keesing's Contemporary Archives.*
175. Ibid.
176. Ibid.
177. Ibid., and M. Adkin, *Urgent Fury* (London: Leo Cooper, 1989) p. 112.
178. Ibid.
179. *Keesing's Contemporary Archives.*
180. Ibid.
181. Ibid.
182. See J. Joliffe, *East Timor: Nationalism and Colonialism* (University of Queensland Press, 1978) *passim*.
183. *Keesing's Contemporary Archives.*
184. Ibid.
185. B. Buzan, 'The Status and Future of the Montreux Convention', *Survival*, November/December 1976.
186. IISS, *Strategic Survey 1976* (London: IISS, 1977).
187. *Keesing's Contemporary Archives.*
188. Lt de Vaisseau Robert L. Cogné, 'France's Global Reach', *United States Naval Institute Proceedings*, March 1987. See also H. Coutau-Bégarie, *Géostratégie de l'Océan Indien* (Paris: Economica, 1993) pp. 87–8.
189. *The Times*, 7 July 1977.
190. *The Review of the River Plate*, 12 July 1978. Grove, op. cit., p. 358.

191. *The Times*, 13 October 1977. See *Journal of S.E. Asian Studies*, March 1979, for earlier history of this dispute.
192. Grove, op. cit., pp. 358–9.
193. *Keesing's Contemporary Archives*.
194. *Daily Telegraph*, 18 January 1978, and *Soviet Analyst*, 26 January 1978.
195. *Keesing's Contemporary Archives*.
196. Ibid.
197. D. Tretiak, article in *Asian Survey*, vol. XIII, no. 16, December 1978.
198. *Keesing's Contemporary Archives*.
199. *Daily Telegraph*.
200. *The Economist*, 8 September 1979.
201. *Daily Telegraph*, 18 October 1979.
202. Cable, *Navies in Violent Peace*, op. cit., pp. 59–60.
203. *Keesing's Contemporary Archives*. See also Z. Brzezinski, *Power and Principle 1977–81* (London: Weidenfeld & Nicolson, 1983) pp. 482–506.
204. J.F. Cooley, *Libyan Sandstorm* (London: Sidgwick & Jackson, 1983) pp. 221–2.
205. Cable, *Navies in Violent Peace*, op. cit., pp. 60–70.
206. C. Weinberger, *Fighting for Peace* (London: Michael Joseph, 1990) pp. 124–5.
207. Cable, *Navies in Violent Peace*, op. cit., p. 61.
208. N. Polmar, 'The Soviet Navy', *United States Naval Institute Proceedings*, January 1987.
209. M. Middlebrook, *Task Force: The Falklands War 1982* (Harmondsworth: Penguin Books, rev. edn 1987) chapter 2.
210. *New York Times*, 3 May 1982. Such exercises were frequent. In 1980, Operation Solid Shield involved forty-two warships and included the landing of 2000 marines at Guantánamo (T. Thorndike, *Grenada* (London: Frances Pinter, 1985) pp. 64–5).
211. *The Times*, 3 December 1982.
212. *The Times*, 20 January 1983.
213. J. Cable, *Diplomacy at Sea* (London: Macmillan, 1985) p. 29.
214. *The Times*, 6 August 1983.
215. *Keesing's Contemporary Archives*.
216. See Chapter 2 and Cable, *Navies in Violent Peace*, op. cit., pp. 49–56; also *The Sunday Times*, 18 October 1990.
217. *The Times*, 8 March 1984.
218. *The Times*, 4 April 1984.
219. J. Cable, 'Outside Navies in the Gulf', *International Relations*, May 1988.
220. Captain T.C. Pullen, 'What Price Canadian Sovereignty?', *United States Naval Institute Proceedings*, September 1987.
221. See Chapter 6.
222. 'Report of Proceedings', *Royal Navy Broadsheet 86* (London: HMSO, 1986).
223. Lt Commander R.E. Stumpf USN, 'Air War with Libya', *United States Naval Institute Proceedings*, August 1986.
224. *The Times*, 18 September 1986.
225. *The Times*, 20 October 1986, and *Guardian*, 1 November 1986.

226. *The Times*, 21 and 22 May 1987.
227. *Naval Forces*, no. VI, 1987, p. 65.
228. *The Times*, 19 August 1987, and Cable, *Navies in Violent Peace*, op. cit., p. 86.
229. *The Times*, 3 August 1987.
230. *The Times*, 23 September 1987.
231. Cable, *Navies in Violent Peace*, op. cit., p. 68.
232. Ibid.
233. *The Times*, 17 January 1988.
234. Cable, *Navies in Violent Peace*, op. cit., p. 73.
235. *The Times*, 4 June 1988, and B. Cloughley, 'South China Sea Confrontation', *Jane's Defence Weekly*, vol. 9, no. 21, 28 May 1988.
236. Cable, *Navies in Violent Peace*, op. cit., p. 69.
237. *The Times*, 19 April 1988.
238. *The Times*, 23 May 1988.
239. *The Times*, 9 November 1988.
240. *Keesing's Record of World Events* (new title).
241. *The Times*, 28 July 1989.
242. *Keesing's Record of World Events*.
243. *The Times*, 10 January 1990, and *Facts on File.: World News Digest with Index*, published weekly by Facts on File Inc., New York.
244. *The Times*, 1 February 1990.
245. *The Times* and *Independent*, June 1990 *passim*, and Lt Col. T.W. Parker USMC, 'Operation Sharp Edge', *United States Naval Institute Proceedings*, May 1991.
246. 'Report of Proceedings', *Royal Navy Broadsheet 90*.
247. IISS, *Strategic Survey 1990–1991*, and *West Africa* of 23 November 1992. See also J. Luffin, *The World in Conflict 1991* (London: Brassey's, 1991) pp. 141–6.
248. Articles in *United States Naval Institute Proceedings*, May 1992.
249. A 'Report of Proceedings', *Royal Navy Broadsheet 91*.

Select Bibliography

Not all the publications cited in the text and identified in the notes have been included in this bibliography, which lists works frequently consulted as well as those offering significant additional information or alternative opinions. The reader who samples these works should not neglect their footnotes, which have long been the main repository of the neglected history of gunboat diplomacy.

I GENERAL

1 Official Documents

Documents on British Foreign Policy 1919–1939 (London: HMSO).
Documents on German Foreign Policy 1918–1945 (London: HMSO; Washington: US Govt Printing Office).
Papers Relating to the Foreign Relations of the United States (Washington: US Govt Printing Office).

2 Books

Blechman, B.M., and Kaplan, S.S., *Force Without War* (Washington: Brookings Institution, 1978).
Booth, K., *Navies and Foreign Policy* (London: Croom Helm, 1977).
Booth, K., *Law, Force and Diplomacy at Sea* (London: George Allen & Unwin, 1985).
Cable, J., *Diplomacy at Sea* (London: Macmillan, 1985).
Cable, J., *Navies in Violent Peace* (Basingstoke: Macmillan, 1989).
Cable, J., 'Naval Strategy in an Altered World', in *Defense Analysis* (Lancaster, December 1992).
Cooney, D.M., *A Chronology of the United States Navy 1775–1965* (New York: Franklin Wait, 1965).
Edwards, K., *The Grey Diplomatists* (London: Rich & Cowan, 1938).
Grove, E.J., *Vanguard to Trident: British Naval Policy Since World War II* (London: Bodley Head, 1987).
Hill, J.R., 'The Rule of Law at Sea', unpublished thesis (London: Kings College, 1972).
Luttwak, E.N., *The Political Uses of Sea Power* (Johns Hopkins University Press, 1974).
O'Connell, D.P., *The Influence of Law on Sea Power* (Manchester: Manchester University Press, 1975).
O'Connel, D.P., *The International Law of the Sea* (Oxford: Clarendon Press, 1982).

Roskill, S., *Naval Policy Between the Wars, Vol. 1 1919–1929* (London: Collins, 1968).
Rouse, Lt Com. F.C. (ed.), *To Use the Sea: Readings in Seapower and Maritime Affairs* (Annapolis: Naval Institute Press, 1977).
Till, G., *Maritime Strategy and the Nuclear Age* (London: Macmillan, 2nd edn 1984).

3 Periodicals (other than daily newspapers)

Annual Register of World Events, London
Defense Analysis, triannual, Lancaster
International Affairs, quarterly, London
International Affairs, monthly, Moscow
International Relations, was biannual, now triannual, London
Janes's Defence Weekly, London
Keesing's Contemporary Archives (now *Record of World Events*), cumulative annual, Bristol to 1973, London to 1988, now Cambridge
Marine Policy, quarterly, Guildford
Military Balance, annual, London
Naval Forces, bimonthly, Farnborough
Naval History, quarterly, Annapolis
Naval Review, quarterly, London
Navy International, monthly, Newdigate
Revue de Défense Nationale, monthly, Paris
Royal Navy Broadsheet, annual, London
Soviet Armed Forces Review Annual, Gulf Breeze
Soviet Military Power, annual, Washington
Statement on the Defence Estimates, annual, London
Strategic Survey, annual, London
Stratégique, irregular, Paris
Survival, bimonthly, London
United States Naval Institute Proceedings (*USNIP*), monthly, Annapolis
World in Conflict: War Annual, London

II PARTICULAR

1 ALTMARK (1940)

Brookes, E., *Prologue to a War* (London: Jarrolds, 1966).
Derry, T.K., *The Campaign in Norway* (London: HMSO, 1952).
Documents on German Foreign Policy 1918–1945, Series D, vol. VIII (Washington: US Govt Printing Office, 1954).
Correspondence Respecting the German Steamer ALTMARK (London: HMSO, Command 8012 of 1950).
Instilling fra Undersøkelseskommisjonen av 1945, Altmark Saken (Oslo 1947).
Moulton, J.L., *The Norwegian Campaign of 1940* (London: Eyre & Spottiswoode, 1966).

Roskill, S.W., *The War at Sea* (London: HMSO, 1954).
Vian, Sir P., *Action This Day* (London: Frederick Muller, 1960).

2 Baltic (1919–21)

Agar, A.W.A., *Baltic Episode* (London: Hodder & Stoughton, 1963).
Bennett, G., *Cowan's War* (London: Collins, 1963).
Jägerskiöld, S., *Riksföreståndaren Gustaf Mannerheim 1919* (Helsingfors: Holger Schildts Förlag, 1969).
Mercer, D.M., 'The Baltic Sea Campaign', *USNIP*, September 1962.
Paasivirta, J., *The Victors in World War I and Finland* (Helsinki: Finnish Historical Society, 1965).
Page, S.W., *The Formation of the Baltic States* (Harvard University Press, 1959).
Pridham, F., *Close of a Dynasty* (London: Allen Wingate, 1956).
Roskill, S.W., *Naval Policy Between the Wars, Vol. I 1919–1929* (London: Collins, 1968).
Ullman, R.H., *Britain and the Russian Civil War* (Princeton University Press, 1968).

3 Caribbean (1919–91)

Adkin, M., *Urgent Fury: The Battle for Grenada* (London: Leo Cooper, 1989).
Aguilar, A., *Pan-Americanism from Monroe to the Present*, tr. Asa Zata (New York: Monthly Review Press, 1968).
Beman, L.T., *Intervention in Latin America* (New York: H.W. Wisson, 1928).
Council on Foreign Relations, *American Relations in the Caribbean* (Yale University Press, 1929).
Davidson, S., *Grenada* (Aldershot: Gower, 1987).
Dunn, P.M., and Watson, W. (eds), *American Intervention in Grenada* (Boulder, Colorado: Westview Press, 1985).
Howland, C.P., *American Relations in the Caribbean* (Yale University Press, 1929).
Kamman, W., *A Search for Stability* (University of Notre Dame Press, 1968).
Langley, L.D., *The Banana Wars: United States Intervention in the Caribbean 1898–1934* (University of Kentucky Press, rev. edn 1985).
Martin, J.B., *Overtaken by Events* (New York: Doubleday, 1966).
Schlesinger, S., and Kinzer, S., *Bitter Fruit* (London: Sinclair, Browne, 1982).
Smith, R.F., *The United States and Cuba* (New Haven: College and University Press, 1960).

4 China and the Far East (1919–91)

Armbrister, T., *A Matter of Accountability: The True Story of the PUEBLO Affair* (London: Barrie & Jenkins, 1970).
Brice, M.H., *The Royal Navy and the Sino-Japanese Incident 1937–41* (London: Ian Allen, 1973).
China Year Book, The (irregular annual of the 1920s and 1930s) (Tientsin Press).

Christopher, S.W., *Conflict in the Far East* (Leiden: E.J. Brill, 1950).
Coutau-Bégarie, H., *Géostratégie du Pacifique* (Paris: Economica, 1987).
Dreyer, Admiral Sir F.C., *The Sea Heritage* (London: Museum Press, 1955).
Ferrell, R.H., *American Diplomacy in the Great Depression* (Yale University Press, 1957).
Fleming, P., *The Siege at Peking* (London: Rupert Hart-Davis, 1959).
Goulden, J.C., *Truth is the First Casualty: The Gulf of Tonkin Affair – Illusion and Reality* (Chicago: Rand McNally, 1969).
Gwynn, Gen. Sir C., *Imperial Policing* (London: Macmillan, 1934).
Hamilton, Com. L., Manuscript Journal, in National Maritime Museum, Greenwich.
Hewlett, Sir W., *Forty Years in China* (London: Macmillan, 1943).
Panikkar, K.M., *Asia and Western Dominance* (London: George Allen & Unwin, 1953).
Perry, H.D., *The PANAY Incident* (Toronto: Macmillan, 1969).
Pollard, R.T., *China's Foreign Relations 1917–1931* (New York: Macmillan, 1933).
Samuels, M.S., *Contest for the South China Sea* (London: Methuen, 1982).
State Department, *United States Relations with China 1944–1949* (Washington: US Govt Printing Office, 1949).
Tang, P.S.H., *Russian and Soviet Policy in Manchuria and Outer Mongolia* (Duke University Press, 1959).
Tang Tsou, *America's Failure in China 1941–1950* (University of Chicago Press, 1963).
Tuleja, Com. T.V., *Statesmen and Admirals: The Quest for a Far Eastern Naval Policy (1922–1941)* (New York: W.W. Norton, 1963).
Tweedie, Admiral Sir H., *The Story of a Naval Life* (London: Rich & Cowan, 1939).
Wheeler, Com. G.E., *Prelude to Pearl Harbor: The US Navy and the Far East (1921–1931)* (Missouri University Press, 1963).

5   Iceland (1940–76)

Beard, C.A., *President Roosevelt and the Coming of the War 1941* (Yale University Press, 1948).
Griffiths, J.C., *Modern Iceland* (London: Pall Mall Press, 1969).
Grove, E.J., *Vanguard to Trident: British Naval Policy Since World War II* (London: Bodley Head, 1987).
Historical Division, HQ US Marine Corps, *The US Marines in Iceland 1941–1942* (Washington, 1970).
Jónnsson, H., *Friends in Conflict* (London: C. Hurst, 1982).
Nuechterlein, D.E., *Iceland: Reluctant Ally* (Cornell University Press, 1961).

6   Lebanon (1958–89)

Chamoun, C., *Crise au Moyen Orient* (Paris: Gallimard, 1963).
Copeland, M., *The Game of Nations* (London: Weidenfeld & Nicolson, 1969).
Eisenhower, D.D., *The White House Years, Vol. III, Waging the Peace* (London: Heinemann, 1966).

Heinl, D., *Soldiers of the Sea* (Annapolis: US Naval Institute, 1962).
Marine Corps Historical Branch, G.3. Division, *Marines in Lebanon 1958* (Washington, 1966).
McClintock, R., 'The US Intervention in Lebanon', *USNIP*, October 1962.
Murphy, R., *Diplomat Among Warriors* (London: Collins, 1964).
Quabain, F.I., *Crisis in Lebanon* (Washington: Middle East Institute, 1961).
Robin, G., *La Diplomatie de Mitterand 1981–1985* (Paris: Editions de la Bièvre, 1985).
Thayer, C.W., *Diplomat* (New York: Harpers, 1959).
Weinberger, C., *Fighting for Peace* (London: Michael Joseph, 1990).

7   Mediterranean (1919–91)

Barker, A.J., *Suez: The Seven Day War* (London: Faber & Faber, 1964).
Barros, J., *The Corfu Incident of 1923* (Princeton University Press, 1965).
Dismukes, B., and McConnell, J. (eds), *Soviet Naval Diplomacy* (New York: Pergamon Press, 1979).
Dowty, A., *Middle East Crisis* (University of California Press, 1984).
Edwards, K., *The Grey Diplomatists* (London: Rich & Cowan, 1938).
Gardiner, L., *The Eagle Spreads His Claws* (Edinburgh: William Blackwood & Sons, 1966).
Grove, E. J., *Vanguard to Trident: British Naval Policy Since World War II* (London: Bodley Head, 1987).
Heckstall-Smith, A., *The Fleet That Faced Both Ways* (London: Anthony Blond, 1963).
Kissinger, H., *Years of Upheaval* (London: Weidenfeld & Nicolson/Michael Joseph, 1982).
Marder, A., 'The Royal Navy and the Ethiopian Crisis of 1935–36', *American Historical Review*, vol. LXXV, no.5, June 1970.
Pearson, A., *Conspiracy of Silence: The Attack on the USS LIBERTY* (London: Quartet Books, 1978).
Reitzel, W., *The Mediterranean: Its Role in America's Foreign Policy* (Port Washington: NY Kennihat Press, 1948).
Thomas, H., *The Suez Affair* (London: Weidenfeld & Nicolson, 1966).
Walder, D., *The Chanak Affair* (London: Hutchinson, 1969).
Wilson, A., *The Aegean Dispute*, Adelphi Paper no. 155 (London: International Institute for Strategic Studies, 1979).

8   Miscellaneous

Anglin, D.C., *The St Pierre and Miquelon Affair of 1941* (University of Toronto Press, 1966).
Brook-Shepherd, G., *The Last Hapsburg* (London: Weidenfeld & Nicolson, 1968).
Cable, J., 'Flicker of an Imperial Flame', *International Relations*, vol. VII, no. 6, 1983.
Cable, J., *Intervention at Abadan* (Basingstoke: Macmillan, 1991).
Moseley, L., *On Borrowed Time* (London: Weidenfeld & Nicolson, 1969) (for Memel 1939).

238 *Select Bibliography*

Muselier, Vice-Admiral, *De Gaulle Contre le Gaullisme* (Paris: Editions du Chêne, 1946).
Paget, J., *Last Post: Aden 1964–1967* (London: Faber & Faber, 1969).

9 Soviet Union (1919–91)

Coutau-Bégarie, H., *La Puissance Maritime Soviétique* (Paris: Economica, 1983).
Dismukes, B., and McConnell, J. (eds), *Soviet Naval Diplomacy* (New York: Pergamon Press, 1979).
Edmonds, R., *Soviet Foreign Policy: The Brezhnev Years* (Oxford: Oxford University Press, 1983).
Gorshkov, Admiral S., *The Sea Power of the State* (London: Pergamon Press, 1979).
Kaplan, S.S., *Diplomacy of Power* (Washington: Brookings Institution, 1981).
Ranft, B., and Till, G., *The Sea in Soviet Strategy* (Basingstoke: Macmillan, 2nd edn 1989).
Watson, B., *Red Navy at Sea: Soviet Naval Operations on the High Seas 1956–1980* (Boulder, Colorado: Westview Press, 1982).
Weinland, R.G., MccGwire, M.K., and McConnell, J., *Admiral Gorshkov on 'Navies in War and Peace'* (Arlington, Virginia: Center for Naval Analyses, 1974).

10 Spanish Civil War (1936–39)

Cable, J., *The Royal Navy and the Siege of Bilbao* (Cambridge: Cambridge University Press, 1979)
Cervera, V., and Almirante, J., *Memorias de Guerra* (Madrid: Editorial Nacional, 1968).
Eden, A., *Facing the Dictators* (London: Cassell, 1962).
Edwards, J., *The British Government and the Spanish Civil War 1936–1939* (London: Macmillan, 1979).
Edwards, K., *The Grey Diplomatists* (London: Rich & Cowan, 1938).
HMSO, *Documents on German Foreign Policy*, Series D, vol. III, (London, 1951).
HMS ROYAL OAK 1936–1938 Commission: Executive Officer's Log, manuscript in National Maritime Museum, Greenwich
Jackson, G., *The Spanish Republic and the Civil War* (Princeton University Press, 1965).
Moreno, Almirante D. Francisco, *La Guerra en el Mar* (Barcelona: Editorial Ahr, 1959).
Padelford, N.J., *International Law and Diplomacy in the Spanish Civil Strife* (New York: Macmillan, 1939).
Puzzo, D. A., *Spain and the Great Powers 1936–1941* (Columbia University Press, 1962).
Steer, G.L., *The Tree of Gernika* (London: Hodder & Stoughton, 1938).
Thomas, II., *The Spanish Civil War* (London: Eyre & Spottiswoode, 1961).
Toynbee, A.J., *Survey of International Affairs 1937*, vol. II (London: Royal Institute of International Affairs and Oxford University Press, 1938).

Index

Ships mentioned in the text are listed under *Named Ships*.